**W9-BSZ-499**

# Economics of Knowledge

# Economics of Knowledge

Dominique Foray

**WITHDRAWN**

The MIT Press
Cambridge, Massachusetts
London, England

*L'économie de la connaissance*

© Editions La DECOUVERTE, Paris, 2000

© 2004 Massachusetts Institute of Technology

This book was set in Palatino by SNP Best-set Typesetter Ltd., Hong, Kong and was printed and bound in the United States of America.

Library of Congress Cataloging-in-Publication Data

Foray, Dominique.
  [Economie de la connaissance. English]
  Economics of knowledge / Dominique Foray.
     p. cm.
  Rev. and enlarged translation of: L'économie de la connaissance.
  Includes bibliographical references and index.
  ISBN 0-262-06239-9
     1. Knowledge management—Economic aspects. 2. Information technology—Economic aspects. 3. Technological innovations—Economic aspects. I. Title.

HD30.2.F66   2004
338'.064—dc22

10  9  8  7  6  5  4  3  2

# Contents

Acknowledgments    vii

Introduction    ix

1 An Original Discipline    1

2 Macro- and Microeconomic References: Continuity and Breaks    21

3 Production of Knowledge    49

4 Reproduction of Knowledge    71

5 Knowledge Spillovers    91

6 Knowledge as a Public Good    113

7 Intellectual Property Rights in the Knowledge Economy    131

8 Knowledge Openness and Economic Incentives    165

9 On the Uneven Development of Knowledge across Sectors    189

10 A New Organizational Capability: Knowledge Management    207

11 The Public Dimension of the Knowledge Economy    225

Conclusion    247

**Postscript**    251

Notes    253
References    255
Index    271

# Acknowledgments

I acknowledge with gratitude the support that I received for my research during 1999/2000, when I held a fellowship at the International Center for Economic Research (ICER, Turin), as well as the continuous support that I received from the Institut pour le Management de la Recherche et de l'Innovation (IMRI) at the University Paris Dauphine. I am particularly grateful to Valérie Fleurette and Stephanie Pitoun.

In the course of the preparation of this book, I enjoyed many stimulating discussions with a number of friends and colleagues. I am particularly grateful to my colleagues Maurice Cassier, Robin Cowan, Paul David, Jacques Mairesse, Ed Steinmueller, and Eric von Hippel for great discussions, detailed suggestions, and challenging exchanges. Many other friends and colleagues have been involved at various stages of the preparation of this book. They all have contributed to make the writing of this book an enjoyable and memorable enterprise. Warm thanks to Norbert Alter, Cristiano Antonelli, Rémi Barré, Eric Brousseau, Michel Callon, Uwe Cantner, Ann Carter, Iain Cockburn, Patrick Cohendet, Jean-Michel Dalle, Albert David, Louise Earl, David Encaoua, Emmanuelle Fauchart, Maryann Feldman, Chris Freeman, Pierre Garrouste, Fred Gault, Arnulf Gruebler, Dominique Guellec, Bronwyn Hall, David Hargreaves, Armand Hatchuel, Liliane Hilaire Perez, Ali Kazancigil, Max Keilbach, John King, Alice Lam, Patrick Llerena, Bengt Ake Lundvall, Franco Malerba, Frieder Meyer Krahmer, David Mowery, Richard Nelson, Francis-Luc Perret, Luc Soete, Kevin Styroh, Peter Swann, Morris Teubal, Manuel Trajtenberg, Xavier Vence, Jean Benoît Zimmerman, and Ehud Zuscovitch.

At a late stage in the preparation of this manuscript, Brian Kahin was very helpful for many reasons. I thank him warmly. I am also grateful to the four anonymous reviewers who made very sharp comments that helped me to adjust some parts of the book at the last minute. Thanks to Liz Carey-Libbrecht for translation and editorial assistance. Our excellent collaboration without a single face-to-face meeting (even at the start) shows that some of the issues raised in the book are not pure fiction!

This book is an extended and largely revised version of a book published in French: *L'économie de la connaissance* (Paris: La Découverte, 2000).

# Introduction

Just as industrial economics as a discipline was founded with the advent of industrialization in around 1820, so the economics of knowledge developed as knowledge-based economies gradually came into being. By knowledge-based economies I mean, essentially, economies in which the proportion of knowledge-intensive jobs is high, the economic weight of information sectors is a determining factor, and the share of intangible capital is greater than that of tangible capital in the overall stock of real capital. These developments are reflected in an ever-increasing proliferation of jobs in the production, processing, and transfer of knowledge and information. This evolution is not just confined to the high-technology and information and communication service sectors; it has gradually spread across the entire economy since first coming to light as early as the 1970s. Society as a whole, then, is shifting to knowledge-intensive activities.

Some, who had thought that the concepts of a new economy and a knowledge-based economy related to more or less the same phenomenon, logically concluded that the bursting of the speculative high-tech bubble sealed the fate of a short-lived knowledge-based economy. My conception is different. I think that the term "knowledge-based economy" is still valid insofar as it characterizes a possible scenario of structural transformations of our economies. This is, moreover, the conception of major international organizations such as the World Bank and the Organisation for Economic Cooperation and Development (OECD).

## The Knowledge-Based Economy as a Plausible Scenario of Structural Transformation

In the scenario under consideration, the rapid creation of new knowledge and the improvement of access to the knowledge bases thus constituted, in every possible way (education, training, transfer of technological knowledge, diffusion of innovations), are factors increasing economic efficiency, innovation, the quality of goods and services, and equity between individuals, social categories, and generations.[1] Realization of this scenario enjoys a number of structural conditions that have progressively been set in place. Two phenomena in particular will be considered: first, a long-standing trend, reflected in the expansion of "knowledge-related" investments and activities; and second, a unique technological revolution that radically changed the conditions of production and transmission of knowledge and information. The collision between these two phenomena has spawned a unique economy, characterized essentially by (1) the accelerating (and unprecedented) speed at which knowledge is created and accumulated and, in all likelihood, at which it depreciates in terms of economic relevance and value as well as (2) a substantial decrease in the costs of codification, transmission, and acquisition of knowledge. This creates the potential for a massive growth of knowledge flows and externalities. Indeed, the strength of such externalities (and hence the importance of the problems they pose) is historically dependent on technological and organizational conditions that have never been met as well as they are today.

Yet this scenario, in which the rapid creation of knowledge and easy access to knowledge bases enhances efficiency, quality, and equity, is still highly uncertain. While it may be plausible and even probable for certain types of activity and even certain countries as a whole, it is far more uncertain and even unrealistic in many other cases.

These basic underlying trends must not be allowed to obscure the growing importance of science- and technology-related activities. Knowledge-based economies are not, of course, restricted to the realm of high technology, but science and technology tend to be central to the new sectors giving momentum to the upward growth of the economy as a whole over the past few decades (pharmaceuticals and scientific instrumentation, information and communication technologies, aeronautics, new materials).

The term *knowledge-based economy* also enables readers to fully understand a qualitative innovation in the organization and conduct of modern economic life—namely, the factors determining the success of firms and national economies are more dependent than ever on the capacity to produce and use knowledge. The immediate result of this new situation can be found in particular forms of polarization in labor markets, reflecting a bias in favor of qualified workers. Whether one looks at the polarization of labor in the United States or polarization in terms of unemployment in Europe, it is always the qualified workers who come out on top (Greenan, Horty, and Mairesse 2002). This observation is confirmed by studies showing that net job creation is taking place in the "knowledge-intensive" parts of our economies (see Foray and Lundvall 1996 for an overview).

## Outline of the Book

This volume focuses on two new developments: a scientific development corresponding to the emergence of a new economic subdiscipline of which the research object—knowledge—poses new theoretical and empirical problems; and a historical development heralding the advent of a particular period in the growth and organization of economic activities. I stress the importance of this twofold change, which some authors fail to recognize. For them, the only new development of any relevance is theoretical, and the historical period in which they are living follows earlier periods without any discontinuity whatsoever. Because one believes, on the contrary, in the dual nature of the economics of knowledge—as a discipline and as a historical period—it is naturally around that duality that this volume is organized.

By convention, so as not to confuse the two phenomena, I call the discipline "the economics of knowledge" and the historical period "the knowledge-based economy." The book alternates between an analysis of the transformations and challenges of knowledge-based economies and an examination of the concepts and tools of the discipline.

Chapter 1 focuses on the scope of the discipline, which obviously has to be defined in relation to the definition of "knowledge" as an economic good.

Chapter 2 tries to capture the main historical characteristics of the knowledge-based economies and focuses on the broad implications of the historical encounter between a long-standing trend toward the increase in resources devoted to the production and transmission of knowledge (research and development or R&D, education, training, organization) and a major technological event (the advent of new information and communication technologies).

Next I develop a conceptual framework to illuminate various issues and problems arising from the organization of the process of knowledge creation, accumulation, and diffusion. Chapter 3 focuses on the main forms of knowledge production. The increasing importance of three sources of knowledge—scientific research, learning-by-doing, and industrial coordination—is considered to be a major step in the historical emergence of the knowledge-based economy. Chapter 4 analyzes in detail the issue of knowledge reproduction (transfer, transmission) and emphasizes one of the essential factors of the knowledge-based economy at the microeconomic level—namely, the trend toward the codification of knowledge, related to the emergence and diffusion of information and communication technologies. Chapter 5 addresses the issue of (intended and unintended) knowledge spillovers and assesses the role they play in the knowledge economy.

I then consider issues of incentives and institutions that can be relied upon to produce and exploit knowledge in an efficient manner. Chapter 6 addresses the problem of public good and presents the different systems designed to organize the production of knowledge and to strike a balance between the goal of providing ideal motivation to the private producer and the social goal of efficient use of knowledge once it has been produced. Chapter 7 examines the case of private markets based on the protection of intellectual property rights, while chapter 8 studies the "open" organization of knowledge.

Finally, I address policy issues regarding the unbalanced nature of knowledge development across sectors (chapter 9), knowledge management as a new organizational capability (chapter 10), and the public dimension of the knowledge-based economy (chapter 11).

　　　　　　　　　　An Original Discipline

*Economists have, of course, always recognized the dominant role that increasingly knowledge plays in economic processes but have, for the most part, found the whole subject of knowledge too slippery to handle.*

—E. Penrose, *The Theory of the Growth of the Firm*

The economics of knowledge as a discipline should not be confused with the economics of research, for its main focus is not the formal production of technological knowledge; nor should it be seen as the economics of innovation, for it is not centered exclusively on the study of the conditions, modalities, and effects of technological and organizational change. It should also not be likened to the economics of information, since the object of the economics of knowledge is knowledge (and not information) as an economic good. Its field of analysis covers the properties of that economic good governing its production and reproduction as well as the historical and institutional conditions (such as information technology or patent rights) determining its treatment and processing in a decentralized economy.

## Scope of the Economics of Knowledge

### Some Modern Precursors

Apart from historical figures—Smith, Marx, and Schumpeter who all dealt with knowledge, its creation and division, its use and appropriation—the latter-day pioneers in the general economics of knowledge (i.e., not confined to science and technology) are unquestionably Simon, Hayek, Arrow, and Machlup. Simon (1982) has studied numerous subjects pertaining to the economics of knowledge, such as the role of memorization in the learning process, and can be considered as the real precursor of the economics of information technology. Hayek (1945) examined problems posed by the mass dissemination of knowledge and the impossibility of transferring knowledge to a central planning agency. Arrow, in two seminal articles published in the same year (1962a, b), developed the economics of knowledge creation that was to lay the foundations for two main strands of research (on problems of allocating resources to the creation of knowledge, defined as a public good, and on endogenous technical change).

Machlup's work covers a vast domain. Its dimensions are the consequence of an extremely broad conception of the economics of knowledge, encompassing the economics of information, in particular, and consequently theoretical problems of decision making. Defining information as "a certain type of knowledge," Machlup (1984) is naturally led to extend the economics of knowledge to include not only an analysis of information sectors and industry, an examination of the production of new knowledge, and a study of mechanisms of skills acquisition and transfer, but also an exploration of the vast domain of economic theory of choices and expectations in situations of uncertainty and incomplete information. In this respect Machlup's approach is similar to that of Hayek who uses the terms *knowledge* and *information* interchangeably, especially when studying the role of the pricing system as a mechanism in the communication of information. For Richardson (1960) the problem is similarly that of the availability of technological information for improving the coordination of activities in the market. All these authors see human decision making as being at the heart of economics, and the presence or absence of knowledge and information as factors that crucially determine the conditions in which decisions are made. There is no real difference between knowledge and information, which means that the scope of the economics of knowledge is defined very broadly (a quick look at the seventeen subject groups listed by Machlup (1984, chap. 10) gives an idea of just how broad it is).

A more restrictive conception of the economics of knowledge excludes problems of economic choice in situations of incomplete and uncertain information and focuses more specifically on what I would call "expertise"—namely, knowledge. Here, knowledge is above all a cognitive capacity, which is what distinguishes it clearly from information. This conception was developed in France, in particular, by J. L. Maunoury whose book *Economie du Savoir*, published in 1972, was unquestionably the precursor. Maunoury focused essentially on the system of production and acquisition of knowledge, of which

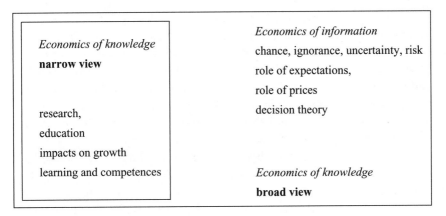

**Figure 1.1**
The scope of the discipline (narrow and broad view)

research and education are the two mainstays, and on the relationship between this system and economic growth.

Choosing between these two conceptions is difficult. Finding one's way between the very broad definition of the economics of knowledge, encompassing the economics of information and theory of choice, and the narrower definition consisting essentially of analyzing education and research, is no simple matter—especially since the economics of knowledge in a narrow sense has expanded since Maunoury's day. It now includes not only deliberate forms of knowledge production and acquisition, corresponding to the main education and research institutions, but also the vast domain of learning processes that describe increasingly numerous situations in which expertise is produced in the framework of "regular" production and use of goods and services. By extension, this economics of knowledge encompasses the notion of competence and the capacity to learn (Garrouste 2001).

The definition of the scope of the discipline (figure 1.1) depends on one's conception of knowledge and information, which I now consider more closely.

**Exploring the Black Box of Knowledge**
For a long time economic analysis equated knowledge with information. Based on this amalgam, economic analysis adopts a particular approach to knowledge information—namely, the universe can be described by a finite (but very large) set of states to which probabilities

can be assigned (Laffont 1989). Knowledge improves when the probability of a particular state is estimated more accurately. Knowledge can therefore be expressed by a vector of probabilities relating to a predetermined set of states. Of course there is a huge practical advantage in adopting this type of approach, but it still does not enable economists to grasp phenomena as important as learning and cognition.

In my conception, knowledge has something more than information: knowledge—in whatever field—empowers its possessors with the capacity for intellectual or physical action. What I mean by knowledge is fundamentally a matter of cognitive capability. Information, on the other hand, takes the shape of structured and formatted data that remain passive and inert until used by those with the knowledge needed to interpret and process them. The full meaning of this distinction becomes clear when one looks into the conditions governing the reproduction of knowledge and information. While the cost of replicating information amounts to no more than the price of making copies (i.e., next to nothing, thanks to modern technology), reproducing knowledge is a far more expensive process because cognitive capabilities are not easy to articulate explicitly or to transfer to others: "we can know more than we can tell" (Polanyi 1966, 4). Knowledge reproduction has therefore long hinged on the "master-apprentice" system (where a young person's capacity is molded by watching, listening, and imitating) or on interpersonal transactions among members of the same profession or community of practice. These means of reproducing knowledge may remain at the heart of many professions and traditions, but they can easily fail to operate when social ties unravel, when contact is broken between older and younger generations, and when professional communities lose their capacity to act in stabilizing, preserving, and transmitting knowledge. In such cases, reproduction grinds to a halt and the knowledge in question is in imminent danger of being lost and forgotten.

Therefore, the reproduction of knowledge and the reproduction of information are clearly different phenomena. While one takes place through learning, the other takes place simply through duplication. Mobilization of a cognitive resource is always necessary for the reproduction of knowledge, while information can be reproduced by a photocopy machine.

As observed by Steinmueller (2002a), by failing to differentiate between knowledge and information, economics—a discipline that often has an imperialistic attitude toward the other social sciences—

has, quite surprisingly, left a vast field open to other disciplines. This field consists of the subjects "learning" and "cognition," two central themes in my conception of knowledge.

A further complication is the fact that knowledge can be codified— so articulated and clarified that it can be expressed in a particular language and recorded on a particular medium. Codification involves the exteriorization of memory (Favereau 2001). It hinges on a range of increasingly complex actions such as using a natural language to write a cooking recipe, applying industrial design techniques to draft a scale drawing of a piece of machinery, creating an expert system from the formalized rules of inference underlying the sequence of stages geared to problem solving, and so on. As such, knowledge is detached from the individual, and the memory and communication capacity created is made independent of human beings (as long as the medium upon which the knowledge is stored is safeguarded and the language in which it is expressed is remembered). Learning programs are then produced that partially replace the person who holds and teaches knowledge.

When knowledge is differentiated from information, economic problems relating to the two can be distinguished. Where knowledge is concerned, the main economic problem is its reproduction (problem of learning), while the reproduction of information poses no real problem (the marginal cost of reproduction is close to nothing). The economic problem of information is essentially its protection and disclosure, that is, a problem of public goods. However, the codification of knowledge creates an ambiguous good. This good has certain properties of information (public good) but its reproduction as knowledge requires the mobilization of cognitive resources.

**Example of a Paradox Resolved by the Distinction between Knowledge and Information**  Paradoxically, in view of the enormous advances in information and communication technologies, many trades and professions are experiencing a crisis regarding the transmission of expertise and knowledge, both vertically between masters and apprentices, and horizontally between experienced practitioners (see OECD 1999a on the case of education and health). The paradox disappears, however, when one distinguishes between problems of reproduction of knowledge and those of transmission of information. Moreover, in all the occupations concerned it is shortcomings in the social networks (which previously played the part of transmitting and building on expertise—see chapter 4) that explain these problems of reproduction of knowledge, and there is nothing obvious about offsetting these weaknesses with new communication technologies.

**What Is the Meaning of the French (German and Spanish) Distinction between *Connaissance* ("Kenntnis," "conocer") and *Savoir* ("Wissen," "saber")?** The French language offers a distinction between *savoir* and *connaissance* that has no real equivalent in English, though it can be conveyed by adding the qualifier *certified*. Certified knowledge ("savoir") means knowledge that has been legitimized by some institutional mechanism (be it scientific peer review or any kind of rituals and belief systems in oral societies). Other forms of knowledge ("connaissance") also enable action (knowing how to do the gardening) but have not been put through the same tests as certified knowledge. What separates the two has less to do with a contrast between the scientific and nonscientific than with whether or not the knowledge has been subjected to institutional testing: "gardening knowledge" is reliable, wide-ranging, and relatively decontextualized, but each gardener has his or her own local (and locality-specific) knowledge. Yet the economics of knowledge does not preclude either form, meaning that it is not devoted solely to the analysis of formal production of "certified knowledge."

**Narrowing the Scope of the Discipline**   In view of this conception of knowledge and information, I now turn away from the economics of information and decision theory and focus essentially on knowledge in the strict sense of the word (as a cognitive capacity). I am thus opting for a narrow conception of the economics of knowledge, although the field I wish to study—research, learning processes, positive externalities, problems of coordination of innovative activities, and codified and tacit knowledge—is vast and covers many areas as yet unexplored.

**Economists' Difficulties Concerning the Economics of Knowledge**

**Categories that No Longer Fit**
To apprehend knowledge, economists constructed a "comfortable world" in which only some agents, institutions, and sectors were specialized in the production of knowledge. R&D laboratories at the corporate level and "knowledge industries" at the level of the economy

were the main categories of a "world" that excluded a large part of all activities and agents, considered not to be stakeholders in the economics of knowledge.

**Economists' Comfortable World**   With regard to innovation in enterprise, economists reduced knowledge production to the function of R&D, defined as the activity specifically devoted to invention and innovation. This representation can be credited with the generation of the immensely useful and extensive collection of data and production of statistics at the international level. But analysis of R&D covers only a small part of all innovation and knowledge production activities.

Economists similarly delimited a number of sectors in the economy, specifically devoted to the production and manipulation of knowledge and information. Machlup (1962), rightly seen as the founder of this tradition, studied the economic importance of the knowledge-based economy, identified as a specialized sector and consisting primarily of activities relating to communication, education, the media, and computing and information-related services. This statistical frame of analysis generated abundant research, commissioned mainly by the OECD. Despite significant methodological variations, all these studies were grounded in the same basic logic of defining a specialized sector covering all activities related to the production and processing of information.

Representations were therefore produced to deal with problems of indicators and quantification on the basis of stabilized information and knowledge and skillfully used measurement tools. But the price to pay is high: representations formed in this way fail, to a large extent, to explain knowledge-based economies.

**From R&D to Learning Processes**   Of course all knowledge produced in a firm cannot be attributed to formal research activities. Depending on the sector and the firm, the share of formal research in knowledge production can range from "huge" to "minute." Other major activities can also play a part.

First, design and engineering play an important role in the growth of knowledge. This role has been clearly identified by Vicenti (1990) who shows that design is an essential locus for the autonomous production of knowledge. The articulation between research and design then raises a series of important questions, since the idea of autonomous production of knowledge implies that design and technology are not subordinate to science and R&D (they are not "applied science").

Second, any activity involving the production or use of a good (or service) can generate learning and hence knowledge production. In other words, in many activities knowledge production is not the goal but may nevertheless occur. Knowledge is a by-product of the activity of production or use. This is where we find the well-known forms of "learning by doing" and "learning by using," concepts formulated by Arrow (1962b) and Rosenberg (1982), respectively. These studies progressively revealed that this type of learning process occupies an essential place in the economics of knowledge. It became more and more evident that certain types of strongly "motivated" and explicitly cognitive learning had economic effects that could go much further than just the consequence of doing one's job better by repeating the same actions. But measuring knowledge produced by learning is difficult.

**From Specialized Sectors to the Entire Economy**   Eliasson (1990) developed an important innovation when he broke away from Machlup's tradition which basically defined a specialized sector encompassing all activities related to the production and processing of knowledge, and measured its contribution to the gross domestic product (GDP). Eliasson considers that knowledge production and information processing are located in all economic activities, including in low technology–intensive sectors. In other words, the advent of the knowledge-based economy is manifested less in the continuous expansion of a specialized sector than in the proliferation of knowledge-intensive activities throughout all sectors of the economy. But here again measurement is complicated. I return to this point in the next chapter.

Both approaches—the analysis of either a specialized sector or of the generalization of knowledge-intensive activities throughout the entire economy—have their pros and cons. However, using the former exclusively may produce serious policy failures. For example, if the conclusion that net job creation takes place only in knowledge-intensive parts of the economy were interpreted in the framework of an approach that reduced the knowledge-based economy to a specialized sector, it could lead to bad choices being made in education policy.

## Unobservable Phenomena and Problems of Measurement

Yet traditional categories—R&D in the corporate world and the information sectors in the national economy, which, as mentioned earlier, could not contain all knowledge-producing activities—had a big advantage. They provided a way of measuring by facilitating the identification of knowledge-intensive activities. This in itself is ample justification for the category, because most phenomena relating to knowledge are largely unmeasurable. Apart from the question of the definition of knowledge, mentioned earlier, the main problems involved in measurement include:

1. Elements of knowledge are heterogenous. No comparison can possibly be made between the invention of writing and the discovery of a new distant star.

2. Knowledge is largely unobservable. The observation of knowledge (and especially tacit knowledge; see chapter 4) seems simply impossible. The most distinctive feature of tacit knowledge is its incorporation in thoughts and deeds, and its invisibility, even for those who possess it and use it "automatically." Knowledge appears only when it is expressed and written and when it becomes possible to attach a property right to it. Yet tacit knowledge is constantly being reconstituted, so that a vast world remains perpetually invisible.

3. There is no stable model that can be used to convert inputs (into the creation of knowledge) and outputs (economic effects). There is no stable formula such as the one used ceteris paribus to link an increase in the quantity of steel to growth in car production. Knowledge, unlike classic capital goods, has no fixed capacity in terms of impact of an additional quantity on the economy. Depending on the prevailing spirit of initiative, the situation of competition or the social organization, a new idea can trigger huge change or have no effect (see Quah 1999, who thus explains China's technological stagnation from the fourteenth century onwards). Thus, there is no production function that can be used to forecast, even approximately, the effect that a unit of knowledge will have on economic performance. Conversely, it is very difficulty to impute an economic effect to particular knowledge. Effects of externality and cumulativity do not make it possible to identify with any certainty an element of knowledge as being behind a particular improvement in the economy. Or else that imputation is at a very general level (e.g., "information technology is at the origin of a particular effect on the economy").

4. Finally, measuring stocks, already difficult in the case of physical capital, becomes an impossible undertaking in the case of knowledge. How could the composition of a stock be defined? What should be selected or rejected in this vast domain encompassing practical, intellectual, and spiritual knowledge: knowledge of perpetual value and significance, and knowledge of fleeting importance; knowledge which is important for many and that which is valued by very few?

Moreover, from a theoretical point of view, serious problems of additivity appear when we want to measure the stock of an entire society (or social group). In the economy of tangible goods, this problem of addition is governed by laws which link a prototype to various scales of mass-produced products, or an original to a small or large number of copies. But knowledge defies both of these laws. There is neither a prototype nor an original, so that the notion of an additional unit is meaningless. It is as if one were trying to measure a stock of flames. Each neighbor can take fire from the others without reducing the size of the fire of the person who had it first. Thus, in a sense, when knowledge appears it is potentially available to all. There is no difference between the situation in which one theorem of Pythagoras exists and one in which a billion such theorems exist. Yet we cannot consider that anyone in the world has the means or opportunity to have access to this element of knowledge. It is knowledge that is useful to some, useless to others, and an impenetrable mystery to others still. We thus arrive at the notion of the absorptive capacity (or learning capacity) of a society, the importance of which is variable for each type of knowledge and probably brings us closer to the measurement of stock.

Finally, the depreciation of knowledge is governed by a wide variety of "laws" (forgetfulness, obsolescence), and it seems that no one rule can adequately account for it (Machlup 1984).

It is possible to observe and measure the resources allocated to knowledge production activities (primarily R&D spending) as well as the results of these activities expressed either in the form of specific outputs (patents, publications, software, new products) or of economic variables, thought to be related to the production of new knowledge. The difficulties mentioned earlier disappear to a large extent when we measure contributions to knowledge (R&D, human resources, patents, and publications) and the product of knowledge (social and private outputs, innovation).

**Table 1.1**
Framework for Indicators in the Economics of Knowledge; Application to the Health
Sector

| Category | Concepts | Indicators |
| --- | --- | --- |
| Inputs | Person-years, equipment-years | Expenditures |
| | Organizational capacity | Use of particular organizational practices |
| Outputs | Ideas, discoveries | Papers, prizes |
| | New products | Patents, new drug applications |
| Outcomes or impacts | Broad advance of human knowledge | Papers, citations, expert evaluations |
| | Improvements in health status and length of life | Outcome studies, life expectancy |
| | Reduction in healthcare expenditures | Outcome studies, statistical analyses of healthcare expenditures |
| | Economic output | Revenue growth, revenue from new products, profitability |
| | Productivity improvements | Productivity studies |

*Source:* Jaffe (1999).

But this is proximation, which does not directly measure knowledge. Very recent and extremely sophisticated studies have therefore tried to measure flows of knowledge (Jaffe and Trajtenberg 1996) or even the degree to which certain knowledge is fundamental (Henderson, Jaffe, and Trajtenberg 1998). In order to do so the authors use what is observable, namely, patents and citations.

These indicators, summarized in table 1.1 for the health sector, are therefore necessary. Yet they illuminate only a small fraction of all economic activity in a sector producing or exploiting new knowledge.

For many sectors (e.g., education), the part of the economics of knowledge that remains unknown is far greater than the part that is known. That is generally the case with sectors in which R&D plays a relatively small role compared to multiple learning experiences that are difficult to grasp. As A. Carter (1996) put it, the indicators in table 1.1 basically shed light on the tip of the iceberg only. That is why use and interpretation of these indicators for exploring and measuring the economics of knowledge always require the economist to have a certain degree of faith.

But if we cannot measure knowledge itself, why not add up the values of knowledge-related transactions (the method usually applied in many cases when there is no clearly defined unit of output)? Unfortunately, our market institutions face daunting problems when a price has to be set for knowledge. The reasons are interesting:

• the seller—by selling knowledge—does not lose anything; knowledge is acquired definitively, even if it is shared or sold afterward;

• the buyer does not need to buy the same knowledge several times, even if it is to be used several times;

• the buyer cannot really assess the value of knowledge without actually acquiring it.

For these reasons (the first two of which will be considered in chapter 5 because they express the "nonrival" property of knowledge) the prices fixed are unique and specific and can never be used as consistent and reliable indicators. Insofar as prices have to be determined, they can vary widely from one transaction to the next. A huge proportion of knowledge is not traded in the framework of monetary transactions; it is accumulated in firms, other organizations, and actor networks without any value being attributed to it.

**Modeling Knowledge**
It is toward growth models that endogenize technological change that we naturally turn to evaluate the capacity of neoclassical theory to solve problems of the economics of knowledge. Two aspects of the modelling of endogenous growth are relevant here. First, in these models firms benefit from R&D investments because they are able to control at least part of the resulting productivity growth or product improvement. Second, markets are assumed not to be perfectly competitive. This makes it possible to obtain a market equilibrium in conditions of increasing returns (generated by the production of knowledge; see chapter 3). The endogenization of technological progress in these models was completed by the construction or deduction of other phenomena, for example, creative destruction that captures the process of depreciation of older technologies when new ones appear; or externalities derived from R&D and education. Finally, in many of these models the rate of investment in new plants and equipment affects the regularity of the growth rate. These models therefore afford many angles from which to study why and how growth rates

differ in time and from one country to the next (see Aghion and Howitt 1998, for an overview).

Of course this short presentation hardly does justice to the richness of this research. It helps, however, to show that these studies served to bring formal theoretical work on economic growth closer to what Abramovitz (1989) called the immediate determinants of growth. Yet many other aspects of the economics of knowledge, of the utmost importance in explaining the determinants of growth, are still overlooked or considered only superficially. Nelson (1994) identifies three other issues:

1. Knowledge itself, the vehicle of externalities, is always represented in models of endogenous growth in the form of a written expression, a manual, a computer program, in short, a set of codified instructions which provide access to immediate and free exploitation of the technology. This is of course a huge simplification, with disastrous consequences on our understanding of knowledge-based economies (Dosi 1996). A large share of knowledge does not appear in the form of codified instructions; it is tacit and naturally excludable, which sharply reduces the dimension of externalities.

2. The firm remains a black box. Given the public knowledge infrastructure and the opportunities to invest in private technologies, firms choose their strategies to maximize profits, taking into account market conditions. But mastery of a new technology or new knowledge is an extremely complex process that each firm will succeed in to a greater or lesser degree, depending on its organization and forms of management and strategy. Economists of innovation, as well as specialists of corporate history and management, use the term *corporate capability* or *corporate competence* to convey these different aspects (Dosi, Teece, and Winter 1992). Yet very few economists of endogenous growth seem prepared to take into consideration the diversity in firms' capacities to innovate as a key element explaining economic growth.

3. Finally, the corporate environment, apart from the market, plays an essential role which, once again, is seldom recognized in endogenous growth models. Many aspects of that environment are determining factors in economic growth, including relations with universities, the quality of the intellectual property rights (IPR) system or of the functioning of the financial market, and laws governing the labor market. The concept of a national innovation system (Carlsson and Stankiewicz 1991; Foray and Freeman 1992; Lundvall 1992; Nelson 1993; Edquist

1997) helps to explain those clusters of institutions which, at the national level, strongly influence firms' innovation strategies and performance. This concept is more relevant than ever at a time of knowledge-based economies.

This brief review is intended primarily to highlight the importance, for economic research, of constant dialogue and mutual attentiveness between the formal theory of growth and what is called *appreciative theories*. Recent work by Keely and Quah (1998) on formal theory shows just how fruitful such dialogue can be.

## Economic Issues

In order to understand better the "economics of knowledge" I broadly outline the general problems of the discipline. It starts with the analysis of the peculiar properties of knowledge as an economic good and proceeds to the normative analysis of resource allocation mechanisms in the field of knowledge production and distribution and, more generally, socioeconomic institutions that can be relied upon to produce, mediate, and use knowledge efficiently.

I simply point out some features which are problematic, not only because they make it difficult to observe and measure knowledge but because they complicate the issues of building efficient mechanisms of resource allocation in both static and dynamic worlds.

## Knowledge Creation

**New Knowledge Stems from a Discovery or Invention**   Much knowledge is produced by invention, that is, it does not exist as such in nature and is "produced" by man. Other types of knowledge stem from discoveries, that is, the accurate recognition of something which already existed but which was concealed. Invention is the result of production; discovery the result of revealing. This distinction, although it may seem vague in many cases (the hammer is an invention but the use of the first hammer, an appropriately shaped stone, was probably a discovery), has many implications for the economics of knowledge. In terms of incentives, one can claim an intellectual property right on an invention, not a discovery. One can patent a new machine but one cannot patent a fresh water spring even if one has "discovered" it. As a result, recurrent debate on the nature of novelty in certain disciplines such as mathematics—is it an invention or a discovery?—has extensive economic implications.

This distinction is also important in terms of the mode of development of knowledge. If knowledge stems from successive discoveries, there must be constants in research activities—like explorers who discover the same land and write different accounts about it containing common points. If, on the other hand, it stems from inventions, one can expect noteworthy differences, even if a number of socioeconomic forces lead toward the convergence of inventions.

**Knowledge Is Often a Joint Product**   Knowledge is very often produced in a context of activities in which other motivations (the manufacturing of a good or the provision of a service) are predominant. People learn by doing or by using (chapter 3). There is learning-by-doing or learning-by-using because knowledge is not absolute but must be defined in relation to a specific physical context (Tyre and von Hippel 1997). Such a characteristic gives many activities an important potential value in terms of knowledge production and innovation: those activities related, for instance, to the introduction of a novel type of equipment, organization, or method. There are, however, inherent limitations to the production of knowledge in this kind of context. Constraints and limitations are due to the basic tension and conflict between the "doing" aspect (the performance to be achieved at the end of the day) and the "learning" aspect (the experiment that is carried out as a consequence of "doing"). Maximizing learning benefits implies tolerating a certain degree of deterioration of static efficiency.

## On Some Properties that Magnify the Social Benefits of Knowledge Creation

**Knowledge Is Partially Nonexcludable and Nonrival**   These properties are investigated in depth in chapter 5 and their welfare economic aspects are discussed in chapter 6. At this point, it is enough to say that making knowledge exclusive and controlling it privately are difficult and costly. Knowledge continuously escapes from the entities producing it. Second, knowledge is nonrival, meaning that economic agents are not rival users of knowledge. Knowledge can theoretically be used by a million people at no additional cost because its use by an additional agent does not imply the production of an additional copy of that knowledge. This characteristic is a form of nonconvexity or an extreme form of decreasing marginal costs as the scale of use is increased. The aforementioned properties define what is meant by a pure public good and, as such, create a difference between the private and the social return in the domain of knowledge production. Recipients of knowledge largely extend beyond those who have produced it and can be multiplied ad infinitum, both geographically, in space, and historically, in time.

**Knowledge Is (Often) Cumulative**  Those external benefits can be made even stronger in the case of "cumulative" knowledge. It is the attribute of cumulativeness that distinguishes knowledge as consumption capital (enabling people to undertake "final" action: I know how to garden; I know how to paint) and knowledge as an intellectual input (enabling people to create new knowledge and thus to broaden the spectrum of possible future actions). Most knowledge in mathematics is cumulative because it may give rise to new ideas and open new lines of research.

**The "Comedy of the Knowledge Commons"**  Owing to these three properties, the production of knowledge has the potential to create a "combinatorial explosion." This is a good which is difficult to control and which can be used infinitely, to produce other knowledge which in turn is nonexcludable, nonrival and cumulative, and so on. In many cases knowledge is also deliberately disclosed and organized in order to facilitate its access and reproduction by others. All these processes give rise to the creation and expansion of "knowledge commons." "Knowledge commons" are not subject to the classic tragedy of commons that describes the case where exhaustible resources (such as a pasture or a shoal of fish) are subject to destruction by unregulated access and exploitation (see chapter 8). Knowledge may be used concurrently by many, without diminishing its availability to any of the users, and will not become "depleted" through intensive use. As Paul David writes (2001, 56), "Knowledge is not like forage, depleted by use for consumption; knowledge is not subject to being "overgrazed" but instead is likely to be enriched and rendered more accurate the more researchers, engineers or craft workers are allowed to comb through it." The properties of nonexcludability, nonrivalry, and cumulativeness have features akin to quasiinfinite increasing returns. Thus, the commons is not tragic, but comedic, in the classical sense of a story with a happy outcome (Rose 1986). Managing the "knowledge commons" requires social regulations that are entirely different to the social arrangements used to regulate ecological systems of exhaustible resources.

## On Some Properties of Knowledge that Impede the Full Realization of Social Benefits

Social benefits stemming from the full exploitation of the "knowledge commons" are, however, neither obvious nor automatic. New knowledge is most often partially localized and weakly persistent, tacit and sticky, dispersed and divided.

**Knowledge Is Partially Localized and Weakly Persistent**   Apart from strategic choices of private agents who are inclined to impose exclusivity on their knowledge (through secrecy and intellectual property rights), new knowledge is most often not of general value for the economy because it has been produced in a local context for particular purposes. A large body of literature argues that the production of knowledge is at least partially localized: learning that improves one technology may have little or no effect on other technologies (Atkinson and Stiglitz 1969; Antonelli 1999, 2001). The process toward generalization of knowledge is a very difficult one. It involves, for instance, the creation of theoretical knowledge that can fit in many local situations, or the search for analogic links among fields and disciplines, or the identification of similarities between the professional knowledge of various occupations. However, the degree of standardization and maturation of technology and knowledge can mitigate these difficulties (Cowan et al. 2002).

Moreover, knowledge is weakly persistent. Evidence in the psychological literature show that people forget. If the practice of a task is interrupted, forgetting occurs. Hirsch (1952) found that when performance was resumed after an interruption it was lower than the level achieved prior to the interruption. Moreover, knowledge can be depreciated (through deterioration and obsolescence). Communities that are in possession of it can break up, resulting in the disintegration of their collective knowledge.

**New Knowledge Is Tacit and "Sticky"**   Typically, new knowledge and expertise have a broad tacit dimension, meaning that they are neither articulated nor codified. Tacit knowledge resides in people, institutions, or routines. Tacitness makes knowledge difficult to transport, memorize, recombine, and learn. Such difficulties can be overcome when the number of people possessing the tacit knowledge is high. In this case there will be a labor market that can be used to transport and transfer tacit knowledge. If the number of people is too small, tacitness increases the risk of "accidental uninvention" and hampers the full exploitation of knowledge. Given tacitness, knowledge is costly to transfer from one site to another in useable form. As von Hippel put it, knowledge is sticky (von Hippel 1994). Stickiness raises a number of issues in terms of the organization of knowledge production, product design, and system integration.

**Knowledge Is Dispersed and Divided**   There is a natural tendency for knowledge to fragment as it becomes subject to more in-depth division and dispersion (Machlup 1984). The division of knowledge stems from divisions of labor and increasing specialization in the field of knowledge production. Its dispersion is related to local situations in which knowledge is produced (a site, a workshop, a laboratory). The result is an extremely fragmented knowledge base, which makes it difficult to form a broad and integrated view of things. This can have disastrous consequences. At the level of global policy making, knowledge that can help resolve a particular problem may exist without being "visible." It can go unnoticed by the decision maker. Knowledge of the greenhouse effect, for instance, has been in the public domain since 1886, thanks to the study by Svente Arrenhuis, but failed to capture the attention of the political system for another hundred years. There is a big difference between the existence of knowledge in some or other place, and its availability to the right people in the right place at the right time. The crux of the matter is knowing how to integrate and organize fragmented, scattered, and thinly spread knowledge.

**Conclusion: The Aim of the Economics of Knowledge**

The aim of the economics of knowledge is thus to analyze and discuss institutions, technologies, and social regulations that can facilitate the efficient production and use of knowledge. Given the peculiar properties and features of knowledge as an economic good, most of the usual resource allocation mechanisms used in the world of tangible goods do not work properly to maximize knowledge creation and diffusion. In this perspective, the most important institutions are of two kinds: those which enable economic agents to appropriate the fruit of their intellectual creation, and those that make it possible to preserve, consolidate, and exploit "knowledge commons." The complexity of the institutional problem derives from the fact that these two objectives are both contradictory and indissociable. Moreover, depending on the nature of the knowledge, the "optimum solution" could vary widely. Thus, this problem is addressed differently in relation to the following three categories:

• knowledge is reducible to "consumption capital" (Machlup 1984)

• it constitutes productive capital (notion of cumulativeness presented earlier)

• it represents a piece of strategic information (notion of "aforeknowledge" developed by Hirshleifer 1971).

In this set of questions, only one agent knows that a particular event is going to occur and that it will change the structure of prices; he can therefore speculate on a given factor. For example, I know that an epidemic is likely to wipe out the entire bee population, so I stock honey.

This question is studied at length in chapter 6. The goal of the economics of knowledge is therefore to develop a framework in order to devise and compare socioeconomic institutions that can be relied upon to create and exploit knowledge in an efficient manner; that is, institutions that can sustain an efficient production and allocation of knowledge of all kinds.

# 2    Macro- and Microeconomic References: Continuity and Breaks

With the notion of knowledge-based economy, economists wish to introduce the idea of a break in growth processes and modes of organization of the economy. It can therefore give rise to skepticism, for knowledge has always been at the heart of economic development. The ability to invent and innovate, that is, to create new knowledge and new ideas that are then embodied in products, processes, and organizations, has always served to fuel development. And there have always been organizations and institutions capable of efficiently creating and disseminating knowledge: from the medieval guilds through to the large companies of the early twentieth century, from the Cistercian abbeys to the royal academies of science that began to emerge in the seventeenth century. The knowledge revolution that some talk about is more an information technology revolution that warrants no more attention than the textile or agricultural revolutions (Howitt 1996). Similarly, there have been no major changes in the macroeconomic functioning of our economies. The role of the new term *knowledge-based economy* is, therefore, to signify a change from the economies of earlier periods, but more a "sea-change" than a sharp discontinuity.

As indicated, this term refers to a development scenario in our economies, in which rapid knowledge creation and easy access to knowledge bases generate greater efficiency, quality, and equity. The realization of this scenario benefits from certain structural (institutional and technological) conditions whose implementation triggers other evolutions, not all desirable. It is this set of structural changes that we consider in this chapter.[2]

## A Slow Trend toward Increasing Resources Devoted to Knowledge Production, Mediation and Transmission

Economic historians point out that nowadays disparities in the productivity and growth of different countries have far less to do with their
abundance (or lack) of natural resources than with the capacity to
improve the quality of human capital and factors of production: in
other words, to create new knowledge and ideas and incorporate them
in equipment and people. Two related characteristics of economic
growth are discussed in the following section: (1) growth of the share
of intangible capital in the stock of real capital; and (2) expansion of
knowledge-intensive activities.

### Growth in the Share of Intangible Capital
A first characteristic of economic growth, that became increasingly
evident from the early twentieth century onward, is the growing relative importance of intangible capital in total productive wealth and
the rising relative share of GDP attributable to intangible capital
(Abramovitz and David 1996). Intangible capital largely falls into two
main categories: on the one hand, investment geared to the production
and dissemination of knowledge (i.e., in training, education, R&D,
information, and coordination); on the other, investment geared to sus-
taining the physical state of human capital (health expenditure). In
the United States the current value of the stock of intangible capital
(devoted to knowledge creation and human capital) began to outweigh
that of tangible capital (physical infrastructure and equipment, inven-
tories, natural resources) at the end of the 1960s.

Table 2.1
Stock of Real Gross Domestic Capital in the United States (in billions of dollars, 1987)

|                                     | 1929  | 1948  | 1973   | 1990   |
|-------------------------------------|-------|-------|--------|--------|
| Conventional tangible: total        | 6,075 | 8,120 | 17,490 | 28,525 |
| Structures and equipment            | 4,585 | 6,181 | 13,935 | 23,144 |
| Inventories                         | 268   | 471   | 1,000  | 1,537  |
| Natural resources                   | 1,222 | 1,468 | 2,555  | 3,843  |
| Nonconventional Nontangible total   | 3,251 | 5,940 | 17,349 | 32,819 |
| Education and training              | 2,647 | 4,879 | 13,564 | 25,359 |
| Health, safety, mobility            | 567   | 892   | 2,527  | 5,133  |
| R&D                                 | 37    | 169   | 1,249  | 2,327  |

Source: Kendrick (1994).

Focusing on economic growth in the United States, Abramovitz and David (1996) clearly show that although technology has advanced in leaps and bounds in the past two centuries, this development has always been biased. The fact that the nature of the bias has changed may be the first clue. Throughout the nineteenth century the bias in favor of tangible capital and general technological developments acted in favor of labor saving. Then from the 1920s technological progress boosted the share of "nonconventional" intangible capital as a factor of production. While the growth of tangible capital per hour of work constituted two-thirds of the growth of labor productivity in the second half of the nineteenth century, it contributed no more than one quarter or one fifth in the twentieth century. The new type of technological change thus identified increases the relative marginal productivity of capital constituted in the form of education and training of the workforce, practical skills acquired through R&D, and organizational structures (managerial structures, systems of information, control, marketing, user services). In particular, Abramovitz and David point out the persistence of high rates of return on education in the context of relatively rapid growth of the stock of capital represented by education and training.

This particular stylization of the history of technological progress is certainly consistent with the more institutional history of capitalism which focuses on (1) the way in which growing problems of industrial coordination at the turn of the century called for new management techniques and organizational structures (Chandler 1992); (2) the significant growth of educational institutions; and (3) the development of large research laboratories (Mowery 1990; Nelson and Wright 1992). However, the professionalization of R&D and the development of research structures in firms are relatively minor events, from the point of view of general economic change, compared to the discontinuity perceived in expenditure on education and training. (In the stock of intangible capital, estimated by Kendrick for the United States, R&D never accounts for more than one-sixteenth.)

**The Great Leap Forward in Learning**   One of the main characteristics distinguishing twentieth-century men and women from their predecessors is their ability to read. The twentieth century was the period of "great learning," to quote a title in *The Economist*. It is obvious, moreover, that this period of transformation is far from over. The frontiers of education are constantly being pushed back in two respects:

education is gradually reaching new fringes of the population and appearing at new stages of life (e.g., adult education and education for retired people). While the twentieth century was one in which decisive advances were made in the former respect, the present century will be characterized by a broadening of education to all stages of life. This switch to lifelong learning will trigger a new quantitative leap forward regarding efforts and resources devoted to education and training.

**The Increase in Knowledge-Related Investments** Recent work by the OECD has helped to produce stable categories of knowledge-related investment for given countries or sectors. Taking the simple yet highly restrictive measure of investment in research and development, public/private education and software, one can see that annual investment rates have grown strongly since the 1980s (at an average annual rate of 3 percent in the OECD countries). Between 1985 and 1992, the OECD countries spent an average of between 8 and 11 percent of their GDP on knowledge-related investments (public education, R&D, and software). The following figure provides most recent data for total investment in knowledge as a percentage of GDP for twenty-four OECD countries (1998). Total investment in knowledge amounts to 8.8 percent of GDP.

However, some studies (Minne 1996) show that the structure of these investments differs from one country to the next. Whereas in Scandinavian countries public education spending is highest (7 percent of the GDP), in the United States the share of investments in industry (R&D, software, computers, advertising) is predominant. More recent studies on Europe are likely to cause some perplexity. While intangible investments have increased substantially, like everywhere else, the actual structure of these investments is a cause for concern. Investments in R&D have dropped by 1.7 percent and remain at a low level. Yet, as readers shall see, knowledge externalities, so important for growth, are unquestionably generated by research.

The rapid increase in information and communications technologies (ICT) investments is another important element. Yet there are discrepancies between the United States, with its fast growing ICT sector, and Europe and Japan where the role of information technologies has remained stable since the early 1990s (OECD 1999b). I consider the role of these technologies in the advent of knowledge-based economies further on in this chapter.

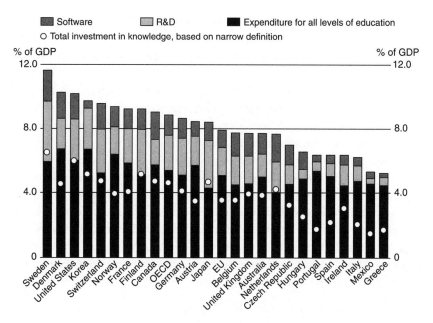

**Figure 2.1**
Knowledge investments (% GDP, 1998). *Source:* Khan (2001).

## Continuous Expansion of Knowledge-Intensive Activities

The trends previously described are reflected in the expansion of knowledge-intensive activities throughout the economy. I have already mentioned work by Machlup (1962), who defines a specialized sector specifically devoted to the production and processing of information. Machlup in further studies (1984) studied the contribution to the GDP and showed that in the United States it rose from 29 percent in 1958 to 34 percent in 1980. The statistical framework thus defined was the subject of many studies, most of which were commissioned by the OECD. All concluded that the information and knowledge industries were expanding regularly (Porat and Rubin 1977; Rubin and Huber 1984). The contribution of these industries to the GDP topped the 50 percent mark in all OECD countries in the mid-1980s.

The OECD has proposed a new unit of measurement, based on the contribution of knowledge-based sectors to the added value of firms (OECD 1998). This measure adds together all high-technology sectors (computing, space, pharmaceuticals, and soon), the ICT sector and related services, financial services and insurance companies, and services to business. In 1997 this category, called the "knowledge-based sectors," accounted for 35 percent of the added value of the business sector (OECD average). This figure has risen steeply in recent years.

Unlike these studies, which identify a sector specialized in knowledge, Eliasson (1990) proposes an important theoretical and methodological innovation. He considers that tasks relating to knowledge production and information processing are situated in all economic activities, including low technology-intensive sectors. In other words, the increase in the knowledge-intensity of the economic system is reflected less in the continuous expansion of a specialized sector than in the proliferation of knowledge-intensive activities in all sectors of the economy. The taxonomy of activities compiled by Eliasson is therefore functional. It records all operations, in all sectors, that contain any amount of production and processing of knowledge. These operations include the following main categories:

- creation of new knowledge: R&D, design
- economic coordination: marketing, distribution, administration
- internal transfer of knowledge: training

In this new framework Eliasson shows that, in the United States in 1980, 45.8 percent of all working hours were devoted to knowledge-intensive activities (as opposed to 30.7 percent in 1950).

Along the same lines as Eliasson's research, some economists propose measurements for growth in the intensity of knowledge in

**Table 2.2**
Labor Use in Different Countries (labor hours in percent of labor force)

|                                    | U.S.  |       |       | U.K.  |       |       | Japan |       |
| ---------------------------------- | ----- | ----- | ----- | ----- | ----- | ----- | ----- | ----- |
|                                    | 1950  | 1958  | 1980  | 1951  | 1971  | 1981  | 1960  | 1975  |
| **Category**                       |       |       |       |       |       |       |       |       |
| Knowledge creation                 | 5.0   | 7.2   | 9.7   | 3.9   | 5.0   | 8.8   | 2.1   | 4.5   |
| Economic coordination              | 23.4  | 29.9  | 31.7  | 20.8  | 27.4  | 27.7  | 13.9  | 22.7  |
| Knowledge and information transfer | 2.3   | 4.0   | 4.4   | 2.0   | 3.2   | 4.3   | 1.9   | 2.4   |
| Total                              | 30.7  | 41.1  | 45.8  | 26.7  | 35.6  | 40.8  | 17.9  | 29.6  |
| Other                              | 69.3  | 58.9  | 54.2  | 73.3  | 64.4  | 59.2  | 82.1  | 70.4  |
| Total                              | 100   | 100   | 100   | 100   | 100   | 100   | 100   | 100   |

*Source:* Eliasson (1990).

each sector. K. Smith (1995), in an attempt to formulate a synthetic measurement that, for a particular sector, takes into account R&D spending, employment rate of graduates, and rate of use of new technologies, shows changes in the intensity of knowledge between 1986 and 1994. He also shows that the increase in this intensity was much stronger during that period whenever the sector under consideration was already knowledge-intensive at the beginning of the period. This leads him to suggest that the gap between sectors is growing, at least in terms of this measurement.

**The Upheaval of Information and Communication Technologies**

In light of the century-old trend toward increases in growth-related investments and knowledge-intensive jobs, it is tempting to treat new ICT as a historic upheaval determining a marked discontinuity. This is not, however, an entirely accurate way of seeing things. It would be more relevant to talk of a continuous acceleration of the innovation rate in the field of ICT over the past fifty years, which is now leading to the famous convergence between informatics and telecommunications. Can we identify the causal links here between the advent of ICT and that of knowledge-based economies? Abramovitz and David (1996) maintain that technological discontinuity can be situated well after the switch of our economies toward knowledge-intensive activities. We must nevertheless agree that with ICT the knowledge-based economy found an appropriate technological base and that there has since been mutual consolidation between the upsurge of knowledge-intensive activities and the production and diffusion of new ICT. This has had three effects on the economy (Steinmueller 2002a):

• it allows productivity gains, particularly in the processing, storage, and exchange of information, a fundamental area in the knowledge-based economy where productivity gains were notoriously slow over the past few centuries (the impact of ICT on the "codification" of knowledge is examined in more detail in chapter 4);

• ICT favor the creation and growth of new industries (multimedia, e-commerce, software);

• they are an incentive to adopt original organizational models, with a view to better exploitation of new possibilities in the distribution and dissemination of information.

It took several decades before the historical upheaval was evident in the statistics. Everyone knows the episode of the productivity paradox. That phase, or at least the aspect of it that is strictly related to the diffusion of ICT, seems to be drawing to a close.

## ICT as a Knowledge Instrument

The ICT revolution is crucial insofar as it involves technologies geared to the production and dissemination of knowledge and information. These new technologies, which first emerged in the 1950s and then really took off with the advent of the Internet, have breathtaking potential. The immense potential for economic change offered by the new ICT system is particularly relevant to situations in which the main object of the transaction can be digitalized. This is the case for knowledge and information, but not for potatoes, for example. One can, of course, order potatoes on the Internet and pay with electronic money, but much of the transaction still depends on traditional ways of delivering goods which, to be efficient, still require a good truck and a skilled driver. By contrast, the full digitization of knowledge (of the codified expression of it) has the potential to generate dramatic changes in the knowledge economy. In addition to transmitting written texts and other digitizable items (music, pictures), the new ICT also allow users to access and work upon knowledge systems from a distance (e.g., remote experimentation), to take distance-learning courses within the framework of interactive teacher-student relations (tele-education) and to have large quantities of information—a sort of universal library—available on their desktops.

Information technologies can affect knowledge creation in a number of different ways. For a start, the mere fact that one has the capacity to create such a wealth of information is truly revolutionary. Imagine how hard it was for people to obtain instruments of knowledge before the modern age. Apart from a handful of marvelous centers of intellectual life such as the ancient library of Alexandria, such instruments were few and far between. The great eleventh century thinker Gerbert d'Aurillac had a library containing no more than twenty books (although that was quite a lot in those days). Even in the somewhat less perilous times of a few decades ago, imagine what a laborious task it was for students to produce a roundup of the "state of the art" in a particular subject or discipline, and the uphill struggle involved in remaining abreast of the latest findings in their field of study.

Development here has been a long, drawn out process punctuated by the invention of the codex and the book (which took over from scrolls), the perfecting of paper, the transformation of the book into a knowledge tool (reduction of size and illumination and, above all, creation of analytical systems such as abbreviations, contents pages, indexes, tables, footnotes, and endnotes (Le Goff 1985)); improvements in the productivity of copymaking (from the "industrial" organization of the scriptorium through to the invention of the printing press, (Eisenstein 1980; David 1988)); the proliferation of modern libraries, and; finally, the advent of increasingly efficient access and communication networks. Do new technologies signal an end to that evolution? Clearly not, for an enormous amount of progress remains to be made in such areas as information search systems. But this might almost be said to be the culmination of what the French medievalist Georges Duby once called the "relentless pursuit of instruments of knowledge" that has preoccupied humankind since the dark ages.

Second, ICT allow more flexibility regarding the constraint of physical proximity in many cognitive activities, such as distance learning and distance experimentation. Access from a distance not only to writing but also to other modes of expression of knowledge (especially gestures and words) revolutionizes possibilities for learning. It is true that many activities cannot be coordinated by virtual means alone. The emulation and spontaneity generated by physical presence and social groupings often remain crucial. Likewise, direct face-to-face exchanges are important when they enable other forms of sensory perception to be stimulated apart from those used within the framework of electronic interactions (Feldman 2002; Olson and Olson 2003). However, the influence of distance is waning now that the technological capacity is available for knowledge sharing, remote access and teamwork, and organizing and coordinating tasks over wide areas (see chapter 5).

Third, ICT are at the base of new modes of knowledge production. They enhance creative interaction not only between scholars and scientists but among product designers, suppliers, and the end customers. The creation of virtual objects that can be modified ad infinitum and instantly accessible to everyone, serves to facilitate collective work and learning and to increase dramatically the speed of prototyping and designing new products. In that respect, the new possibilities opened up by numerical simulation represent a key factor. ICT allow the exploration and analysis of the contents of gigantic databases, which is in itself a potent means of knowledge enhancement (in natural, human, and social sciences, and management alike). Research stimulated by such possibilities has a strong influence in some areas of managerial work.

Fourth, the previously mentioned three ways in which information technologies affect knowledge creation can be combined in the development of large-scale distributed systems for data gathering and calculation and the sharing of findings. Such systems characterize research currently under way in such fields as astronomy and oceanography.

Finally, ICT provide powerful opportunities for collective actions namely, the sharing of "rich" messages among a very large number of people, and, as such, they are the right tools for the creation and expansion of virtual communities (see chapter 8).

In the past fifteen years spectacular advances have been made in some types of jobs which are, in a sense, pioneers in the economics of knowledge. These include researchers, teachers and students, journalists and documentalists, architects, designers and engineers, lawyers, doctors, librarians, archivists, museum directors, and so on. These new information technologies are unquestionably the pedestal of knowledge-based economies insofar as they facilitate access to huge quantities of information and allow a rapid exchange of messages with increasingly rich content (text, image, sound, processes). It seems that new sections of the population, employed in activities less directly related to processes of creation, transmission, and conservation of knowledge, will progressively be affected by these technological advances (depending, fundamentally, on the extension and continuation of the first trend concerning human capital, considered above).

**Production and Adoption of ICT**
For roughly the past twenty-five years the establishment of the ICT technical system has continued relentlessly. Growth in the capacities of computers has gone hand in hand with the shrinking of their size and price. This evolution has been marked, in particular, by the proliferation of software technology and the convergence of informatics and telecommunications. It seems, moreover, that the technical system is still far from saturation (to use a concept of the French historian Bertrand Gille). The most recent technical publications clearly attest to the fact that R&D in ICT is still governed by increasing returns. Thus,

ICT production is one of the most R&D-intensive sectors, in which more new products and processes are expected (e.g., voice recognition systems to replace keyboards) and technological frontiers are being pushed back, extending the limits of miniaturization of silicon chips.

In parallel, the adoption of ICT has followed a classic S curve or, more precisely, a series of S curves corresponding to numerous microrevolutions in general technological development. It seems likely that the dynamics of production adoption will be strengthened by new tendencies to produce simplified, cheap computers whose main function will be access to the Internet and whose limited performance will be more suited to the majority of users' needs.

This dual movement of production and adoption is clearly summarized in table 2.3, taken from the work of Freeman and Soete (1997).

## The "Productivity Paradox"

The productivity paradox, as formulated by Solow—"we see computers everywhere, except in statistics"—is intended to highlight the weak impact of ICT on economic growth in the last three decades of the twentieth century. As economists know, this paradox is partly related to problems peculiar to measurement and data (Mairesse 1998; David 2000a). But it also raises three types of issues.

**Table 2.3**
Estimation of Increase in ICT Capacities

| Area of change | Late 1940s-early 1970s | Early 1970s-mid-1990s | Mid-1990s onwards "optimistic" scenario |
|---|---|---|---|
| OECD installed computer base (number of machines) | 30,000 (1965) | Millions (1985) | Hundred millions (2005) |
| OECD full-time software personnel | >200,000 (1965) | >2,000,000 (1985) | >10,000,000 (2005) |
| Components per microelectronic circuit | 32 (1965) | 1 megabit (1987) | 256 megabit (late 90s) |
| Leading representative computer: instructions per second | $10^3$ (1955) | $10^7$ (1989) | $10^9$ (2000) |
| Cost: computer thousand ops. per $U.S. | $10^5$ (1960s) | $10^8$ (1980s) | $10^{10}$ (2005) |

*Source:* Freeman and Soete (1997).

**On the Diffusion of a General-Purpose Technology**   Freeman and Soete (1997) and David (1991) analyze the diffusion of a new technology as a very long and complex process of both building complementarities at many levels (institutional, organizational, technical) and destroying the old system. Whatever concept is used—general purpose technology or a new techno-economic paradigm—the fact remains that the full realization of the potential of new ICT has been a process that has taken a long time and has been contingent on significant technical, organizational, and institutional adjustments.

Indeed, the establishment of ICT has always created technical, organizational, and managerial problems that subsequent technological generations have tried to solve, thus generating new problems. These difficulties and obstacles—a classic occurrence in any process of diffusion of a new technology—have, in the case of ICT, been particularly numerous and severe. They are part of what Steinmueller (2002a) calls "the hidden dimensions of the productivity paradox." Examples include problems of organizing information in storage units, which can generate substantial costs; problems of preserving information, once again generating substantial costs related to required equipment, apart from the cost of information losses; problems of the perpetual evolution of software which rapidly makes information impossible to decipher and can cause it to be irremediably lost; problems posed by the proliferation of peripheral equipment and constraints of interoperability between them; and problems of education and training that the kilograms of documentation supplied with each new computer certainly cannot help to solve.

Foray and Mairesse's recent book (1998) combines the contributions and reflections of economists, managers, and sociologists, showing the extent to which the exploitation of potential opportunities offered by these new technologies can be hampered by the inertia of forms of organization. There is probably a problem both in the actual creation of organizational knowledge (it is perhaps easier and quicker to increase the number of transistors in a microprocessor than to design a new organizational concept) and in the replacement of existing forms of organization.

In this respect I might suggest that laws of replacement and depreciation are of a different nature for physical capital equipment and forms of organization. While these laws ensure swift technological renewal, they do not allow for such quick renewal of "organizational equipment." This generates new sources of turbulence. Existing organizational systems create opportunities for managers to extract rents, and hence a capacity to resist change (whereas the existing physical equipment does not have such a capacity). These systematic discrepancies between the replacement of technical capital equipment and that of organizational equipment is a strong source of turbulence in the constitution of new technology (David 2000a). A key issue therefore deals with the invention of new forms of organization, the main principle of which is the network. As Coase (1937) forecast, the boundaries of the firm can shift under the impact of new communication technologies: "If the telephone reduces the cost of use of the price mechanism more than it reduces the cost of organization, it will have the effect of reducing the size of firms." ICT thus favor outsourcing and the network-firm model. This model is certainly idealized, for all too often the real costs of coordinating and "disciplining" a profusion of contracting parties and suppliers, whose interests never converge perfectly with those of the principal, are overlooked (Steinmueller 2002a). Yet these models remain viable and persist in all cases where products and services are clearly definable and their differentiation is not at the source of the firm's competitive advantages.

Finally, ICT and, in particular, the specific category of collaborative technologies, play a powerful supportive role in the collective production of knowledge. Thus, new industrial and innovative organizations are built around this network form, strongly based on ICT.

The concepts of technological and organizational trajectories and progressive adjustment of economic and social capacities to a technological revolution therefore seem relevant for explaining that the establishment of new technology takes time and that a long historical transition may occur before the potential advantages of that technology are effectively realized (Freeman and Soete 1997). David (1991), in particular, uses a historical analogy between the establishment of ICT and that of electricity, to underscore the importance of these periods of adjustment. David develops a model highlighting the importance of positive feedback from the increasing diffusion of the technology to the improvement of it. In such a dynamic system context, excess of inertia may occur (when market shares are too weak to provide momentum to both technological improvement and diffusion).

Obviously, such a theory predicts the end of the problem at some point in the future because it is essentially a matter of time. Indeed, the results of recent econometric studies on this subject show the now evident effect of ICT on growth and productivity, especially in individual firms (see Greenan and Mairesse 2000; Mairesse, Cette, and Kocoglu 2000; Brynjolfsson and Kahin 2000, for the most recent collection of empirical and analytical papers on these issues).

**One Sees Computers Everywhere, but Never the Same Ones**  A second argument about the productivity paradox addresses the issue that the general trend toward technological and organizational maturity masks a series of successive revolutions which are the cause of continuous profound changes in the use of ICT, particularly in the corporate environment. Each change, from centralized data processing (dedicated to calculation) to dispersed data processing (management tasks and local automation of tasks) and then network data processing (networking of tasks and expertise), has been an upheaval in forms of integration of ICT and modes of organization of firms.

Thus, another source of concern must be sought in the very specific properties of the general trajectory of ICT, which constantly generates new waves of innovations as sources of endless turbulence. The average life span of a computer is three years and that of software is certainly even less. Constant upgrading of software and hardware, inevitable for the individual user (or entity) due to constraints of interconnectivity and interoperability, creates an atmosphere of continuous change. This observation relates back to the problems posed by the productivity paradox. The key to the paradox is probably less in the time spent on progressive adjustment of economic and social organization to the new technology (which makes it possible to predict the end of the problem in the short term), than in this economy of perpetual and radical change that constantly undermines the base of productivity gains. To be sure, one sees computers everywhere, but never the same ones! The nature of the problem changes, as society shifts from an economy of diffusion of generic technologies to one of constant innovation in which the return to a regular regime seems to be perpetually postponed.

**ICT Skepticism**  Finally, some economists claim that there is no paradox because the potential for economic changes offered by new ICT is not that great, which is why one does not see a big impact in statistics. Somewhat irritated by the Internet gurus who claim the "Internet is the greatest invention since the wheel, and there is a need for a new "economics" to understand how this revolution will change economic laws," some macroeconomists jump too fast from commendable rigor to a crude skepticism. When looking at the data they conclude that this is a conventional story of a technology revolution resulting in economic growth. They claim that the underlying economic relationships themselves have not changed. New technologies are contributing to recent economic gains in ways which are consistent with conventional economic theory (Styroh 2001). All of that looks perfectly reasonable. However, macroeconomists, by training and tradition, do not pay attention to the microlevel details of innovation and new technologies. They therefore fail to develop a proper analysis of the technology itself and its future impact on the organization and conduct of economic activities. And their arguments become less reasonable when claiming that the Internet is an insignificant toy: when the technology bubble bursts on the stock market, its economic benefits will turn out to be no greater than the seventeen century tulip bubble (*The Economist* 2000). Gordon (2000), in particular, develops the argument that the new ICT revolution does not measure up to the great inventions of the late nineteenth and early twentieth centuries.

There is, thus, a danger in moving too fast from a moderate and reasonable interpretation of the new economy to a moderate interpretation of the new technology. The various arguments developed here on new ICT as a significant step in the evolution of knowledge instruments show that there is no inconsistency in being both a new economy skeptic and a new technology enthusiast!

## The Age of Rapid Growth of Knowledge and of Knowledge Flows

The encounter between the two phenomena studied in the previous two sections has spawned a unique economy, characterized essentially by an increase in the number of agents capable of producing, diffusing, and absorbing knowledge, and a substantial decrease in the marginal costs of information and knowledge processing. This twofold phenomenon has resulted in major changes in systems of knowledge creation and distribution.

### The Rapid Growth of Knowledge

One major trend concerns the accelerating speed at which knowledge is created and accumulated, reflecting an intensified pace of scientific and technological progress. Three factors can briefly be noted:

• the role of science in the implementation of scientific knowledge bases, directly useful to industrial innovation;

• the appearance of a system of increasingly decentralized knowledge creation, in which the production of innovations is a more socially distributed function;

• the evolution of industrial architectures toward more complexity and modularity, creating a greater need for new types of knowledge known as *integrative knowledge* (e.g., standards, common architectures).

These factors are explored in more depth in chapter 3.

### The Increasing Production and Use of Codified Knowledge

A key factor of rapid growth of knowledge and learning externalities is the extension of capacities to codify knowledge, that is, to express knowledge independently of the person holding it. This makes it possible to multiply "copies" of knowledge at a very low cost and to create new objects of knowledge (from the list and table to the mathematical formula). These two properties are explored in depth in chapter 4. Abramovitz and David (1996, 35) concluded in their work on the economic history of U.S. growth: "The main characteristic of modern economic growth has been the increasing use of codified knowledge as a basis for the organization and performance of economic activities. While tacit knowledge continues to play a critical part, the codification of knowledge is both the cause and the most common form of expansion of the knowledge base."

### Knowledge Flows and Externalities

The knowledge externalities of interest here are said to be *nonpecuniary*. They denote the fact that knowledge produced by an agent benefits other agents without financial or any other kind of compensation. Since knowledge is difficult to control, its consumption is nonrival and often cumulative.

Knowledge externalities have existed throughout history but have, as a rule, been few and far between and relatively feeble. Their magnitude was historically limited by the high level of the costs of codifying, reproducing, and transmitting knowledge, as well as by the prevailing attitudes that obstructed the widespread disclosure of "Nature's secrets." But knowledge externalities become potentially very strong when codification, reproduction, and transmission costs fall at the margin, depending on the dynamics of ICT as a knowledge instrument and on the increasing resources devoted to knowledge-related investments. This topic is fully developed in chapter 5 and its welfare aspects are discussed in chapter 6.

A new kind of organization is spearheading the phenomenon by providing proper incentive and coordination structures to manage and fully harness the knowledge externalities. I develop, in particular, the notion of "knowledge communities" to grasp the emergence and expansion in the economy of these new organizations which are explicitly devoted to the production and reproduction of knowledge through decentralized and cooperative procedures and an intensive use of new ICT. Although knowledge-driven communities are not the whole story of a knowledge society, and a focus upon them will not uncover everything of interest concerning the economics of knowledge, their organizational forms and functions will become or have already become of wider relevance in a knowledge society. This is evident in the cases of scientific research communities and, more recently, open source software development communities. It is also obvious in many cases of user communities. The value of studying them as new kinds of "machinery of knowing" is therefore particularly high. In such communities and networks, individuals are striving to produce and circulate new knowledge and working for different, even rival, organizations. One sign that a knowledge-based economy is developing is seen when such individuals penetrate conventional organizations, to which their continuing attachment to an "external" knowledge-based community represents a valuable asset. As members of these communities develop their collective expertise, they become agents of change for the economy as a whole (see chapter 8).

It is enough to say now that the knowledge-based economy is clearly an economy in which knowledge externalities are more powerful than ever, consequent to this twofold trend of ICT development and increasing investments in education and learning, and in which new organizational concepts such as knowledge communities are flourishing.

## Change Becomes the Main Economic Activity

One hypothesis regularly put forward to characterize the knowledge-based economy relates to the increasingly important role of change as an economic activity (Carter 1994a, 1994b; Foray and Lundvall 1996; Metcalfe 1998, 1999).

The argument shared by certain economists and managers is that a new regime has replaced the one which traditionally combined brief phases of construction of new capacities with longer ones of exploitation of those capacities. This new regime is said to be one of constant innovation, an economy of continuous change that requires higher levels of training and specific skills in which priority is given to adaptability, mobility, and flexibility. It also demands investment in systems for accessing information (technological, commercial, regulatory) and procedures of complex coordination for R&D and design, production, and marketing. The advent of this new regime might thus explain the prevalence of intangible capital.

**Facts and Measurements**
Can this phenomenon of accelerated change be measured? This is a difficult question because it is not easy to distinguish between an increase in innovation rates and an acceleration in the marketing of new products. How can economists differentiate between faster innovation rates, related to the fact that certain sectors afford numerous opportunities for technological innovations, and the establishment of new modes of management characterized by more forceful and effective marketing procedures (projects are selected better and are less risky, while the connection of the firm to the market becomes an essential element of strategy)?

It is necessary first to clarify the concept of innovation. Are we talking about what is new "under the sun"? If so, change is produced by absolute inventions. If the change is new just for the firm, it is the result of processes of adoption and diffusion. If it is new in the sense of a new application of existing knowledge, it is obtained by transfer and transposition. This question obviously seems important, especially for specifying the link between innovation and growth. It suggests the difficulty of building an aggregate of innovations. But it is secondary if economists simply want to suggest that the knowledge-based economy is one in which the agents have to be prepared to deal with constant change. Whether this change stems from an absolute novelty or the adoption of a technique that has already been diffused by a firm makes no difference. The fact is that there will be upheaval and disturbance.

Some data are useful for studying this phenomenon more closely. For example, significantly increasing investment in innovation (not least in R&D) has sent the numbers of innovations soaring, as evidenced not only by the volume of patents requested and approved (OECD 1999b), but also by the proliferation of new varieties of goods and services that has marked the trend toward "mass customization" as well as the growing share of new products in total sales.

An effort to define new indicators certainly needs to be made. The indicator proposed by Carter (1994a) is a good example, even if it is limited to the manufacturing sectors. This author bases her argument on the assumption that there is a strong relation between the proportion of workers not intervening directly in production and the rate of change in the sector. Workers not directly performing a productive task are defined as "agents of change"; their job is to prepare changes and facilitate the necessary adaptations and adjustments: "It is difficult to imagine what functions managers, technical and even sales and clerical employees would perform if all technologies and consumer buying patterns were fixed over a long period. What problems would they solve? Why keep records if they only document the same old pattern? What remains of the sales function when everyone continues to purchase exactly what he did last time?" (Carter 1994a, 2).

Manufacturing sectors with a low level of innovation are characterized by a 20 percent proportion of this category of employee, while in highly innovative sectors the proportion can be as high as 80 percent. Carter interprets the evolution of the structure of employment in the manufacturing sector in the United States, revealing a sharp increase in the size of this category of employee as an indicator of accelerating change. She thus establishes a hierarchy of "rapidly changing" sectors (with reference not to the intensity of R&D or the total technological intensity, but to the proportion of jobs not directly affected by production). We see that the classification of the thirteen top manufacturing sectors combines nine high-tech industries (notably aerospace, aeronautics, defense electronics, informatics and telecommunications, and pharmaceuticals) and four industries in the publishing and printing sector (newspapers, books, diverse publications, multimedia). These are all rapidly changing sectors, particularly sensitive to progress in ICT, in which innovation costs are explosive.

The proportion of spending on innovation compared to total spending is another way of approaching this question of intensity of change. Carter (1994b) distinguishes intangible investment costs, replacement (and flexibility) costs, and virtual costs of inexperience. The share of these costs increases substantially on average. In certain sectors they are as high as 90 percent of the total costs, while the remaining 10 percent are imputed to tasks that were formerly dominant, consisting of maintaining what already exists.

**The Causes**

Apart from the reasons previously developed (expansion of knowledge-related investments, new ICT and growth of knowledge, and knowledge flows), other factors must be considered. Increasing competition (related to various factors such as globalization, deregulation, and the use of ICT as a tool increasing market efficiency), growing technological and organizational interdependencies, and some kind of hysteresis effects exhibited by a system oriented toward innovation and change, are three other major factors explaining this new phenomenon.

**Increasing Competition**   Trends toward a marked increase in competition have forced companies to adopt much more aggressive innovation strategies. Innovation provides one way of getting out of the competition, which is to say situations in which activities are not very profitable. Innovation indeed provides an opportunity to set oneself apart and temporarily to assume a monopoly position; this provides an opportunity to make a profit either by increasing prices (product innovation and technological competitiveness) or by reducing costs (process innovation and active price competitiveness). There are, of course, other means that can be relied upon to survive and prosper in a market economy. These conventional means rely mainly on geographical distances and transportation costs, the limited capacity of consumers to compare prices and qualities fully, the existence of regulated activities, and the creation of artificial switching costs. All these mechanisms reduce the degree of competition and allow companies to survive even if they do not have the best product or the cheapest price. However, globalization, deregulation, some antitrust policies (making it more difficult artificially to increase switching costs), and the use of ICT are all trends which dramatically erode the effectiveness of those conventional means. Innovative strategies, therefore, appear as the only way to survive and prosper in the new competitive environment.

For instance, ICT renew the material base on which markets function and, in so doing, trigger an acceleration of product innovations (Guellec 1996). These new technologies reduce costs of circulating information and transferring knowledge, and facilitate the efficient storage and retrieval of data on quality and prices. All this creates a new range of constraints for firms—the constraints of a more efficient market. In other words, the opportunity costs of delays or bad performance (in terms of quality or price) are far higher. This increase in opportunity costs related to a failure, management error, or delay in innovation automatically leads to an acceleration of innovation based on product differentiation—the only way of reducing opportunity costs—and an acceleration of convergence and imitation between competitors.

**Growing Interdependencies** The huge increase in technological interdependency is an essential factor in the accelerating pace of innovation.

When entities are composed of closely linked units, in the context of vertical or horizontal technical and organizational relations, an innovation introduced somewhere in the system creates many disturbances. According to Gille (1978, 716), "Once the first discoveries had been made, everything, or almost, stood to reason. Distortions between the various stages of the production process pushed towards complementary inventions. There was then a sort of chain reaction to restore the balances destroyed." No one has described the capacity of innovation to disrupt a system and create the need for other innovations better than Bertrand Gille (1978), in this case with regard to textile techniques in the eighteenth century. Rosenberg (1976, 1982) analyzes similar processes in various industrial contexts. But technological and organizational interdependencies have increased sharply and are at the origin of the phenomenon of mass innovations and generalized adjustments.

Another form of interdependency is generated by systemic innovations. A systemic innovation is one whose value, or private and social "return on investment," depends on its adoption by a number of economic agents, such as the adoption of the experimental method by the scientific community in the nineteenth century, quality standards, new inventory-management practices, and electronic data interchange networks. All these innovations facilitate either intellectual or logistical and physical coordination. In each case, the value of the innovation is therefore highly dependent in its collective adoption. A good illustration is when a large corporation decides to have its subcontractors adopt an electronic data interchange network (David and Foray 1994). Technological standard is a particular form of systemic innovation since its value is dependent on the scope of its adoption.

Greater interdependencies make the system as a whole more sensitive to any perturbation and create the need for constant adjustments to restore the technological balances destroyed.

**Change Breeds Change**   Finally, I wish to mention the hysteresis effects related to growth of the category of jobs not directly concerned with production, namely, "agents of change." Here is a fascinating explanation given by Carter (1994a, 3): "To the extent that non-production workers are change agents, their continued employment is a commitment to continued change. Staffing itself has an essential inertia. Industrial change takes place because engineers, salesmen and managers promote it. Employees who have effected change successfully tend to remain on the payroll and thus to effect more change. Experience builds capability. An engineering, or a sales or a managerial capability is an asset that can provide a stream of benefits. While the stream of solutions or ideas may fluctuate, the continuous employment of individuals capable of solving certain kinds of problems shapes the course of change. This may go a long way toward explaining why change-oriented sectors tend to remain dynamic while others remain relatively static over years or even decades." Firms are part of this self-reinforcing process. To keep employees committed, they have to give them problems to solve. Such a process can result in a dramatic transformation of works in some sectors where problem solving activities are becoming dominant.

Thus, it is just as difficult to exit from an innovation-intensive economy as to enter it. And the issue of exiting can arise.

**Creative Destruction: Costs of Change**
Unquestionably, most of the topics of the economics of knowledge were developed by Schumpeter (see, e.g., Schumpeter 1942). The production and diffusion of knowledge are processes that lie at the heart of Schumpeterian thinking, as does the impact of those processes on economic growth and development. However, what was really novel in Schumpeterian thinking was his emphasis on the destruction and disorder that entrepreneurs caused by their innovation. As I argue now, this is certainly one of the main features of the knowledge-based economy.

Change and innovation are costly. Apart from spending in intangible capital (R&D):

• they disconnect networks, making technical systems incompatible; in short, they untie technical links built up in the past;

• they reduce the value of skills and downgrade equipment;

• they destabilize the organization of production and hugely complicate economic coordination;

• they accentuate asymmetries of information by increasing the complexity of goods and the uncertainty of their quality, making market transactions less efficient.

Certain institutions, occupations, and cognitive resources have always made it possible to limit these costs. But these mechanisms function only for a certain "dose" of change, when it is transitory and the period of turbulence is rapidly superseded by a long period of stability.

Corporate theory has always postulated moderate doses of change—a notion of "normal" change. Indeed, periods of change are those in which the firm is not technologically efficient because it is faced with the problem of initiating a new production process and the issue of learning. These are therefore periods of distortion between the profile of (present) costs and that of (future) income (Amendola and Gaffard 1988). They must necessarily be transitory and rapidly make way for long periods of stability during which costs of change are recovered.

**Problems Due to Obsolescence that Is Too Rapid**
When change is no longer transitory but becomes, in a sense, the regular regime, these problems of coherence in time of costs and income become almost impossible to solve. Other costs and other sources of inefficiency, which cannot be reduced by traditional mechanisms, arise.

1. Innovations no longer spread because they are too rapidly replaced by new ones. This leads to losses of increasing returns to adoption (Arthur 1989).

2. The excess of innovation results in waiting behavior by users who gradually learn that the pioneers (the first buyers) are always penalized. The recent case of France Télécom's "Bi-bop" is, from this point of view, illuminating. Users who bought this new product in 1996 are now being asked by the operator to replace it with the Ola, a model with upgraded functions but a more expensive subscription. The pioneers are trapped because, although they are apparently free to keep their "Bi-bop," it will never again benefit from network externalities since the operator is discontinuing it. Situations of "angry orphans," so well described and named by David (1987), proliferate in contexts of excessive innovation.

3. The pace of depreciation of knowledge is accelerating. Oliner and Sichel (1994) show, for example, that the share of computers in the stock

of active productive capital is very small (around 2% in the United States in 1993), without any relation to the amount of cumulated sales of the product. This is due simply to the fact that we have a glut of computers that are "economically worn out" by rapid change.

4. In enterprise, costs of learning, adjustment and adaptation are rocketing. Hatchuel and Weil (1995, 109), who devoted long passages to this "hidden crisis of industrial expertise," write: "For operators, the dynamics of the variety economy implies memorizing several different protocols, some of which are used only occasionally and unexpectedly, since the specialization of production lines is not always possible. One can easily imagine the type of accumulation of expertise that exists in such contexts of learning. . . . But with a continuous flow of modifications, the risks of opacity and inaccurate interpretations multiply. Furthermore, notions as natural as productivity, yield or workshop capacity become complex and variable; it is then necessary to talk in abstract terms of thousands of work hours, or of equivalent products, when in fact these will obviously vary from one month to another." Alter (2000) writes about the "*weariness*" of operators who have to innovate all the time.

**The Importance of Norms and Standards**   When the pace of change accelerates and becomes the dominant economic activity, traditional institutions and mechanisms are no longer enough to contain the explosion of costs of all kinds under the impact of change on organizations. That is where standardization comes in: it facilitates the creation of temporary stability or lock-in, to enable agents to coordinate their activities in a context of rapid change.[3] Depending on the characteristics of the standards in question (quality standards, compatibility and interchangeability standards), standardization allows the following:

• rapid provision of new technical relations between equipment and between networks (compatibility standards);

• reduction of users' need to acquire new knowledge when they try a new product (interchangeability standards);

• provision of economies of scale and variety in the production of components and subunits, when the final product changes;

• "limiting the damages" when new equipment is introduced and has to coexist with older generations (intergenerational compatibility standards);

• guarantee that transactions maintain a minimal level of efficiency (quality standards such as ISO 9000).

Standardization ensures that the product bought now will evolve in line with the technology race. In so doing, it helps agents to form positive expectations, that is, expectations that will not necessarily result in waiting behavior in contexts of rapid innovation. Of course, standardization often offers nothing more than partial and temporary stability. This depends on the scale of the technological upheavals underway, and, in this respect, there are very strong sectoral disparities.

## Questions about the "Knowledge Workers"

### Increase in Highly Skilled Jobs

The knowledge economy is characterized by an increase in the proportion of highly skilled workers (see figure 2.2). This sudden change in the labor demand has led either to the transfer of jobs "upward" or to growing inequalities—of which the least skilled workers are the main victims—depending on the measures taken to adjust supply (cf., chapter 11 on training and education challenges for the knowledge economy).

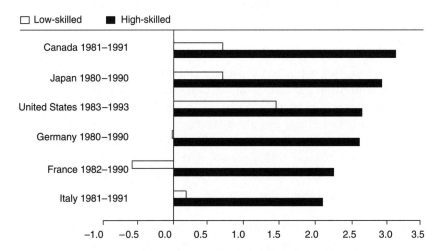

**Figure 2.2**
Shares of highly skilled workers (ISCO-88 groups 1, 2, 3) in total employment (percentage). *Source:* OECD (1996).

While the general trend is clear, the factors responsible for tilting the labor demand toward highly skilled jobs are difficult to define clearly. The technological bias thesis does not seem to explain this development fully. Other factors may also be concerned.

### Are We All Destined to Become Programmers?

The hypothesis often put forward to explain the effects of ICT on employment is the technological bias. ICT favor the substitution of skilled workers for unskilled workers. This hypothesis suggests that the deterioration of the situation of unskilled workers in the job market is the reflection of an upheaval in the labor demand, related to technological change. Yet empirical research on the relationship between investments in ICT and the dynamics of employment in sectors or firms has produced no conclusive results.

Depending on the nature of the technologies introduced and the organizational forms chosen, the effect on unskilled labor varies widely. In a recent article focused entirely on computerization in the tertiary sector, Bresnahan (1999) argues in favor of a moderate technological bias. There are first limited effects of substitution (that have not affected jobs with a high level of cognitive and interactive competence) and effects of the evolution of jobs (a new type of job has appeared, the "data worker"). There are also effects of organizational complementarity (ICT create new functions for managers, especially research in data bases and use of automatic information processing tools). It is, however, difficult to assert that in the near future "We shall all be programmers" (Steinmueller 1997).

Growth of the proportion of highly skilled workers must therefore be related to more general trends than the diffusion of ICT only. It is the actual advent of knowledge-based economies that must be taken into account, including, in particular, the increase in the intensity of innovation (see the previous section). Thus, a recent study in Denmark (Lundvall and Nielsen 1999) shows that the growth of innovation-related activities and the acceleration of change are the source of firms' demands for more skills and competencies.

### Does the Knowledge Economy Demand Specific Skills and Abilities?

It follows that the new skills required for integration into the knowledge economy can hardly be reduced to some higher levels of proficiency needed for the use of information technologies. There appears to be a number of set requirements: teamwork, communication, and learning skills. But these kinds of "soft skills" can hardly be described as new. Indeed, though sidelined during the age of Fordism, they have always, throughout history, been crucial to the development and well-being of individuals in the world of work.

A good many experts underscore the importance of generic learning abilities (learning to learn, knowing what we do not know, being aware of the main forms of heuristic bias that can distort the power of reasoning). It is better to have a firm command of such abilities, they say, than to be able to master a specific repertoire of technical skills. The need to keep up with incessant change is essentially what drives employees to develop new kinds of skills and abilities. These go beyond the constant updating of technical knowledge, for they also pertain to the capacity to understand and anticipate change (see chapter 11).

### Five Years of the "New Economy" from a Historical Perspective

Now that the emergence of knowledge-based economies has been put into historical perspective, the new economy debate can only be viewed with a degree of amusement. It has focused on the possible need for a radical reform of macroeconomics because the dominant tenets of that field appeared to have been surprised by the American economy's performance during the last half-decade of an entire millennium. Overall, this debate will mainly be remembered for the clash between the ultraoptimists and their relatively crude economic thinking, and the skeptical macroeconomists who, despite their usual rigor and prudence, have an extremely partial and truncated view of the impacts of new technologies (Gordon 2000). Yet are the United States and, more recently, European and other Western countries' recent experiences not just part of an accelerating transition to the knowledge-based economy, a process that began quite some time ago but that started gathering momentum only fairly recently, owing to the slow maturation of the new, general-purpose technology of digital information processors and computer-mediated telecommunications (David and Wright 1999; David 2000a)?

# 3                 Production of Knowledge

Knowledge is produced in different ways that can be defined in terms of a dual dichotomy.

First, there are two main ways in which new knowledge comes into being: first, through formal research and development work *off-line* (i.e., "isolated" and "sheltered" from the regular production of goods and services); second, through learning *on-line*, where individuals learn-by-doing and, as a rule, can assess what they learn and hone their practices for what follows. This can be an extremely potent form of knowledge production in many professions when learning-by-doing is not limited to the simple effect of repetition and specialization but rather consists explicitly in performing experiments during the production of goods and services. Formal research may remain the cornerstone of knowledge production in many sectors (for the simple reason that it provides a more or less sheltered domain in which to carry out experiments that would not otherwise be possible in real life), but the knowledge production system is becoming more widely distributed across a host of new places and actors as explicitly cognitive forms of learning-by-doing spread to activities other than "craft trades."

Second, it is useful to create a second dichotomy between two types of knowledge generating activities (Steinmueller 2002b). On the one hand, the generation of knowledge may involve search processes within domains that are relatively unexplored or underexploited. This is the search model of knowledge generation. On the other hand, the processes of increasing complexity in industrial architectures involve somewhat different needs for the systems of knowledge generation. There is a need to produce "integrative knowledge," such as norms, standards, and common platforms. These processes comprise a coordination model of knowledge generation.

**Table 3.1**
Four Forms of Knowledge Production

|                      | Off-line process of knowledge creation | On-line process of knowledge creation |
| -------------------- | --------------------------- | ------------------------ |
| Search model         | R&D                         | Learning-by-doing        |
| Coordination model   | Formal integration          | Informal integration     |

I can thus produce the matrix in table 3.1 describing the different forms of knowledge production explored in the next sections.

## Research: A "Distance" Activity of Production and Consumption

When knowledge is produced through search processes, in some kind of organized and formal way, the concept used to describe it is *research*. The more precise term *research and development* (R&D) is used for intellectual creation undertaken systematically for the purpose of increasing the stock of knowledge. Research centers, scientific academies, and R&D laboratories are the main institutions that have the explicit aim of creating knowledge. The main characteristic of these activities is their situation "at a certain distance" from places of production and consumption. This distance, which can at once be spatial, temporal, and institutional, is needed to nurture the talent of "philosophers or men of speculation, whose trade it is not to do anything, but to observe everything; and who, upon that account, are often capable of combining the powers of the most distant and dissimilar objects. In the progress of society, philosophy or speculation becomes like every other employment, the principal or sole trade and occupation of a particular class of citizens." These were the words of A. Smith (1995, 8) who, from the first chapter of *The Wealth of Nations*, announced the development of research. This notion of distance is essential. It enables us to distinguish researchers from other producers of knowledge, discussed further on. The distance can be large or small—research is far from industry or close to it—and even if it is a source of problems, it has to exist to allow for the division of labor and the development of research-related occupations (Mowery 1990; Nelson and Wright 1992). The twentieth century has thus seen the advent of R&D laboratories in companies and the upsurge of specific occupations and skills. Moreover, even if the share of research in the stock of intangible capital necessarily remained small (see chapter 2), R&D activity has been a mainstay of national innovation systems since the beginning of the twentieth century. This means that the formal production of knowledge is taken seriously by entrepreneurs and decision makers and that it comprises a substantial part of all efforts devoted to innovation. Furthermore, the share of resources poured into this activity has constantly increased since the immediate postwar years. The large contribution of research and development to economic growth is an undisputed fact today.

**Different Types of Research?**
Within the broad category of research and development various functional types may be distinguished (Tassey 1992):

• Basic or fundamental research aims at producing basic knowledge that allows for a fundamental understanding of the laws of nature or society. This first category is like surveying: it generates maps, that is, informational outputs, that raise the return to further investment in exploration and exploitation (David, Mowery, and Steinmueller 1992).

• Applied research and development aims at producing knowledge that facilitates the resolution of practical problems. This second category deals with the practical implementation of basic knowledge that gives rise to applied product and process technologies.

• There is finally a particular class of activity which is functionally different from the first two but is difficult to identify and measure. This category concerns the production of infratechnology, meaning sets of methods, scientific and engineering databases, models, and measurement and quality standards that support and coordinate the investigation of fundamental physical properties of matter and the practical implementation of basic knowledge (Tassey 1992).

Such a definitional framework makes it possible to identify and measure basic research and applied research and development. That has been the purpose of traditional categories on which international surveys on R&D are based. These categories are defined in terms of the extent of their exploratory nature and their distance from commercial application.

Yet such categorization remains imprecise. It does not seem to correspond to the reality of certain sectors in which basic research seems closely related to the market (e.g., the pharmaceutical and biotechnology sectors). It is therefore useful to distinguish two types of basic

**Table 3.2**
Three Types of Research

|  |  | A practical application? | |
| --- | --- | --- | --- |
| Is the research intended for: |  | No | Yes |
| Basic understanding? | Yes | Pure basic research (Bohr) | Use-inspired basic research (Pasteur) |
|  | No |  | Applied research (Edison) |

*Source:* Stoke (1994).

research, in relation to the initial objective of the project: is the goal of the basic research a practical application or is it devoted solely to understanding a fundamental problem? In this way Stoke (1994) identifies not only an applied research domain but also two modes of basic research (top line of table 3.2): pure basic research (without any initial practical goal) and basic research oriented toward a certain area of application. For convenience, Stoke (1994) suggested symbolizing each of these types of research by giving it the name of a famous scientist who practiced it. Thus, Bohr symbolizes pure basic research, Edison applied research, and Pasteur basic research inspired by a particular use. The distinction between these two types of basic research is important because it prepares people's minds for analyzing situations in which basic research is close to the market. Such "short circuit" situations are distinct from the perpetual series of phases separating basic research from the market.

Basic research inspired by an application is at the heart of problems of organization of innovation because of its articulation of activities aimed at understanding basic problems, and activities oriented toward the resolution of practical problems. Tension between different incentive logics is strong in this type of research and the institutional frame in which it must be carried out can vary greatly, depending on the sector and country. In chapter 6 I briefly address these questions which primarily concern the articulation between public and private research.

## Why Is R&D Important?

The notion of "distance" activity, which makes R&D an important functionality in the whole process of knowledge production, has two aspects. First, there is an economic aspect, meaning that R&D

cannot be subjected to the same kind of cost-effective and just-in-time managerial approach as the regular activity of goods and service production. Second, the cognitive aspect means that the distance between the laboratory and the real world makes it possible to undertake experiments while using the lab to control some aspects of the reality.

**Economic Aspect**   The main motivation of explicit R&D activities is the production of knowledge. As such, R&D is not subjected to the same kinds of economic constraint as those characterizing the regular production of goods and services. There are of course cost and time issues. However, an entrepreneur or a policy maker who is launching a R&D program is perfectly aware that this activity is fraught with many uncertainties, by which we mean an inability to predict the outcome of the search process or to predetermine the most efficient path to some particular goal. Given this uncertainty, research activities cannot be managed and outputs evaluated in the same way as in the regular production of goods and services. This creates a sort of "isolated or protected world" for R&D which is less dependent on cost-effectiveness and timely delivery of outputs than are other economic activities. A clear illustration is that even a failure in R&D can be viewed as a useful informational output. Particularly when it happens at the basic research stage, the failure contributes to a better "map" of cognitive opportunities.

Of course, managerial decisions taken under some kind of economic constraint may dramatically erode such a "shelter." Following economic and management analysis of the Japanese-type firm (Aoki 1988), efforts were made to bring the R&D function closer to product development. The aim was to subject processes of knowledge production to the immediate needs of the market. The decline of corporate R&D laboratories, the relocation of research structures and budgets within operating divisions, and the creation of internal markets for research were all trends toward a stronger dependence of research on market needs, emphasis on shorter-term objectives, and introduction of more cost-effective research techniques and practices. But there is a basic confusion between the idea that research is "endogenous" because it is constrained, influenced, and oriented by the economy and society (Rosenberg 1982), and the incorrect idea that all distance must be reduced. By eliminating all distance it seems that one loses the capacity, peculiar to research, to trigger radical changes by conceiving major innovations that will create tomorrow's markets.

The pendulum has probably swung too far toward a research entirely devoted to the solution of current business problems. There are some concerns about the fact that downsizing central laboratories and cutting funding for basic research may erode the basis for innovation and growth over the long term. There is thus a range of issues related to organizational design, capable of finding a sort of optimal balance between short-term and long-term objectives, building good trade-offs between the promotion of cost-effective methods and the freedom to experiment, and creating appropriate conditions for the effective management of research activities for today, tomorrow, and beyond.

**Cognitive Aspect**   Explicit R&D activity is also important because it makes it possible (in most cases) to conceive and carry out well-defined and controlled experimental probes of possible ways to improve technological performance and to get relatively sharp and quick feedback on the results (Nelson 1999). Well-defined and controlled experimental probes require isolation of the technology from its surroundings. Experimentation often uses simplified versions (models) of the object and environment to be tested. Using a model in experimentation is a way of controlling some aspects of reality that would affect the experiment, in order to simplify analysis of the results. The ability to perform exploratory activities that would not otherwise be possible in real life is a key factor supporting rapid knowledge advances.[4]

**The Diffusion of Science-Based Research**
In an increasing number of sectors, the possibility to carry out "experimentations" generates a large scientific knowledge base. The term *scientifically based research* means research that is guided and informed by a science which has reached the predictive stage. As argued by Kline and Rosenberg (1986), only science in the predictive stage provides results, which are usable immediately to advance technological knowledge. Some industrial sectors have used for a long time scientific approaches to create knowledge (electricity, chemicals) (Rosenberg 1992). Yet most major technological breakthroughs were not directly based on science.[5] It has been the slow expansion of the model of science illuminating technology that has spawned innovation in sectors where scientific research rarely or never resulted in innovation.

A scientific approach contributes to innovation in three different ways:

1. It provides a more systematic and effective base for discovery and innovation.

2. It allows for better control (quality, impact, regulation) of the new products and processes introduced.

3. Finally, it may be at the origin of entirely new products or processes.

These scientific approaches seem to conquer new ground all the time, even those sectors that appear a priori to resist them. Drug discovery is a good example of a domain that has recently been characterized by a shift from a random approach through large-scale screening toward a more science-guided approach relying on knowledge of the biological basis of a disease to frame a research strategy.

The main direction of change in financial services is toward scientific approaches. Nightingale (2000) has investigated how the diffusion of Ph.D. physicists into financial services has changed the nature of financial institutions, particularly in the area of risk management. The development of the theory behind financial arbitrage by Modigliani and Miller, and the development of models for pricing contingent claims, based on the Black-Scholes-Merton option pricing model, are contributions to the development of a scientific knowledge base leading to the construction of predictive models.

In the health and pharmaceutical sector, the accepted "gold standard" of evidence is the randomized controlled trial (RCT), in which a new drug is compared with the best existing therapy (or with a placebo, if no treatment is available). Patients are assigned to one arm or the other of such a study at random, ensuring that the only difference between the two groups is the new treatment. The best studies also ensure that neither patient nor physician knows which patient is allocated to which therapy. This "double-blinding" reduces the risk that wishful thinking or other potential biases may influence the outcome. Drug trials must also include enough patients to make it unlikely that chance alone may determine the result. Randomized controlled trial or randomized field trial is the kind of scientific method offering a large potential to generate scientific knowledge and robust evidences on a broad range of topics in various fields of social and educational research (Fitz-Gibbon 2001) (see chapter 9).

This list of examples is certainly heterogeneous (from drugs to financial services and education), but it is precisely that heterogeneity that highlights a general trend, namely, the constitution of scientific knowledge bases directly useful to innovation, in most sectors. The idea is not to rehabilitate the old linear, so-called "science push" innovation model, but to grasp the structure of knowledge systems characterizing areas with the biggest advances in knowledge and know-how. Scientific research enables us to respond more quickly and efficiently to market signals and to the emergence of certain social demands.

The connection of scientific research to innovation has two distinct forms. First, scientific knowledge production upstream from industrial sectors allows more effective innovative research that escapes from empiricism. For example, knowledge of the properties of transition of certain materials renews innovation in the adhesive sector. Second, I note the appearance within the firm itself of scientific investigation tools. Hence, the ability to organize rapidly a large number of virtual experiments is revolutionizing design and development work: "Automotive companies are currently advancing the performance of sophisticated safety systems that measure a passenger's position, weight and height to adjust the force and speed at which airbags deploy. The availability of fast and inexpensive simulation enables massive and rapid experimentation necessary to develop such complex safety devices" (Thomke 2001, 75).

These different developments all point to the idea that any research problem warrants an effort at collecting scientific data, and that appropriate forms of experimentation are necessary and most often possible. As shown by K. Smith (2000), one of the features of the knowledge economy is that many industries are now firmly based on complex scientific knowledge. Quite surprisingly, industries that might at first glance be considered "low-tech" are in fact "complex knowledge-based."

**Research Collaboration**
Classic rationales have been thoroughly analyzed in the literature (see Foray and Steinmueller 2003b). They address the need for sharing research costs and avoiding duplicative projects; the benefit to be harnessed from creating larger pools of knowledge, which in turn generate greater variances from which more promising avenues of research can be selected; and the economic gains to be generated from division of labor in research activities. Those rationales still apply for the collaboration developed in the domain of basic research. My own study on consortia in genomics shows that these consortia provide

opportunities to divide research tasks among several teams. Each team is allocated sections of a chromosome to be decoded, and sends its data to a central data processing laboratory (Cassier and Foray 2000). They are set up to take advantage of the different teams' specializations and to combine them, since no single team has all the expertise required to study the functions of thousands of genes in an organism. Finally, consortia are set up to put together a large enough collection of samples in order to produce knowledge of a better quality, or knowledge which could not be obtained otherwise.

### Increasing Returns in the Production of Knowledge

**Various Forms of Complementarity**   Many forms of complementarity between elements of knowledge are at the base of knowledge production. These complementarities have been studied extensively in the fields of technological knowledge (Maunoury 1972; Gille 1978) and scientific knowledge (David, Mowery, and Steinmueller 1992; Rosenberg 1992). Everywhere, transfers, transpositions, and new combinations allow knowledge to advance. Relations between science and technology are also characterized by strong complementarities: by improving the informational basis for decisions at the applied research and development level, a scientific theory improves the effectiveness with which the resources devoted to technological development can be allocated among competing alternatives (David, Mowery, and Steinmueller 1992), while technological advances (instrumentations) reduce the cost of basic and applied research. Finally, the linkages facilitating transfers and transpositions of knowledge between fields can be identified. For example, analogical links are important because "nature is conservative in the use of concepts and structures" (David, Mowery, and Steinmueller 1992). The notion of "homotopic mapping" describes another kind of linkage structure between various fields (David, Mowery, and Steinmueller 1992). In some science it is possible to examine a portion of an entire system of interrelated phenomena and make useful generalizations and applications in other areas: results obtained at one level or in a particular domain may be homotopically mapped onto other levels or into other domains.

**Increasing Returns**   This notion of complementarity in knowledge production is a way of saying that I do not share the argument that exploitation of a knowledge field is governed by the law of decreasing returns that applies in the world of exhaustible resources. In terms of that law, the more one invents the less there remains to invent, so that it is necessary to devote more resources to obtain a result at best equivalent to past achievements. Naturally, it is the law of increasing returns that predominates:

• The different types of complementarity between knowledge implies that it is profitable to allocate resources to many different strands of research whose advances are mutually beneficial, while a particular invention can suddenly cause the costs of research to drop (or the domain to expand) in a particular area. At the very least, information about where others have failed to make a discovery will be valuable in guiding the explorer's own research.

• The effects of indivisibility in knowledge production processes also act in favor of increasing returns.

Yet there are limits to the effect of complementarities and indivisibilities; knowledge production can enter into a zone of decreasing returns. That is where basic research and the creation of generic knowledge come in, for they can trigger a shift in the productive function which pushes back the point at which decreasing returns start. We could even consider that such assaults on the research front happen very often and that consequently the productive function is continuously shifting. This should allow a constant increase in research activity, without moving too deeply into the domain of decreasing returns. Everything depends on the articulation and balance between pure basic research and applied research and between public-sector and private-sector research (chapter 6).

### Learning-by-Doing: a "Joint" Activity Related to Both Production and Use

Learning-by-doing is a form of learning that takes place at the manufacturing (and/or utilization) stage after the product has been designed (i.e., after the learning in the R&D stages has been completed). It leads to many kinds of productivity improvements, often individually small but cumulatively very large, that can be identified as a result of direct involvement in the productive process. Thus, learning-by-doing constitutes the basis for a relationship between productive experience (the accumulation of "doing") and the improvement of productive performance. A learning process takes place, and it is argued that this is the result of the development of increasing skill in production attained by learning-by-doing and by using. It is therefore a source of innovation that is not recognized as a component of the R&D process and receives no direct expenditures.

### Learning-by-Doing

The very notion of learning-by-doing expresses a central proposition that the long-term evolution of a technology is governed by accumulated experience. The starting point of this proposition is the concept of the progress function (also called the learning curve): the productivity of a plant gradually picks up as it becomes possible to remedy various bottlenecks in its operation through the accumulation of relevant experience. The unit cost of producing manufactured goods tends to decline significantly as more are produced. The phenomenon was first observed in the aircraft industry where the direct labor input per airframe was found to decrease at a uniform rate with increase in cumulative output. Beginning with Wright in a paper published in 1936, a host of analyses have confirmed the systematic nature of this relationship. These empirical studies showing the existence of a systematic relationship between some measure of productive experience and improvement in productive performance shaped the formulation of Arrow's (1962a) contribution to the theory of endogenous technical change.

To understand learning processes, economists have (somewhat over-cautiously) hidden behind the learning curve that describes a functional relationship between cumulated production and productivity gains. They have thus left psychology, education science, and cognitive science to answer the question of why this relationship exists.

Owing to more recent empirical work on technological learning (Cantley and Sahal 1980; Adler and Clark 1991; von Hippel and Tyre 1995; Pisano 1996), it is clearer now what happens at the very heart of the technological learning process. The interest of these studies is that they show how the process itself, which creates no apparent break in the production program, consists of a series of experiments. These experiments are the result of unexpected problems in the design stage or expected problems that have not been solved.

### The Main Economic Issue

Learning-by-doing should not be confused with incremental innovation. In fact, while learning-by-doing generates only technological or

organizational increments, most incremental innovations are not produced only through learning-by-doing mechanisms. Indeed, a large
part of R&D is actually devoted to incremental improvements.

At the microeconomic level, learning-by-doing can be related to a
particular locus of innovation and knowledge production. This is a
process which occurs in the field and not in the R&D laboratory. It is
an "on-line" activity as opposed to "off-line" R&D. On-line learning
means that there are both cognitive opportunities and economic
constraints.

Opportunities are related to the situated character of learning-
by-doing (Tyre and von Hippel 1997). The physical context within
which activities are undertaken as well as the interactions between
people and physical equipment or between the service provider and
the "client" generate problems that create cognitive opportunities for
learning. Constraints come from the need to keep the regular activity
going: You cannot stop it to run an experiment. The regular activity
must continue while the learning takes place. In this context, learning
is a joint activity and knowledge a joint product. Knowledge creation
is not the intentional goal but may nevertheless occur as a by-product
of the activity.

This idea of learning as a joint activity has been effectively developed by Arrow (1969a, 31) who said: "The motivation for engaging in
the activity is the physical output, but there is an additional gain which
may be relatively small in information yet which reduces the cost of
further production."

The economics of learning-by-doing appears, therefore, to be an area
in which the conflict between static and dynamic efficiency is particularly important. There is a tension between the normal performance
expected at the end of the day and the learning aspect. "In most
instances of learning-by-doing, the feedback from experience to
inferred understanding is severely constrained. The doers have limited
facilities for accurately observing and recording process outcomes or
for hypothesizing about the structure of the process they are trying to
control. Advances in knowledge that are empirically grounded upon
inferences from trial-and-error in a myopic control process cannot be a
big help when they are restricted in both the number of trials they can
undertake, and the states of the world they can imagine as worth considering" (David 1999, 130). This tension (and how it can be solved
within "learning organizations") raises the most interesting issues in
the economics of learning-by-doing.

## Learning as Experimentation during Production

The notion of learning as a by-product (as something which is not the main motivation of the economic activity) should not preclude a distinction between first order and second order learning. The pure mechanism—the so-called Horndhall effect (by which Arrow means a long lasting increase of productivity as a pure function of cumulated production, without any technical and organizational changes during the period)—is based on repetition and the associated incremental development of expertise: By repeating a task, one becomes more effective in executing that task. Learning of a routine nature, resulting from the repetition of action, is universal insofar as everyone can take advantage of it, from the artisan to the artist, the doctor to the nurse.

Another level of learning is "explicitly cognitive" in the sense that it consists of performing experiments during the production of goods or services. The goal is to test and select a better strategy or a better design for the next period. Through these experiments new options are spawned and variety emerges. This is learning based on an experimental concept, where data is collected so that the best strategy for future activities can be selected. Technical and organizational changes are then introduced as a consequence of learning-by-doing. The locus of the learning process is not the R&D lab but the manufacturing plant or site of use. In other words, explicitly cognitive learning-by-doing consists of "on-line experiments." The concept can be traced back to A. Smith (1995, 76–77), who mentions a little boy who repeatedly opens and closes the valve between a boiler and a cylinder, and who thus discovers a device enabling the valve to open and close automatically: "One of the greatest improvements that has been made upon this machine, since it was first invented, was in this manner the discovery of a boy who wanted to save his own labour."

The importance of experimental learning depends strongly on the nature of the activity: there are high-risk activities in which the agents have to limit their experiments because they could conflict with the "normal performance" that has to be achieved. Airline pilots or surgeons cannot learn in this way. Similarly, people managing a marshaling yard or regulating the flow of traffic in the underground will avoid any type of experiment in the normal course of their work. By contrast, a teacher can carry out educational experiments and a craftsman can look for new solutions to a particular problem during the production process. The error element of their professional trial-and-error is rarely consequential. The fact of being able to carry out this type of learning depends on the nature of the risk and the immediacy (or delay) of the sanction. Thus, explicitly cognitive learning consists of a series of planned but weakly controlled (because "on-line") experiments.

## Users at the Heart of Knowledge Production

One particular case of explicitly cognitive learning-by-doing has been documented by N. Rosenberg (1982) who emphasizes learning-by-doing related to the use of a product or process: using generates problems; problem-solving capacities are deployed and learning occurs (von Hippel and Tyre 1995). Faced with new and unexpected local situations, users have to solve problems that designers failed to anticipate, and are thus in a position to teach and inform those who design systems. It is because there are limits to the perfect reproduction of the environment during R&D phases that problems arise in the course of normal production and use. These unplanned experiments produce learning. Learning-by-using cannot be dissociated from the existence of lead users, that category of actors who, through their degree of autonomy and leeway in searching for the best use of a complex product (a medical instrument, software, a machine), play a decisive role in knowledge production (von Hippel 1988a).

This learning-by-using process has two aspects:

• Final users learn how to use the product. This learning process can be extremely important when use of the product involves complex tasks, including maintenance, operating procedures, and optimal control. This first aspect leads to what Rosenberg calls disembodied knowledge: Prolonged experience with hardware reveals information about performance and operating characteristics that in turn leads to new practices that increase the productivity of the hardware;

• Final users learn about the performance characteristics of the product, which are higly uncertain before the product has been used for a long period. This improved understanding of the relationship between specific design and performance can generate knowledge that can then be used to design adjustments. The feedback loops in the development stage leading to some kind of optimal design after many iterations are crucial. In this case, when learning-by-using results in design modification, Rosenberg uses the notion of embodied knowledge.

This engagement of users in innovative activities is related to three factors:

• The first factor deals with a particular kind of agency problem (von Hippel 2001b): the user—as a direct beneficiary of specific improvements in the design of a product—will be motivated to find a solution that will fit exactly with his or her specific needs and circumstances. In contrast, the supplier may have an incentive to create solutions that are "good enough" for a wider range of potential users.

• The second factor is related to the "situated" nature of learning (Tyre and von Hippel 1997). Users in a very broad sense acquire a certain kind of knowledge that is particular to a specific site and/or usage. This is the case for the user of a machine tool or a medical instrument and for the "user" of a valley or beach (the inhabitant has a particular knowledge about the environmental impact of the traffic on the local vegetation).

• The third factor involves the impact of "sticky" knowledge (von Hippel 1994). When knowledge is costly to transfer (e.g., knowledge about some particular circumstances of the user), the locus of problem-solving activity can shift from supplier to user.

Users' engagement in innovation has three forms.

• The creation of technical and organizational systems through which the producer leaves it up to users to make adjustments and develop the design that suits them best (von Hippel 2001a). Such a partial transfer of design capabilities should occur under the following circumstances (Thomke and von Hippel 2002): when market segments are shrinking and customers increasingly ask for customized products, when costs are increasing, without much possibility of passing those costs on to customers, and when producers and users need many iterations before a solution can be found.

• The emergence and upsurge of user cooperatives which take over the function of innovation (e.g., open software and sports equipment): users participate in the community, design, and build innovative products for their own use, and freely reveal their design to others. Others then replicate and improve the innovation that has been revealed, and freely reveal their improvements in turn. Some of these communities are not only complementary with commercial systems of manufacturing and distribution, they may even compete with them (von Hippel 2001b) (see chapter 8).

• The activities of very particular types of users (e.g., users of medical technology, users of the environment) who become experts on their own situations and may be involved in the process of knowledge creation (Callon 1999).

## Maximizing Learning Potential

A difficult challenge for an organization (a firm or research center) is to reveal, capture, and turn to account the knowledge thus produced on the job. However, very often knowledge produced unintentionally remains invisible, neither recognized nor memorized, and economic agents' efforts to overcome a particular problem are largely wasted.

Maximizing learning potential requires the conflict between static and dynamic efficiency to be dealt with in a certain way. First, in a "doing" context, maximizing the learning benefit requires the addition of instrumentation in order to take advantage of observational opportunities on the production line, or the slowing down of the production stream for the purpose of eliciting new knowledge that could not be obtained otherwise. Explicitly implementing cognitive learning implies toleration, to a certain degree, of reduced productivity. A great deal of added value in terms of knowledge may be obtained at very low cost with little sacrifice of product (or service) output by adding a certain amount of instrumentation and extra observing and reporting personnel to an otherwise routine production operation.

Evolution of knowledge production systems toward such objectives may make the boundaries between off-line (R&D) and on-line experiments blurred. One witnesses, for example, research activities performed on production lines, which weakens this dichotomy between off-line and on-line forms of production of knowledge. Each time a production workshop is fitted with sensors and instruments for research, handled by researchers, or a production line is intentionally slowed down to test a process, there is a new situation, a sort of "on-the-job R&D" that is no longer distant and therefore demands that the firm compromise on productivity.

Second, organizational design matters. Extreme technical specialization is of course detrimental to cognitive learning. Gilbreth, a disciple of Taylor, tried to break up any elementary function (such as picking up a tool) to the point beyond which any further reduction seemed impossible. He called those elementary micromovements "therbligs" and identified seventeen basic therbligs. For example, signing a letter is a process characterized by nine therbligs. Such a level of specialization has of course substantial costs in terms of individuals' learning potential. Practice-based learning environments appear to be broadening out from situations where Taylorist and Fordist divisions of labor in offices and factories reduced the individual's scope of activity and, hence, opportunity to learn. This, in turn, is fostering ever greater possibilities for explicitly cognitive learning. Another important issue deals with the notion of organization robustness. Because errors and mistakes are inherently associated with experimental learning (experiments may fail), one can lessen the consequences of failures by making the organization more robust, less dependent on possible errors. The design of fault-tolerant organizations (or computers) is thus an important prerequisite of the promotion of experimental learning. Thanks to fault-tolerant organizational designs, errors and failures are not consequential and will not result in totally blocking the system.

Third, it is important to create special incentive structures and organizational forms to support learners and encourage them to reveal new knowledge (acquired by doing), to create documents and thus generate knowledge objects, and to memorize and share that knowledge. These sets of incentives and organizational structures are captured in the notion of "knowledge management" to which chapter 10 is entirely devoted.

**An Important Transition toward the Knowledge Economy**
The possibility of moving on to explicitly cognitive learning in activities other than "craft trades" represents an important transition in the historical emergence of the knowledge-based economy. As long as an activity remains fundamentally reliant on learning processes that are procedures of routine adaptation and leave no room for deliberate planning of experiments during economic activity, the gap between those who deliberately produce knowledge and those who use and exploit it remains wide. When an activity moves on to higher forms of learning where the individual can plan experiments and draw conclusions, knowledge production becomes far more collectively distributed.

However, experts who consider only this trend—the expansion of cognitive forms of learning-by-doing—and disregard the latter (the development of science-based research), are making the serious mistake of believing that the knowledge creation system has become so distributed and scattered between a growing number of "intelligent agents" that there is no more R&D in the sense of professional scientific research. Defining research today with a little "r," as "the structured acquisition of knowledge and support for learning across the total process of creating, making, selling, and supporting innovative and efficient products and services" (Myers and Rosenbloom 1998, 5), is a way of saying that everyone does research. According to this definition, all those who are involved in experimental learning in their jobs are researchers (Gibbons et al. 1994). In our view, however, specialization and division of labor remain important. Even if they are producers of knowledge, doctors, architects, teachers, and artisans are not researchers just because they produce knowledge in the course of their regular activity of producing goods or providing services.

A more accurate understanding of current trends reveals a complex process. Whereas the knowledge production system is indeed becoming more distributed and democratic, the weight of scientific research performed in isolation, by professionals in laboratories, is increasing.

## The Growing Importance of the Coordination Model of Knowledge Production

### The Evolution of Industrial Architecture

The expanding role of science in the innovation process, and the increasing contribution of users to the improvement of product and service design, are significant trends making the system of knowledge production more complex and more widely distributed.

A further element of complexity relates to the evolution of products. New products are rarely stand-alone items; they are more often components of broader systems or structures. In modern technology, modularity is an objective that increasing numbers of firms are pursuing in order to benefit from the specialized division of labor and to create proper conditions for innovation. Modularity is both a solution to growing complexity and a method for innovation management (Aoki and Takizawa 2002). Module designers are free to try out a wide range of approaches as long as they obey the design rules ensuring that the models fit together (Baldwin and Clark 1997). The definition of specifications for the interfaces and organization of integration are thus becoming an essential aspect of product development as well as providing opportunities for creating specific types of knowledge. A significant share of knowledge generation occurs in the process of interface design and system integration (Steinmueller 2002b).

## "Integrative Knowledge"

The appearance of increasingly complex coordination problems affords an opportunity to produce "integrative knowledge," that is, norms, standards, infratechnologies, and common product development platforms. Integrative knowledge is used temporarily to guarantee compatibility, interoperability, and interconnectivity between subsystems and modules. It is thus at the base of new forms of division of work, allowing the exploitation of network externalities and creating a new regime of variety of goods. The consumer can combine different modules to obtain a singular good. The abundant literature on the economics of interface standards (cf. David 1987; David and Greenstein 1990; David and Steinmueller 1996) and on infratechnologies (see Tassey 1992; Kahin 2002) attests to the importance of this phenomenon.

## Another Rationale for Collaboration in Knowledge Production

It follows that the increasing importance of collaboration in knowledge production cannot be explained only by the usual rationales provided by the economics of R&D. When integration is the issue, a possible rationale for collaboration concerns the need for reducing uncertainties and ambiguities in modular technologies and loosely coupled systems. This is a usual rationale in sectors such as automobiles, other transport technologies, and jet engines. The traditional solution relied on vertical integration, but this practice has now been revised in favor of outsourcing and collaboration, requiring strong coordination mechanisms. The Covisint venture, for instance, involving many car companies (DaimlerChrysler, Ford, GM, Renault, Nissan) supports cooperation in engineering and system design with a view to standardizing parts, as well as supply chain management and procurement functions. Another rationale for "integration-oriented collaboration" relates to the strategy of forming a tribe and building a coalition to create a standard.

## Conclusion: Three Models of Innovation in the Knowledge Economy

The three sources of innovation or models of knowledge production that seem to be gaining in importance are as follows:

• The first major trend concerns the increasingly scientific nature of research methods. In more and more sectors, the "epistemic culture" of science for knowledge production is growing in importance (see chapter 9).

• Users' increasingly marked engagement in knowledge production represents a second trend.

• Finally, the increasing complexity and modularity of industrial architecture make it more critical than ever to produce "integrative knowledge," such as standards, norms, common architectures, and platforms.

These three forms are summarized in table 3.3.

Yet these ideal types are rarely identifiable in a pure form. They are born at certain points in history, in specific limited domains. Their importance grows as they combine and hybrids are formed. Many "real" innovation processes are the result of combinations between the different models already described.

I am thinking particularly of the combination between model 1 and model 2, that is, innovations based both on science and on users' (or laypersons') knowledge. This category of innovation has been analyzed in depth by Callon (1999). The crucial factor is the participation of "layexperts" in the production (and use) of scientific knowledge. Some areas, in which laypersons unquestionably possess knowledge of use to scientific investigation, are particularly well-suited to this type of innovation. The perfect example is health. The environment can also afford opportunities for close collaboration between layexperts and scientists.

The combination between model 1 and model 3 corresponds to innovation resulting from a technological break, based both on scientific progress and the ability to solve coordination problems posed by complex technological systems. The archetype here is innovation in

**Table 3.3**
Three Critical Models of Innovation

|                                              | Model 1                                           | Model 2                                  | Model 3                                                                          |
| -------------------------------------------- | ------------------------------------------------- | ---------------------------------------- | -------------------------------------------------------------------------------- |
| Innovative opportunities                     | Scientific advances                               | User needs and capabilities              | Problems raised by integration in complex technological systems                  |
| Critical relations, Crucial organizations    | University-industries, *startups*, large integrated firms | Users-producers Users communities | Architect and module designers Strategic and standardization consortia           |

transport technologies. A recent study of Swissmétro, a revolutionary land transport technology, clearly shows the importance of both aspects in this type of innovation (IMRI 2001).

Finally, a last trend has been highlighted, concerning the increasing role of collaboration, not only for basic research purposes but also for solving increasingly complex problems raised by design and integration. Such coproduction of knowledge may take various forms beyond basic research consortia, from establishing a strong relationship between a supplier and user to creating a complex set of coproducers based on the modularity of the product or to cooperatively establishing a technical standard.

# 4                    Reproduction of Knowledge

As the reproduction of a cognitive capacity, the reproduction of knowledge poses a problem that constantly recurs both in technology transfer and in the succession and transmission of occupational or educational skills.[6]

## Three Forms of Reproduction

Polanyi (1966), who introduced us to the concept of tacit knowledge, points out an essential aspect of knowledge that makes its reproduction difficult. Tacit knowledge cannot be expressed outside the action of the person who has it. In general, we are not even aware of the fact that we have such knowledge, or else we simply disregard it. I can use the example of the rugby player who tries to describe all the gestures and know-how required to score a goal: "My method, my routine? Heel the circle and then the hollow. Always put the ball so that the valve is turned slightly to the left, like that, and then lean the nose of the ball slightly towards the goal post to give more momentum. Take aim, calmly. Note the wind. Stand straight. The left foot barely touching the ball, the right just behind it. Visualize the kick. Eye and foot on the same line. Rub your hands. Take exactly four steps back. Stop. Check. Visualize. Then two steps to the left if it's a Mitre ball like those we use in Bristol, one and a half if it's a Gilbert ball at Twickenham. They need more control, although they go further. Imagine the feeling in your foot." At the end of this long description, the player concludes: "If you tried to write down exactly, with absolute certainty, everything you do when you kick a ball between two posts, it would be impossible, you'd still be here in a thousand years. But you just need to have done it once and your body-and-mind have the exact formula, ready to be repeated" (interview with J. Webb, British journalist, quoted in Mangolte 1997,

123; my translation). It is only when the player is prompted to describe in detail what he does that he becomes aware of all the gestures he made and the intentions he had "without thinking."

For this very reason, tacit knowledge is a good that is difficult to make explicit for transfer and reproduction.

The reproduction of knowledge primarily involves the composition, delivery, and use of a script, that is, a "set of rules similar to those given to an actor who is asked to improvise on a particular theme" (Weizenbaum 1976, 5). Three main forms of elaboration and transmission of scripts can be distinguished.

Form (a) consists in demonstration which takes place primarily in the context of relations between master and apprentice or teacher and learner. The teacher lays down a set of rules which he or she transmits to the learner through gestures and speech (Perriault 1993).

Form (b) is that of codification, in which the script is detached from the person in possession of the knowledge, with a view to inscribing it

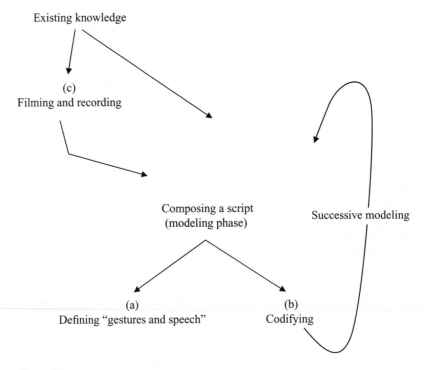

**Figure 4.1**
Three forms of reproduction of knowledge

in a medium. This form may require successive modeling phases and the mobilization of languages other than natural language. In form (b) the script may be imperfect (e.g., the operating manual for a machine) but it has the virtues of a public good (it is a nonrival good that can be copied and distributed at a very low cost).

Both forms (a) and (b) imply the elaboration and presentation of the script, a phase in the modeling of tacit knowledge (Hatchuel and Weil 1995). It is a difficult and costly process. Take, for example, a tennis teacher who wants to transmit his knowledge. Whether he wants to write a book or provide teaching on the court, he has to create a model consisting of breaking down the gesture into micromovements.

Codification (form (b)) would probably require additional modelling phases, although not necessarily. For instance, codification of a cooking recipe would involve knowledge modeling very similar to that required for its demonstration.

Form (c) consists of an audiovisual recording of the action. The recording of voices and images provides a means for facsimile reproduction, which allows the memorization and analysis of knowledge mobilized during that action. It is the notion of technical reproducibility, studied by philosopher Walter Benjamin, in particular. In this case, the script is not really created, but the subject matter is there, faithfully memorized, available to be worked on in constructing the script. One can, for example, show a scene in slow motion or enlarge a photo to study a particular mechanism better.

These three forms are currently available, and the aim of this chapter is to study their respective developments in order to show the essential role of codification in the context of our knowledge-based economies.

## Codification

When knowledge is tacit it can be reproduced in form (b). Tacit knowledge is a good, the very nature of which creates strict dependence between the potential value of the intellectual asset (e.g., for a firm or other organization) and the good will of individuals who have the knowledge comprising that asset. The exchange, diffusion, and learning of tacit knowledge require those who have it to take deliberate or voluntary action to share it. These operations are therefore difficult and costly to implement. The storage and memorization of tacit knowledge are contingent on the renewal of generation after generation of people who have such knowledge. In many fields, including those that seem the most rational and systematized, the risk of "disinvention" is great. As MacKenzie and Spinardi (1995) show, and contrary to common sense, it is possible to "disinvent" the bomb. In the field of nuclear weapons, studied by these researchers, tacit knowledge is so important that a break of a single generation of engineers would be enough to lose a large number of procedures and simply forget "how it's done." Last but not least, research on elements of complementary knowledge, related to a particular project, is severely limited by their tacit nature. Tacit knowledge can be neither classified nor systematically recorded. Even if the notion of "good will" of people is in fact structured and framed by institutions such as the internal job market, the corporation or the community of practice, the firm remains dependent on whoever has the knowledge. Such dependence can become unbearable when institutions which regulate and control individual knowledge are in crisis.

Knowledge can, however, be codified; that is to say, it can be expressed in a particular language and recorded on a particular medium. As such, it is detached from the individual, and the memory and communication capacity created is made independent of human beings.

Although it involves high fixed costs (as discussed in the next paragraph), codification also enables agents to perform a number of operations at a very low marginal cost. It reduces the costs and improves the reliability of storage and memorization. As long as the medium remains legible and the code has not been forgotten, codified knowledge can, theoretically, be stored and retrieved indefinitely. Other aspects of transmission—such as transport, transferral, reproduction, and even access and search—are functions whose costs always decrease with codification. Because codified knowledge is easy to reproduce, the number of copies can be multiplied. This makes it easier to retrieve and transport (Simon 1982).

A second aspect of codification relates to the fact that codified knowledge is similar to a commodity. It can be described and defined more specifically in terms of intellectual property. When knowledge is codified it becomes transferable, independently of the transfer of other resources such as people in whom tacit knowledge is embedded. This improves the efficiency of knowledge market transactions.

A lesser effect concerns the impact of codification on spatial organization and the division of labor. The ability to codify knowledge enables firms to externalize knowledge production and to acquire larger quantities of knowledge at a given cost. It is no longer necessary to develop knowledge internally, for it can be bought. This effect is at the root of the growing trend toward outsourcing in many industries. Not only is the production of elements and components externalized, even their design can be bought.

### Systems of Codification

As in any situation of demonstration of tacit knowledge (form (a)), its codification involves the composition of a script, expressed in natural language. But the process of inscription in a medium external to the individual requires the mobilization of tools and additional structures.

Codification results in the formulation of a message imprinted on a base or medium. This process involves the mobilization of imprinting tools and techniques. From the invention of writing to its mechanization and from copyists to the electronic printer, progress in printing technologies has been enormous.

Codification can also require additional modelling phases (apart from the initial composition of the script) and the mobilization of artificial languages, especially when the knowledge concerned is complex.

Consider the codification of an expert's knowledge, as described by Hatchuel and Weil (1995). The modeling of that knowledge is crucial. It may be so important that several stages of codification are needed to reach a level of modelling required to make the expertise automatic. In the case of an expert responsible for the maintenance of a flexible manufacturing system, the first stage of codification involves the writing of a maintenance manual that helps to clarify certain ambiguities and to reveal the most frequent operating sequences. This initial formalization is then used to write the rules of dynamic questioning at the base of the expert system. In other words, the first stage of codification provides the level of modeling required by the final objective of codification. Two generations of scripts are involved in this process: one, relatively simple and incomplete, is limited to describing operative sequences monitored by the expert; the other, more complex, allows a degree of automation of investigative procedures.

Thus, existing codified knowledge (the maintenance manual) serves as an input for the second process, that is, as a basis for the development of languages and models required for the production of the expert system. By breaking down codification into different stages—each of which produces an output that in itself is useful—it is possible to

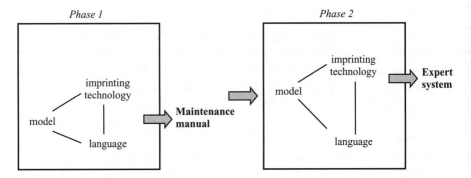

**Figure 4.2**
Two phases for the codification of procedural knowledge

reduce the costs of the final stage. Moreover, this also reduces the cost of using the final system. Users of expert systems have to learn the language in which the knowledge is expressed and to understand certain dimensions of the modeling. In that respect, the user who has read and remembered the maintenance manual has already accomplished a part of the learning.

**The Two Functions of Codification**   Basically, knowledge codification has two functions. The first is the function of storage and "transfer" that permits signaling over time and space and provides humans with marking, mnemonic, and recording capabilities. When codifying became common, as Goody (1977, 37) writes, "No longer did the problem of memory storage dominate man's intellectual life."

Traditional forms of codified knowledge had unique properties related to their use of symbolic representation. The ability to manipulate symbolic representations to reorder, juxtapose, visualize, and manipulate provides a basis for transforming the knowledge they represent. This is the second function of literacy and knowledge codification; it is the basis for their second-order effects. As I shall demonstrate, the second-order effects may dominate the first order effects, partly because of the forces favoring new types of codification activities.

**The "Visible" Function: Creating Memory, Communication, and Learning Program**
The codification of a certain kind of knowledge (know-how) generates new opportunities for knowledge reproduction. For example, a written

recipe is a "learning program" enabling people who are not in direct contact with those who possess the knowledge to reproduce it at a "lower" cost. Goody (1997, 143) writes: "The written recipe serves in part to fill the gap created by the absence of Granny, Nanna or Mémé (who has been left behind in the village, or in the town before last)."

*In part* is the important term here. Naturally, codification mutilates knowledge. Getting the written recipe does not totally eliminate the learning costs. What is expressed and recorded is not complete knowledge; it is a learning program that helps to reproduce knowledge. When a young technician receives a user's manual, he or she is not directly given knowledge on "how to run the machine." That said, the manual is helpful and will serve to reduce the costs of knowledge reproduction.

In many cases, when technicians have "learned to learn" and are dealing with a more or less standard machine, knowledge reproduction becomes almost instantaneous and assumes characteristics close to those of information reproduction. In more complex cases, however, the codified knowledge, while certainly useful, will provide only partial assistance. Knowledge reproduction will then occur through training, practice, and simulation techniques (aircraft pilots, surgeons).

The other aspect of the first function of codification concerns the locus of power in social institutions. Once again, Goody (1977) offers acute observations. Codification depersonalizes knowledge. The written recipe acquires independence from those who teach it. It becomes more general and universal. It reduces the relation of subordination between master and apprentice, and this "liberation" has at least two implications: from a social point of view, the apprentice can learn when he or she decides to do so and does not need to wait until the master is willing to teach. From a cognitive point of view, "The human mind [is] freed to study static text (rather than [being] limited by participation in the dynamic 'utterance')" (Goody 1977, 37).

A further aspect of this evolution is, however, the weakening of subcultures and local practices since, as Goody writes, "the 'secrets' of one group [are] made public to all others" (Goody 1977, 142) or at least are expressed in a form that predisposes them to becoming public. To be sure, one can codify knowledge by means of an enigmatic language to protect the secret, as in the case of alchemists: "I am revealing my secrets to you figuratively, speaking with enigmatic examples and signs" (Secretum Secretorum, qtd. in Eamon 1985, 324). However, this attitude is limited by the intrinsic nature of language as a public good.

Private production and use of a language are by nature economically inefficient.

The important aspect of this initial function is economic. Once a recipe has been written, it can be disseminated at a very low cost or even virtually free of cost, owing to new information technologies. This means that although the production cost of the first copy (basically, the codification cost) may be very high, the cost of all subsequent copies will rapidly decrease so that the codified knowledge can be reproduced and disseminated ad infinitum. It is clearly the codification of knowledge that changes the conditions of its circulation and that constitutes the condition on which advances in information technology can serve to improve that circulation until it is almost perfect.

**The First Function Can Be Achieved in Oral Societies**  Oral societies have alternative reproduction technologies to support memory, communication, and learning. In particular, they develop powerful cognitive mechanisms to create and support individual and collective memory. This is what anthropologists show in their descriptions of the rituals and customs that oral societies apply to preserve memories. Dagognet (1995, 182) explains: "To form a series of places in the memory, Quintilien says that one should think of a building, one that is as gracious and varied as possible, with an atrium, a living room, bedrooms and lounges." Severi (1994), in a text aptly entitled "Paroles durables, écritures perdues" (literally, "Enduring talk, lost writings"), concluded his study of cuna pictographic techniques by noting that memory can effectively be socialized within rigorous ritualization procedures, and that the memory of the spoken word can be supported, in this context, by things other than linguistic signs.

By creating a repertoire of "mnemotechnics," these societies generate cognitive tools which provide individuals with effective ways to memorize knowledge and information, and give the society as a whole the means to maintain a sound and robust intergenerational collective memory.

In a contemporary context, the recording of voices and images provides a means of "facsimile" reproduction (referred to as form (c) in figure 4.1). As such, facsimile recording involves no "higher level" codification of the structure or meaning of the recording. The important new ICT-based features that permit "illustration" of these recordings, their deeper, second-order inscription, suggest new possibilities for the transmission of and distant access to all kinds of knowledge, far beyond the traditional forms of codified knowledge and written instructions. According to the French cognitive scientist Pierre Levy (1997), "New ICTs are closing the brackets of centuries of knowledge transmission through writing."

There is, thus, a sort of convergence (of course, far ahead of us) between various kinds of knowledge in terms of marginal cost of storage and transfer. In this sense, the traditional forms of codified knowledge are losing their singularity as a category of knowledge that is more appropriate than others for achieving the operations of storage and transfer at low marginal costs.

**The Invisible Function**
This is why it is important to consider the second function, the ability to manipulate symbolic representations by their reordering, juxtaposition, visualization, and manipulation. This is what makes codification unique compared to simple facsimile representation.

In particular, codification makes it possible to arrange and examine knowledge in different ways. Lists, tables, formulae, blueprints, and virtual models are cases of progressively more complex knowledge objects that codification is capable of creating. A "simple" list could not be created without some kind of codification. Likewise, tables open the path toward taxonomic and hierarchical structures (Slaughter 1985). While such structures can be created by oral means, they do not work well as tools for the extension and reordering of knowledge. Tables and formulae, which are the basis for mathematical constructions, become meaningful when they can be visualized and manipulated in a space. These capabilities are inherent in codification and essentially absent in facsimile recording.

Codification provides a spatial device to screen and classify information, opening new opportunities for the modeling or representation of knowledge, a condition for rapid knowledge production and accumulation. Knowledge modeling is made as a prelude to the act of codification, while acts of codification shape the nature and appropriateness of knowledge modeling. One may therefore learn more about the processes of codification by examining the variety and evolution of knowledge modeling.

In particular, as illustrated by the contrasts between oral and literate societies, the type of code has cognitive implications. Several different types of knowledge modeling and their associated codes may be identified for purposes of illustration.

1. Natural languages based on the alphabetic system as well as written ideographic symbols can support knowledge accumulation. Natural languages are particularly demanding on the "absorptive" capacities of the receiver because of the extremely complex network of cognitive associations that are evoked by the idea of the "native speaker" and, still further, the "educated native speaker." In practice, the codification of knowledge using natural language often involves the creation of written discourse in which interpretation and comparison provide the cognitive clues for reconstructing knowledge. Even the most straightforward and "instrumental" usage of natural language is likely to generate discourse. For example, as Goody (1977) indicates with respect to the "recipe," natural language encoding is often supplemented by comment and addition. Second, discourse occurs through individual experiment, assessment, and isolation of common elements.

2. Formal logical structures, such as software languages, dramatically reduce the complexity of associations inherent in natural language, with the aim of eliminating ambiguity. As all those who have produced software have learned, the absence of ambiguity makes knowledge modeling a tedious process.

3. The development of specialized software for representing knowledge structures has been heralded as a means to fill the gap between natural language and formal logical structures. Most commonly called "expert systems," these systems create rule-based inference systems that can incorporate a degree of formalized ambiguity. They have proven to be valuable in highly situated contexts, such as the reproduction of experience in chemotherapy for treating cancer. The shortcomings of these systems lie in their cognitive structure. Since the system is not able to recognize "relatedness" except through enumeration, the resulting knowledge modeling is exceedingly complex and discards most of the advantages of other simpler forms of codification which are far more flexible in both content and structure.

4. The development of simulation technologies for virtual representations of real world structures constitutes an alternative and complementary path for knowledge modeling. A good simulation model for a system or artifact makes it possible to manipulate elements in order to examine their interactions. Current techniques in simulation modelling make it possible to create new knowledge, namely, knowledge that was not explicitly codified in the design of the simulation, through the use of simulation models. Although simulation models are still relatively expensive to create, they are becoming an essential tool for the

design and study of a vast range of systems. In many cases, effective knowledge acquisition can be accomplished through experience in the use of simulation models. The training of commercial pilots to fly new types of jet aircraft involves a predominance of simulator over "real world" experience.

5. During the last few years a particularly promising structure for knowledge representation, the World Wide Web, has emerged. The advantage of this representation technology is that it simultaneously provides a means for expressing information as "quanta," and establishing interrelations between that information. This feature, first referred to as "hypertext," is now better labeled "hypermedia" in light of the possibilities to incorporate audiovisual representations as information quanta and "maps" of interrelationships. It offers an extremely flexible system for knowledge representation which also supports useful divisions of labor in entering and validating data. It incorporates means of representing all known forms of graphical information representation.

One may see these examples as successive attempts to address specific problems in knowledge modeling with the aim of improving the opportunities for codifying knowledge. In each case, the codification technology is related to a specific means of reproduction, such as reading a text, executing a program, operating an expert system, or using the World Wide Web. In each case, the person interacting with the information resource is engaged in a process of learning. The people who are designing these information resources have an ever greater variety of tools available for representing knowledge, including a growing capacity to "link up" with the efforts of others.

**Codification Has Two Facets**
Codification has always had two facets: it is a state in which knowledge (the script) is presented, and it is a tool for constructing new knowledge. The trend previously described shows that the second aspect (codification as a creative tool) tends to play an increasingly decisive role.

**Direct and Indirect Costs of Codification and Endogenous Nature of Economic Choices**
I have considered the effects of codification at length, regarding learning, memory, and communication capacities as well as cognitive dynamics.

Codification costs depend on the adaptation of existing languages and models to the type of knowledge to be codified. When this infrastructure exists, direct costs of codification are reduced to those of printing (writing and other). They diminish very fast with the evolution of information technologies. When no infrastructure exists, the fixed costs are immense and will often be borne by several generations (Konrad and Thum 1993).

There are also indirect costs of codification. At least three kinds of issues concern such indirect costs:

• The first involves the fragility of digital memory. I address this issue in the final chapter, as one of the most interesting problems raised by the knowledge economy.

• The second issue pertains to the problem of organizing information in storage units, which can generate substantial costs (see Steinmueller 2000a, for an analysis and overview of this problem). If the net benefits of codification increase, we are likely to find ourselves faced with more of it, or at least want to have useful access to more of it. This demands as yet unknown organizational abilities or technologies. How to enter knowledge or information into our non-mental memories—both data-entry and data-storage technology— becomes more important in our codification activities and their economics.

• The third issue concerns the organizational rigidity that codification can generate while increasing communication and transaction efficiency. Codification can become a source of "lock-in" to obsolete conceptual schemes and the technological and organizational systems built around them. Because of the investments needed to create both codified knowledge and a community of users of it, a certain amount of path dependence will emerge. It can be difficult to switch from one mode of operation to a different one that better suits both internal and external contemporary realities (Arrow 1974).

Of course, costs and benefits will explain the decision to codify only in the case of codifiable knowledge. The economic question is therefore the following: how do economic agents decide whether or not to codify "codifiable but not yet codified knowledge" (Nelson and Winter 1982)? This is where price considerations come in. If, instead, one takes the case of tacit, noncodifiable knowledge (considering the state of printing, modeling, and language technologies), for example, knowledge concerning the recognition of a perfume, there is obviously no possible choice or discussion on costs. For the firm, the only way of managing knowledge is by resorting to the internal labor market. If this firm has a vision of its future it will be able to allocate resources to an R&D program for developing the complex tools to make this knowledge codifiable in the long term. There is already an artificial nose capable of recognizing and analyzing smells. But in the short-term the knowledge remains tacit, without being the consequence of an economic choice. By contrast, a computer technician may choose either to codify his or her knowledge in the form of a manual or expert system and then to exploit its dissemination, or else to keep it tacit so that users carry on buying the technician's repair services.

Thus, the economic analysis of the choice to codify concerns only that which is codifiable in a given historical context. This "codifiability" depends on the existence of appropriate languages, printing technologies, and modeling capabilities for the knowledge under consideration.

## Current Transformations in the Economics of Knowledge Reproduction

### The Uncertain Evolution of Reproduction by Demonstration

This mode of reproduction—the master prepares and presents the script to his apprentice—predominated for a long time. Its efficiency depended on a sufficiently large and stable population of "masters" who retained, and in many cases, captured the tacit knowledge. In large companies and industrial clusters it was the internal labor market that for a long time had the function of memorizing, transferring, and accumulating knowledge (Lam 2000). Some centuries before, the craft guild played the same role (Epstein 1998). The stability of employees and their mobility in a clearly delimited area are essential elements in such a system of memorization, accumulation, and transfer of knowledge. A sort of community of fate that linked the expert to the firm according to a principle of life employment implied that the employee had to devote the last part of his or her professional life to the transmission of know-how. For example, large companies used to bring in a replacement two years before an engineer was due to retire, so that the transmission of expertise took place smoothly between teacher and learner. In such cases, the conditions were propitious for ensuring that the professional community itself took care of the memorization and transmission of knowledge from one generation to the next.

Internal labor markets, however, are approaching a state of crisis in which increasing externalization, turnover, and mobility are making traditional methods of knowledge management, based upon localization of tacit skills transfer, ever more uncertain.

Today young engineers often arrive just a week before their predecessors leave. As a result, other ways of transmitting expertise have to be found, for those based on the teacher-learner relationship no longer function. Furthermore, the evolution of these labor markets, from broadly defined jobs and continuous careers toward narrowly defined jobs and stratified careers, is making the accomplishment of knowledge management functions by these markets more difficult (Lam 2000). Some new attempts to reconstruct an internal labor market at a more agregated level exist. A case in point is the IK project driven by Saab in Sweden. IK is a grouping of sixty-five firms. Its purpose is to mutualize high-tech jobs. This mechanism recreates the conditions for a large stable community in which the circulation and transmission of knowledge can take place.

**Advantages and Shortcomings of Facsimile Reproduction**
In the first analysis, the advantages of technical reproducibility (form (c) in figure 4.1) are obvious. It affords a mode of memorization and learning which seems better than codification. Making a film on a traditional craft technique allows people to store and have access to interesting knowledge. The creation of this information is subject to increasing returns in the sense that there are high fixed costs to produce the first copy and very low marginal costs to produce and diffuse additional copies. But this is a first degree of codification that does not involve any generation of new knowledge structures and representations. This form of knowledge representation has shortcomings even compared to the more primitive instruction manual. Although the user may be able to memorize individual components more rapidly by viewing visual representations, a simple visual representation will provide little or no cognitive structure for understanding the information, whereas all but the very worst instruction manuals are capable of delivering such clues.

Exchanging images or learning by images are pleasant and useful activities but an increasing use of this mode of knowledge representation could limit cognitive advances obtained via representations based on the condification of scripts.

## Current Transformations in Codification

New ICT have had a decisive impact by substantially expanding the fields of codifiability and increasing the profitability of codification. They have three effects on the codification of knowledge: effects on the process of codification, its outcomes, and incentives to codify.

1. By generating progress in printing techniques (computers and printers, graphics software, and so on) ICT reduce the cost of codification of simple knowledge.

2. By requiring the formulation of new languages (for artificial intelligence) and substantially increasing the capacity to model complex phenomena, ITC allow the codification of more complex knowledge (expertise). As previously noted, these developments give codification ever greater importance in terms of the creation of new knowledge and automation of more or less routine procedures. Take, for example, the evolution of the "blueprint," previously a method of codifying knowledge about dimensions and relationships among the components of an artifact (Foray and Steinmueller 2003a). Blueprints involve graphical expression and a limited amount of writing. Most of the blueprint created in the 1980s were simply a visual representation of a real or planned artifact. The transformation of blueprints into artifacts or artifacts into blueprints involved a considerable repertoire of skills, many of which were not scripted in any explicit fashion, but acquired through experience. Thus, the blueprint of that time was an "incomplete" script for the reproduction of an artifact. Since 1982 the meaning of the term "blueprint" has evolved considerably. Contemporary engineering diagrams are capable of incorporating precise information about curvature, sufficient data to allow the visual representation of the artifact from any viewing angle, and the possibility of additional information allowing virtual simulation of the artifact's performance under various environmental conditions. Furthermore, it is possible to link "blueprint" data for some artifacts to fabrication equipment capable of creating the artifact from the blueprint and *conversely* to digitize the surfaces and dimensions of artifacts in order to create a blueprint. The most advanced example of this capability is the design software for integrated circuit devices that allows the

production of the most complex artifacts yet known to human beings to proceed entirely automatically from computer-aided design "blueprints."

3. The third effect concerns incentives: by providing a medium for a new electronic communication infrastructure, ICT enhance the economic value of codification since codified knowledge can circulate easily on these networks.

These effects can help to introduce dynamic interdependence between the growth of ICT capacities and the increase in resources allocated to codification. ICT raise the value of codified knowledge, which increases private incentives to codify knowledge and results in an expansion of the codified knowledge base. This can, in turn, affect the supply and demand of ICT, and so on. A virtuous circle of positive feedback is established.

It is, however, advisable to qualify this view of the impact of technological progress on the value of codification (see the previous discussion on costs).

As argued there is a general trend toward the increasing codifiability of knowledge. This trend, however, is largely unbalanced. Technological change related to the evolution of ICT has varying impacts on the codifiability of different types of knowledge. To clarify this last point, I use the typology that distinguishes among factual knowledge (know-what), procedural types of knowledge (know-how), and knowledge providing access to other knowledge (know-who) (Foray and Lundvall 1996). The field of codifiability depends strongly on the type of knowledge considered.

**The Codifiability of Factual Knowledge**    As far as factual knowledge is concerned, the successive inventions of paper, books and, the printing press were essential developments allowing the codification of this type of knowledge. Full codification was thus obtained very early in the historical process of the knowledge instrument's development. Indeed, factual knowledge has a structure which makes its codification a relatively simple task. Later developments of knowledge instruments (e.g., the ability to store a large quantity of information on a CD-Rom) therefore improved the codifiability of factual knowledge only marginally.

However, the so-called electronic book represents a major breakthrough. The historian R. Chartier (1994, 2000) identifies the three lines of transformation that have constantly disrupted the economy of writing and the codification of factual knowledge:

• Transformations relative to material mediums: the scroll was followed by the codex, a book composed of folded, assembled, and bound pages. The creation of the book with a structure still used today constituted the basic starting point for a sequence of inventions relating to the quality of paper, the reduction in the size and importance of illuminations and, above all, the creation of analytical systems—foliation and indexing—making it easier to find one's way in a text. All this gradually turned the book into a knowledge instrument and opened the age of manuals (Le Goff 1985).

• Transformations relative to the production of writing, from the manual copy workshop to the advent of printing and its mechanization (Eisenstein 1980; David 1988).

• Transformations relative to the reader's relationship with the book: "With the new materiality of the book, formerly impossible practices such as writing while reading or flipping through a book became possible, and the use of texts was thus transformed" (Chartier 2000).

Chartier notes that changes at the three levels have never really coincided in history. For example, the book retained the same basic structure before and after Gutenberg. Very few inventions produced simultaneous changes at all three levels. It is in this sense that the electronic book is unique. It appears as a threefold revolution since it is causing an upheaval in the materiality of the text, its mode of production, and the reader's relationship with it.

**The Codifiability of Procedural Knowledge**   The field of know-how and procedural-type knowledge is very different. The literary description of occupations, tricks of the trade, and expertise offers only very partial codification. In this field crucial technological changes were to occur only much later and, in most cases, still lie ahead of us. It is expert systems, based on the invention of new languages, models, and techniques, that greatly improve the codifiability of procedural know-how. Moreover, this know-how comes in a whole range of different forms (Hatchuel and Weil 1995), from the artisan's know-how (consisting in the mobilization of a sum of known and memorized processes) to that of the repairer (which amounts to unravelling a mystery) and, finally, that of the strategist (consisting in defining a tactic by simultaneously reconstructing ends and means, depending on the circumstances). Cowan (2001) has explored the codifiability of knowledge in those three cases:

• Planning and executing a linear process with a fixed goal is relatively easy to automate with an expert system. The steps of the process and the stages in planning it have simple interaction, with no feedback, to that "backward chaining" from the fixed goal through the various stages needed to reach it is feasible. Modern expert systems handle this task well. It is the fixity of the goal and the linearity of the process to achieve it that make this possible.

• Pattern recognition, categorization, and generalization are more difficult. The industrial processes in which these activities are most prominent lie in faulty diagnosis or repair. Expert systems developed for faulty diagnosis are moderately successful but have great difficulty when they encounter situations that are significantly different from those they have seen in the past. The difficulty here lies in the novelty of situations and in trying to draw analogies to other situations. What makes a repairer good is that he has internalized some of the logic of the system he is repairing and can use this in drawing the analogies he needs when faced with new situations. But this logic is highly abstract and difficult to codify. Current technology is still weak at drawing analogy, so it remains something at which human agents are better.

• Finally, there is activity which does not involve stable goals. In a sense, any firm's final goal is fixed, namely to maximize profit. But often the link between actions that can be taken immediately and the final goal of profit maximization is highly tenuous and difficult to discern. In this case, intermediate goals are put in place, to which the connection is closer. For instance, maximizing profits of a conglomerate is reduced to maximizing the profits of its subsidiaries. But when this is done, the intermediate goals can, and often do, conflict. Part of the process of deciding which actions to take involves negotiation (whether actual or metaphoric) over the different intermediate goals. The activity here involves a simultaneous definition of means and ends which, as yet, is not within our technological capabilities and must therefore remain in the hands of human experts and thus part of the body of uncodifiable knowledge.

Although the artisan's know-how can now be codified relatively satisfactorily by means of an expert system, more complex know-how still largely defies expert system technology and is therefore part of the field of uncodifiable knowledge.

**The Codifiability of the "Know-Who" Type of Knowledge**   Finally, knowledge that allows access to other knowledge has remained largely uncodifiable for a long time. Address books or Yellow Pages are used to structure information without codifying the "know-how-to-find-information." It is only with the development of artificial exploration agents operating on electronic networks that this type of complex knowledge becomes more efficiently codifiable. Its full codifiability is thus something of the distant future. The best agents would not only have to be efficient in finding all the information corresponding to a certain question, they would also have to take into account the peculiarities of the user and the situation. In this sense, an agent should fill the role of what some experts call a "digital sister-in-law": when I want to go out to the movies, I ask my sister-in-law who is an expert on movies and an expert on me. Thus she will not inform me about the thousand movies showing this week in Paris but about the ten that she knows I would enjoy seeing. "In fact, a useful agent is often one where expertise on a certain topic is mixed with knowledge of you. A good travel agent blends knowledge about hotels with knowledge of you" (Bradshaw 1997, 6). And that of course puts strong limitations to the codifiability of this kind of knowledge.

Table 4.1 shows how the same technical change can determine the codifiability of one type of knowledge far more than that of another.

**Table 4.1**
Technical Changes and the Codifiability of Different Types of Knowledge

| Evolution of ITs* | Books/Manuals | Printing | Computing | Digitization |
|---|---|---|---|---|
| **Types of knowledge** Factual | | *Advanced Technologies* | | |
| | Encyclopedia | | | CD-ROMs; e-book |
| Processes and Procedures | Encyclopedia | Operating Manual | | Expert systems |
| Access to other knowledge | "Yellow Pages" | | | "Digital sister-in- law" |
| | | *Primitive Technologies* | | |

*Technologies are defined as "advanced" above the diagonal and "primitive" below it. Thus the same technology (e.g., encyclopedia) can be both advanced for a certain type of knowledge and primitive for another type.

**Codification at the Heart of the Advent of Knowledge-Based Economies**

My study on current changes in the different modes of reproduction of knowledge confirms what Steinmueller (2000a) has said: "Codification has become the very essence of economic activity." In this respect I think of the prime importance not only of the visible function of codification (memory, communication, and learning) but also of its invisible function—the other side of the coin—which induces and facilitates the elaboration of new cognitive devices (from the table to the formula) and, as such, is a potent tool for abstraction and intellectual creation.

# 5        Knowledge Spillovers

In this chapter I examine the three properties that qualify knowledge as an economic good and create "knowledge spillovers": any original, valuable knowledge generated somewhere that becomes accessible to external agents, whether it be knowledge fully characterizing an innovation or knowledge of a more intermediate sort. This knowledge is absorbed by an individual or group other than the originator (Appleyard 1996; Antonelli 1999). In order to fully grasp the implications of each aspect, I first consider the extreme case of codified knowledge (appearing in the form of a manual of codified instructions) and then progressively move on to other situations.[7]

## Three Properties of Knowledge as an Economic Good

Knowledge is a strange good, with properties that differ from those characterizing conventional tangible goods. These properties are ambiguous, for while on the one hand activities concerning knowledge production generally have a very high "social return" and are therefore a powerful mechanism in economic growth, they also pose daunting problems of resource allocation and economic coordination.

### A Good that Is Difficult to Control
Knowledge is a nonexcludable good; in other words, it is difficult to make it exclusive or to control it privately. It is a fluid and portable good. Knowledge can, of course, be kept secret, yet as soon as it is revealed it slips out of one's grasp. In that respect, it is a good that differs from jewels that one wears, for example, or that one shows but of which one remains the sole owner.

A firm finds it far more difficult to control its knowledge than its machines, for numerous opportunities for leaks and spillovers arise.

Information and knowledge continuously escape from the entities producing them, and can thus be used freely by rivals. The literature uses the generic term "positive externalities" to denote this positive impact on third parties, from whom it is technically difficult to obtain compensation. Knowledge or information externalities, of interest to readers here, are said to be "nonpecuniary." They denote the fact that knowledge produced by an agent benefits other agents without financial or any other kind of compensation. They are different from so-called "pecuniary" externalities that relate to cases in which inventors are unable to recover from buyers the full value derived from the innovation in terms of lower costs or better quality.

Knowledge leaks out in multiple ways, some of which have been the subject of an abundant literature. Von Hippel (1988b), in particular, analyzed the role of informal networks of cooperation and exchange of experiences between engineers in different—sometimes even rival—companies. But simply the marketing of high-tech products that competitors can disassemble is an important source of technological knowledge.

The significance of these spillovers has been evaluated by Mansfield (1985) who shows that information on R&D decisions is known to rivals within six months, while technical details are known within a year. As we know, however, the harnessing of knowledge by other firms also depends on their learning capacity.

**A Good that Is Nonrival**
The generation of positive externalities by knowledge-producing activities is a fairly general property that economists encounter in many situations. For example, a fruit farmer provides a positive externality to his neighbor the beekeeper, whose bees gather pollen in the orchard; a musician does the same thing for her neighbor who loves music. In all such cases the characteristic of a total lack of control enables one to account for situations in which services are accidentally provided to third parties, without any financial compensation. The fact remains, however, that in these cases the externality is limited since the resource concerned is either exhaustible or difficult to access (congestion). The beekeeper can set up a dozen hives to take full advantage of the orchard, but if he set up a thousand hives most of the bees would not have access to them. The music lover on her own can enjoy her neighbor's music, but a thousand people wanting to listen to it would hear nothing.

This is where knowledge differs from situations in which positive externalities are limited. As a resource, knowledge can be characterized by its inexhaustibility. Why? Because unlike bees in the orchard, economic agents are not rival users of a resource when that resource is knowledge (Romer 1993). The use of existing knowledge by an additional agent does not imply the production of an additional copy of that knowledge. The author does not have to produce an additional unit of knowledge every time its use is extended.

To explain this strange property to economics students, the following example is often used. A teacher gives his watch to a student in the class. This operation changes nothing regarding the aggregate: There are still $n$ watches in the classroom. It is a rival good insofar as the students are rivals for its consumption. But if the teacher just gives the time (assuming that only the teacher has a watch and that there is no clock on the wall), we immediately see that transmission has a completely different meaning: the aggregate changes completely. Whereas only one person had the information in the beginning, the entire class now has it and the fact of having transmitted it does not deprive the teacher of anything. It is a nonrival good insofar as people do not have to compete for its use.

One thus sees that transmitting knowledge is a positive sum game that multiplies the number of owners of that knowledge indefinitely (as opposed to transmitting a watch which is a zero-sum game).

Instead of the term "nonrivalry," some authors prefer "infinite expansibility" (David 1993; Keely and Quah 1998). They justify their choice with the idea of describing this property by means of a positive term, and also with the following reference to a great thinker, T. Jefferson who, in 1813, wrote: "That ideas should freely spread from one to another over the globe, for the moral and mutual instruction of man, and improvement of his condition, seems to have been peculiarly and benevolently designed by nature, when she made them, like fire *expansible over all space, without lessening their density in any point,* and like the air in which we breathe, move, and have our physical being, incapable of confinement or exclusive appropriation" (qtd. in David 1993, 26; my emphasis). Jefferson thus highlighted the two characteristics underlying the power of positive externalities in the case of knowledge production: the difficulty of private control and nonrivalry.

It is important to note that the codified knowledge received by each party or individual is neither an additional piece in a mass production program nor a copy of an original good (as one can possess a copy of a work of art). It is not a copy of Pythagoras's theorem that you use but the theorem itself. The implications of the property of nonrivalry regarding costs and prices are important. Since the marginal cost of use is nil, economics cannot comply with the rules of cost-based pricing. According to those rules, the use of existing knowledge is free, and it would be impossible to compensate financially for the fact that a piece of knowledge is used many times. This problem concerns more than just scientific and technological knowledge; it affects all knowledge expressed in the form of texts, books, journals, music scores, drawings, and graphs. Television and radio program also belong to this category of goods.

**The Two Dimensions of Nonrivalry**   The property of nonrivalry has two dimensions: an individual dimension and a collective dimension. First, agents can use the same knowledge an infinite number of times to reproduce an action, without it costing them anything. That is the individual dimension. Second, an infinite number of agents can use the same knowledge without depriving anyone of it. That is the collective dimension. Thus, on the one hand, the same quantity of knowledge used to realize $m$ units of output will serve to make $m + 1$ units and, on the other hand, the same knowledge used by $n$ people can be exploited by $n + 1$ people. In these two dimensions there is no additional cost of use, once the knowledge has been acquired.

**A Good that Is Cumulative**
Knowledge is cumulative when it is an intellectual input likely to spawn new ideas and new goods. In the field of science and technology, knowledge is most often cumulative and progressive. This means that externalities enhance not only consumers' enjoyment but also, and above all, the accumulation of knowledge and collective progress; it is the possibility for some to "stand on the shoulders of giants." In other words, what spreads and can be used an infinite number of times is not only a consumer good (say, a piece of music) but essentially an intellectual input likely to spawn new goods that will also be usable an infinite number of times. Jefferson, a particularly insightful thinker, wrote: "The fact is, that one new idea leads to another, that to a third, and so on through a course of time until someone, with whom no one of these ideas was original, combines it all together, and produces what is justly called a new invention" (qtd. in David 1993, 28). It is this

cumulativeness that distinguishes "small talk and pass time," as Machlup (1984) put it, from scientific and technological knowledge. In the new knowledge economy many types of knowledge are strongly cumulative, such as data bases (the international DNA data base), research tools (a simulation software package), or generic knowledge (a blueprint to build a micro array robot). These stand in contrast with noncumulative knowledge (consumption goods), such as songs, poems, entertainment programs, or galleries of photographs available on the Internet.

**Temporal Dimension of Cumulativeness**   To characterize "models" of cumulativeness, it is important to take into account the temporal dimension. On the one hand, some cumulative process covers a very long period of time. Rosenberg (1992) has given many historical examples illustrating very long periods of time and the entanglement of relations and affiliation between pure basic research and commercial application. His favorite example is the sequence of discoveries from Faraday's phenomenon of electromagnetic induction (1831) to Maxwell's theories (around 1875), Hertz's experimental research (1887) and Marconi's use of radio waves for long-distance communication (1901). On the other hand, cumulativeness can be very fast, almost instantaneous, and involves recombination and reuse of pieces of knowledge which are all available. These two models (the second characterizing, for instance, the kind of cumulativeness found in the software industry) imply very different modes of coordination and management of knowledge.

**Involuntary Spillovers and Absorptive Capacities**
Involuntary spillovers result from the fact that an organization or an individual cannot capture all the benefits resulting from its inventive activity. Involuntary spillovers are a feature of market competition. Competition not only creates incentives to produce new knowledge but it also forces the other agents to increase their own performance through imitation, adoption, and absorption of the new knowledge created elsewhere, in order not to be excluded from the market. This encourages economic agents to build and develop absorptive capacities (Cohen and Levinthal 1989). An immediate effect of the creation of effective absorptive capacities is that involuntary information and knowledge spillovers may increase at the system level. Because

knowledge is difficult to control privately and private agents develop effective absorptive capacities, competitive markets are a very potent way in which to generate involuntary spillovers, namely, a knowledge infrastructure that creates private as well as social gains. Hence, there is a "pool of knowledge" which is automatically maintained by the involuntary spillovers, which are themselves a result of competition. Several scholars stress an important trend on many competitive markets, which is increasing importance of capabilities for imitating, adapting, and reproducing knowledge generated elsewhere (see, e.g., Steinmueller 1996). In sectors that are not fully part of the market, such as education and health, the diffusion of knowledge is less automatic, and administrative measures or "reforms" aimed at disseminating knowledge and new practices will fail to have as much impact as competitive markets. Thus, knowledge spillovers are considerably more significant in competitive sectors of the economy.

### Combinatorial Explosion and Increasing Returns in the Use of Knowledge

It is basically the uncontrollability, nonrivalry, and cumulativeness threesome that is at the origin of the huge size of potential externalities associated with the production of knowledge. Potential externalities are becoming effective when agents develop and maintain absorptive capacities. Knowledge production has, therefore, the potential to create a combinatorial explosion. This is a good which is difficult to control and which can be used infinitely to produce other knowledge, which in turn is nonexcludable, nonrival, cumulative, and so forth.

### A Few Phenomena that Reduce the Dimensions of Spillovers

A whole series of phenomena exists that, naturally or intentionally, reduce the dimension of externalities. Yet technological developments under way seem rather to compound the problem.

### Qualifying the Argument of Uncontrollability

Until now we have treated only one extreme case, knowledge expressed in an appropriate form for its diffusion (writing, computer programs, digital image, film). But a knowledge base—that of a firm, institution or even sector—is not reducible to pure "codified" knowledge. It is composed of tacit knowledge, know-how, and practical experience, such as knowing how to conduct an experiment, as well as research materials, instruments, and tools, all of which are more easily controllable goods.

Thus, very few research results, inventions, or new technological practices are formalized from the start to the point of being a "simple" set of codified instructions which, if scrupulously followed, allow experiments and results to be reproduced (in the way that anyone, by reading the manual, can get their new washing machine going). When knowledge is expressed completely in this form of codified instruction (of which software is the most interesting example), it is indeed practically impossible to control it, at least in the community of specialists and practitioners able to understand and interpret the instructions. In reality, however, knowledge and results are far more often presented as a combination of formalized instructions and tacit knowledge, based on practical experience that can be acquired only in the laboratory where the discovery was made. An excellent example has recently been provided in the scientific world, where about thirty teams from different countries competed in the race for zero Kelvin degrees. To date only one of them has managed, and reproduction of the experiment requires know-how that is kept largely secret. Thus, the tacit dimension of knowledge affords those who have it a degree of control, since only voluntary demonstration and learning on site allow its acquisition.

Hence, there is a sort of natural excludability that this tacit dimension bestows on knowledge (Zucker, Darby, and Armstrong 1994). This represents a temporary source of intellectual capital, producing rents for scientists who have the know-how. They benefit from it until the new knowledge is sufficiently codified, articulated, clarified, and hence diffused so that the rents dwindle away.

This temporary tacit dimension is therefore a way of controlling access to new knowledge, but it is not a solution that can be used systematically by firms. Many technological and organizational issues today—such as transfer, communication, and learning between scattered sites; capitalization and memorization of skills; effective use of new information technologies; and acquisition of a quality label—demand a degree of formalization and codification of knowledge (see chapters 4 and 10).

The same reasoning applies to the implementation of technologies and organization aimed at keeping "manufacturing secrets." It concerns a solution that has to be found to the problem of knowledge leaks by anyone wanting to protect themselves in the absence of property rights. Yet the cost of keeping a secret can become so exorbitant that only certain types of organizations can afford it.

**Complementary Assets**   Another aspect of controllability relates to the role of complementary assets. Very often the exploitation of new knowledge requires specific capacities that only the inventor has, such as technological capacities needed to implement the innovation. Even if the idea is harnessed by others, only those who have the required capacities are able to exploit it. Moreover, apart from highly advanced technological capacities that have to be mastered in order to exploit the new knowledge, control of a particular market is a kind of complementary asset essential to the exploitation of an innovation. In all these cases, the externality is artificial. Although knowledge is diffused, the profits associated with its implementation remain internal.

### Qualifying the Argument of Nonrivalry
The capacity of knowledge to be used infinitely, which strengthens positive externalities is limited when costs of accessing, reproducing, and transmitting that knowledge are high. Even if the cost of using existing knowledge is nil, this does not mean that there are no costs for reproducing, transmitting, and acquiring it.

   The term *acquisition costs* is used to refer to the costs of intellectual investment needed for people to be capable of understanding and exploiting knowledge. Without these investments (absorptive capacities) the value of nonrivalry of knowledge is nil, as Callon (1994) suggests in his critical analysis of the economics of science. For the property of nonrivalry to be actually exploited, there has to be a collective capable of understanding and using that knowledge. This collective may be tiny, as in the case of using the last theorem in an extremely specialized branch of mathematics. In that instance the economic value of nonrivalry is relatively low. On the other hand, the collective may be almost universal when the knowledge in question concerns an elementary technique or know-how. The bigger the community of agents with the "intellectual equipment" to understand the knowledge, the greater the economic value attached to the property of nonrivalry will be and, consequently, the greater the social return of the knowledge. By taking into account acquisition costs it is possible to distinguish between a fairly specific or specialized nonrival good and a more general or universal nonrival good. This distinction, which must of course be represented on a continuum, depends on the investments that communities of agents make to enable them to use and exploit a particular type of knowledge. Acquisition costs also include search costs, which are the costs of retrieving, screening, and selecting relevant and reliable knowledge. These costs are expected to increase in a world of information abundance.

Apart from these costs for training and the maintenance of intellectual equipment and search capabilities, we also identify costs for reproducing knowledge, which relate essentially to costs for producing a script (and possibly codifying it) (see chapter 4) and to costs for physical transmission.

### Qualifying the Argument of Cumulativeness

Limits and obstacles to cumulativeness stem from the same factors: if knowledge is kept secret or if the costs of formatting, transmission, and acquisition are high, cumulativeness will be reduced or even nil. But there are also specific obstacles that hinder cognitive processes at the basis of the cumulativeness of knowledge.

First, the cumulativeness of knowledge implies a degree of trust in the validity of existing knowledge. Cumulativeness is not possible when there is doubt and uncertainty. That is why cumulativeness is contingent on the adoption of systematic codes and forms of expression as well as procedures of verification and evaluation of knowledge, agreed and observed by all. It appears, however, that these conditions are far from being self-evident. In the Middle Ages the alchemist was symbolic of the absence of cumulativeness of knowledge. Books written by alchemists used allusive, obscure terminology so that, as Rossi (1999, 43) so eloquently put it, "Alchemy was a science that never progressed. One had to redo alone what others had done throughout the centuries." Sixteenth-century engineers complained of the same problem. "We find many books on the subject but they are all vague, for the authors do not refer to things by their names but use strange words of their own invention," Agricola wrote regarding technical books of his time. This observation provided his impetus to develop a systematic technical vocabulary (qtd. in Rossi 1999, 47).

The difference is of course very slight between a secret that allows control and allusive terminology that is an obstacle to progress. Yet it enables us to show that disclosure itself is nothing; it must be accompanied by an effort to systematize and clarify. It was after a long time only that awareness grew of the importance of technical names and systematic classifications used by all. People protested against the (deliberate) lack of clarity, the instability of terminology, the "play on words" of alchemists. During the Renaissance engineers started to codify technical processes and develop a systematic technical vocabulary in order to reduce the imprecision and ambiguity of existing vocabulary (Long 1991). A basic factor was also the adoption of a single standard of scientific reliability, based on observation, reason, experience, and the possibility of replicating experimental work. This standard enables scientists to use the results of other laboratories and even other disciplines.

Second, the dynamics of knowledge is marked by phenomena of obsolescence. As a consequence of the appearance of new knowledge, older expertise loses its value and the cumulative process is weakened. The extent of this depreciation (the economic consequence of obsolescence) depends on the field in question and of course on the historical period. Mathematical truths and theorems, for example, hardly become dated; some even last for centuries. By contrast, in other domains frequent changes of paradigm constantly depreciate knowledge.

### Knowledge: A Good that Is Fragmented, Partially Localized, and Weakly Persistent

Finally, apart from all these subtle differences—and particularly the fact that economic agents must be endowed with a learning capacity to absorb knowledge—externalities are not "ready to use." The introductory chapter has already considered these properties:

For one, knowledge is divided and dispersed (Machlup 1984). Knowledge is a good that is most often presented in a fragmented form, scattered over sites and disciplines, territories, or institutions. Its structures constantly need to be rebuilt.

Second, externalities are most often localized within the space of technologies; that is to say, learning that improves one technology may have little effect on other technologies (Antonelli 1999, 2001; Atkinson and Stiglitz 1969).

Finally, knowledge is weakly persistent. A small number of studies have examined the effect of an interruption in production and learning. Argote, Beckman, and Epple (1990) use a data base on the construction of the Liberty Ship in sixteen different shipyards during World War II. They produced 2,708 ships. They adopted a standard design and produced minor variations in all the yards. Argote, Beckman, and Epple discover a remarkable lack of learning persistence: the knowledge derived from learning-by-doing quickly loses its value and, from a stock of knowledge available at the beginning of a year, only 3.2 percent would remain one year later. Thus, if the stock of knowledge were not replenished by continuing production, it would depreciate rapidly. This very weak memory is due to three factors: high turnover (people leave), technological change (depreciation of existing knowledge); and failure of human memory (people forget). These three factors are reinforced by the absence of memorization/codification systems of the knowledge acquired.

### Knowledge Spillovers and the Geography of Innovation

The notion of "localized spillovers" has another meaning which is related to geographical space and the role of "real" distances, namely, the ability to absorb knowledge spillovers is influenced by the distance from the knowledge source. Thus, geography matters in two senses:

1. Marginal costs of reproduction and transmission of knowledge are sufficiently high to create a space in which distance and proximity play an important role in shaping knowledge and information spillovers. There is therefore a law of decreasing importance of spillovers, in direct relation to increasing geographical distance;

2. Collocation of people engaged in a collective process of intellectual creation has its own merits when it comes to knowledge exchange (see table 5.1).

In view of these merits, face-to-face contact and real meetings have an unquestionable advantage in the field of knowledge exchange and collective intellectual creation.

Thus, spatial clusters of activities are at least partially explained by the advantage of proximity and the necessity of collocation in the process of knowledge creation (Audrestch and Feldman 1996; Audrestch and Stephan 1996). The fact that geography matters in explaining the importance of spillovers is therefore undisputable. This argument must, however, be qualified in three respects:

1. First, many other factors play a role in explaining the formation of geographical clusters of activities. The mere fact that the concentration of physical activities may generate large private and social returns (owing to economies of scale and indivisibilities in physical infrastructures) is an important factor (Bresnahan, Gambardella, and Saxenian 2002). Purely political factors are also important. Some cases of clusters of activities have very little to do with spatial effects. For

**Table 5.1**
Key Characteristics of Collocated Synchronous Interactions

| Characteristics | Description | Implications |
| --- | --- | --- |
| Rapid feedback | As interactions flow, feedback is as rapid as it can be | Quick corrections possible when there are noticed misunderstandings or disagreements |
| Multiple channels | Information among participants flows in many channels—voice, facial expressions, gesture, body posture, and so on. | There are many ways to convey a subtle or complex message; also provides redundancy |
| Personal information | The identity of contributors to conversation is usually known | The characteristics of the source can be taken into account |
| Nuanced information | The kind of information that flows is often analog or continuous, with many subtle dimensions (e.g., gestures) | Very small differences in meaning can be conveyed; information can easily be modulated |
| Shared local context | Participants have a similar situation (time of day, local events) | A shared frame on the activites; allows for easy socializing as well as mutual understanding about what's on each others' minds |
| Informal "hall" time before and after | Impromptu interactions take place among subsets of participants upon arrival and departure | Opportunistic information exchanges take place, and important social bonding occurs |
| Coreference | Ease of establishing joint reference to objects | Gaze and gesture can easily identify the referent of deictic terms |
| Individual control | Each participant can freely choose what to attend to, and change the focus of attention easily | Rich, flexible monitoring of how all of the participants are reacting to whatever is going on |
| Implicit cues | A variety of cues as to what is going on are available in the periphery | Natural operations of human attention provide access to important contextual information |
| Spatiality of reference | People and work objects are located in space | Both people and ideas can be referred to spatially; "air boards" |

*Source:* Olson and Olson (2003).

instance, Leslie and Kargon (1993) contrasted the Princeton cluster of scientific activities (involving Washington, DC, and Los Alamos, which is a pure political cluster based on an "imaginary geography") and the Stanford cluster, in which the local environment matters a lot.

2. Second, the potential of ICT to reduce spatial and proximity constraints has to be seriously considered.

3. Finally, proximity in itself is irrelevant. It is the way in which professional communities use it to combine their tangible and intangible assets that counts. Depending on the dynamic created, proximity remains a purely geographical phenomenon or becomes an effective organizational structure (combining incentives and coordination) for knowledge creation (Feldman and Francis 2001). Thus, Silicon Valley is not only a territory, it is above all "A set of collaborative practices that blur the boundaries between local firms, and between firms and local educational and financial institutions" (Saxenian 2001, 3).

## The Age of a Massive Growth of Knowledge Externalities

Clearly, situations with full spillovers correspond to a fictive world in which knowledge is codified (and not tacit); costs of acquisition, codification, and transmission are low; and knowledge is highly cumulative. Knowledge externalities are a constant in history because the three properties identified are the intrinsic characteristics of knowledge. Their magnitude, however, was historically limited by the high costs of accessing, formatting, and transmitting knowledge. It is therefore

**Table 5.2**
Structure of Costs of Knowledge

| Knowledge Cost Structure |
| --- |
| *Production* |
| Learning, R&D |
| *Use and Reuse* |
| Knowledge is nonrival |
| *Acquisition (and Search)* |
| The cost of intellectual investment needed for people to be capable of understanding and exploiting knowledge (cost of training and maintenance of intellectual equipment and search capabilities) |
| *Reproduction* |
| Production of scripts, codification and articulation of various kinds |
| *Copy and Transmission* |
| Physical infrastructure |

very important to think about the structure of these costs, for it can change not the nature but the degree of the problem of externality.

In this structure I differentiate between reproduction costs (the cost of producing the script and codifying it) and acquisition costs (the cost of educating people, training, and maintaining intellectual equipment and capabilities). This difference makes the point that there is a cost to produce and absorb a script. Even the best codified script (providing a good articulation of the knowledge) has no value if it is lost in the jungle, and very little value if it is on my desk and deals with very complex mathematical knowledge. The evolution of acquisition costs are related to human capital investments.

The argument developed in this section is that the knowledge economy is an economy which is approaching the hypothetical world, as already described:

• in which the marginal cost of acquiring, reproducing, and transmitting knowledge constantly decreases;

• in which geographical constraints are mitigated; and

• in which attitudes shift away from prevailing behaviors that obstruct knowledge disclosure.

A world in which a "combinatorial explosion" is likely to occur.

### The Decrease of Marginal Costs of Knowledge Reproduction and Transmission in the Digital Age, and the Less Predictable Evolution of Acquisition Costs

**Rachid and Joe**    The following fable highlights the significance of the use of new technologies for decreasing marginal costs in the reproduction and transmission of knowledge. Compare the experiences of two scholars: Rachid, a seventeenth century astronomer from the beautiful town of Fez, and Joe, a young postdoctoral engineering student working in a Stanford University laboratory in the late twentieth century.

Rachid invents a new telescope and wants to transmit the details of his discovery to colleagues in Cordoba, Padua, and Salamanca. (I was inspired by an Arab novel, translated into French: *Le télescope de Rachid*; see Majhoub 2000). This is an arduous task because this kind of knowledge has not yet been codified; only manual writing exists as a codification technology. Moreover, Rachid cannot use engineering drawing techniques, such as orthographic projection, because they have not yet been invented. He therefore entrusts his precious documents to the northbound caravans, in the hope that they will one day be delivered to his colleagues. There is little certainty of that happening.

More problematic still are the situations in which knowledge is basically memorized and passed on by word of mouth (accompanied by somewhat incomplete papers intended to assist recall), because the circle of effective users typically remains confined to direct, personal contacts. As that circle widens, there is an increasing risk of the content becoming distorted in the course of oral transmission and successive copying. Only recurring communication back-and-forth among each of the pairs participating in such a network of transmission would be able to limit the propagation of "copying errors." The likelihood of that occurring, however, diminishes as the number of links in the human chain of communication increases.

Hence, there are physical limitations preventing expansion of the community of people who can harness new knowledge and possibly further improve upon Rachid's design. Knowledge flows have existed throughout history but, as a rule, they have been few and far between and relatively weak. As historians know, the main exceptions were permitted by the maintenance of dense interpersonal communication networks, such as those that linked the Cistercian abbeys of medieval Europe. This has checked the development of cumulative momentum in the growth of the stock of reliable knowledge.

The *marginal* cost structure of that knowledge can be studied. The *marginal* cost of production is, of course, very high and the *marginal* cost of reproduction is zero (nonrival good). The *marginal* cost of knowledge reproduction is very high because at the time of Rachid's invention, codification is a costly and painful process. Finally the *marginal* cost of transmission is very high. Thus, Rachid's invention is nonrival and cumulative knowledge but has no actual audience. The externalities produced are very weak, probably nil.

Now take the case of a student at Stanford, Joe de Risi, who posts a document called the Mguide on the Web. This is a document telling the reader how to build a micro array robot and listing all the necessary parts, suppliers and prices (*Science* 1999). Wishing to inform his community, he quickly produces the relevant documents and plans with the help of graphic design software. The files are then copied and dispatched as email attachments to a list of selected addresses. Within seconds, they are received by dozens of laboratories throughout the world and hundreds of researchers can begin reproducing the knowledge and sending back their comments, criticisms, and suggestions. The cost of production of this piece of knowledge is still very high and the cost of reuse is still zero. But knowledge codification and transmission costs here are very low i.e., Joe's marginal costs of codifying and transmitting the knowledge in question, given the fixed infrastructure, and his training costs.

We have already noted that tacit knowledge transmission costs also fall at the margin. Many cognitive scientists argue that the combination of digital technologies and new networks of electronic transmission makes remote access to and remote learning of tacit knowledge feasible (see chapter 4). Tacit knowledge will no longer remain a factor limiting the scope of externalities.

**Do Acquisition Costs Also Fall at the Margin?** What can be said now about the evolution of the marginal cost of knowledge acquisition? In the case of Rachid the *marginal* cost of acquisition is very high: this is extremely specialized knowledge in an almost esoteric branch of astronomy and only very few other people around the world are able to understand and exploit it.

In the case of Joe, the cost of acquisition is quite high but thousands of biologists have the "intellectual equipment" to benefit from that knowledge. This is the case when the invention itself remains within the framework of knowledge with which the community's members are familiar: the people receiving the file have "learned to learn" this kind of knowledge and the attached document provides a detailed learning program. For that fairly large number of scientists, the marginal cost of acquisition is low.

**Table 5.3**
A Comparison of Marginal Cost Structures

| Cost structure (marginal cost) | In Rachid's world | In Joe's world |
|---|---|---|
| Production | Very high | Very high |
| Use and reuse | 0 | 0 |
| Acquisition (including search) | Very high | Lower |
| Reproduction (including codification) | Very high | Low |
| Transmission | Very high | Very low |
| Externalities | No externality | Massive |

**Summary**  Comparison with knowledge *marginal* cost structures introduces us to an understanding of the significance of the knowledge economy: when acquisition, transmission, and reproduction costs fall the externality becomes very strong. In the case of Joe's invention, externalities are huge. Several dozen labs around the world, including those in China, Japan, Australia, and Eastern Europe, have acquired that knowledge and developed the robot.

Thus, we can consider that, as a rule, formatting and transmission costs drop steeply with time, depending on the dynamics of information and communication technologies. By contrast, the development of acquisition costs is far less predictable. They remain very high for specialized knowledge but the increase in education and training investments causes them to decline over time. Note, however, that without search capabilities (see chapter 11), the cost of congestion (information overload) would exceed the benefits provided by information abundance. Thus, the development of search capabilities is a critical factor in order to limit search costs as a part of acquisition costs.

### The Reduction of Geographical Constraints

In Joe's world the physical constraint is greatly reduced. Even the argument of tacit knowledge transmission making it necessary to maintain face-to-face contact is losing its force, for tacit knowledge transmission costs also fall at the margin (see chapter 4). Given how efficiently knowledge can travel when codified, and the fact that the costs of moving people are still very high (and are rising with the growth in size of urban areas), one may well have grounds for believing that clusters of activity are now less necessary to absorb knowledge spillovers, while the other explanations (indivisibility of physical infrastructures and political factors) are still highly relevant. In other words, in locational problems characterized by the centrality of the relative costs of moving knowledge, as opposed to moving people, one can expect the relative decrease of clustering of activities in case of intensive use of the new ICT (Mokyr 2000).

The geography of innovation is now structured primarily by the existence or absence of professional communities, while their spatial dispersion is no longer particularly relevant. This is typically what tells us the story of Joe, in which the kind of knowledge considered is not so simple. Many cases of scientific communities, open source users, and communities of practices fall into this category of situation, where the collective process of innovation is relieved of geographical constraints. However, locational advantages remain an important issue in many other cases, when the long-distance transfer of codified knowledge is not enough for people to acquire the knowledge necessary to undertake a collective action. Returning to table 5.1, Olson and Olson (2003) show that most of the virtuous characteristics of collocated synchronous interactions are only poorly supported by ICT or even not supported at all. A distinction that may be useful in this respect is between "collective adoption"—which the "Joe model" describes so well—and "collective creation of knowledge"—which covers processes where the characteristics described in table 5.1 are very important and still poorly supported by the technology infrastructure.

The fact remains that, on the whole, individuals and organizations have far more room to choose between travelling themselves or moving knowledge between various geographically distributed sites. They have far more room to "imagine" geography.

### Departing from Prevailing Attitudes that Obstructed Knowledge Openness

Apart from improvements to technologies for the reproduction and transmission of knowledge, and investments in human capital which swell the communities capable of reproducing that knowledge, another major development, which has contributed to the growth of knowledge externalities, relates to the progressive construction of norms and institutions facilitating the sharing and circulation of knowledge. To be sure, before the seventeenth century, prevailing attitudes in the West obstructing the widespread disclosure of "Nature's secrets" were perhaps more important than limitations of community technology in impeding effective cooperation in the pursuit of knowledge.

With the exception of very particular local situations (exchange between two scientists or engineers bound by close relations of trust) or communities created explicitly to facilitate the transmission of stabilized knowledge, and which institute a sufficiently strong boundary with the rest of the world to be able to shelter practices of disclosure (e.g., the craft guilds) (Epstein 1998), knowledge is neither shared nor revealed. Insofar as revealing or demonstrating are actions which offer knowledge to others, in the absence of intellectual property rights everyone prefers keeping their secrets. In 1421 when an Italian engineer, Brunelleschi, designed a new type of ship he wrote (referring to himself in the third person): "He refuses to make such a machine available to the public in order that the fruit of his genius and skill may not be reaped by another without his will and consent, and that, if he enjoyed some prerogative concerning this, he would open up what he is hiding and would disclose it all" (Eamon 1985, 327). When knowledge was codified to be memorized, it was expressed in the enigmatic form of "books of secrets."

The creation of intellectual property rights—of which the main aim was to attract foreign inventors—made it possible to reconcile the action of disclosing knowledge with the protection of private rights to that knowledge. It is therefore a fundamental institution, facilitating the circulation of knowledge (see chapter 7). But this was only one aspect in a gradual process of transformation of attitudes that encompassed other changes:

• the gradual shift of knowledge from the domain of the divine and sacred (which is not revealed) to that of experimental and natural science—a shift that laid the foundations for the development of a critique of "hidden" knowledge, spearheaded by Francis Bacon in particular (Eamon 1985);

• the enhanced importance of technical change in the world of industry and thus of cooperation, which paved the way for a critique of obscurantist attitudes. As Long (1991, 353) states in a discussion of the sixteenth-century authors who decided to disclose their knowledge in clear and well-diffused articles: "Despite their diversity, these authors shared the context provided by the capitalist expansion of mining. As a result, they elaborated a group of seemingly unrelated attitudes from a remarkably consistent point of view. Their affirmation that knowledge should be transmitted openly was closely associated with beliefs related to early modern mine and metallurgical capitalism: wealth is a positive good; investment in mining should be encouraged and will pay off in riches; clear technical language and precise assaying, and practical skill are all necessary to high productivity. They criticized alchemy not on the basis of whether transmutation occurred, but in terms of the criteria of clarity, honesty and productivity";

• finally, the evolution of knowledge toward modes of increasing technical elaboration and expression which no longer allowed the "protective Prince" himself to judge the work of those striving for his glory (as in the case of composers, writers, and painters). Asymmetries of information thus generated called for a system of peer evaluation, the invisible college which, to function, implied the diffusion of knowledge in order to be scrutinized and reproduced by other scientists (David 1998a).

All these changes, which did not coincide historically, resulted in a complete change in attitudes and in the creation and consolidation of institutions and norms favorable to the transmission of knowledge. These institutions, whose strength lay in their making the transmission of knowledge compatible with the encouragement and promotion of individual inventors, is examined in chapter 8. I discuss the oldest and probably most robust institution, open science, as well as many forms of collective invention which developed with the advent of the industrial world, and which are often linked to an occupation or territory.

These changes should not be interpreted as the expression of an inexorable tendency toward the sharing and circulation of knowledge. On the contrary, the institutions and norms that I briefly mention are extremely vulnerable and can rapidly disappear when opportunities for the commercialization of knowledge become too great and competitive private markets are formed. Yet a decisive change has taken place, relative to the growing awareness of the progressiveness and cumulativeness of knowledge, and hence of the critical role of "the community" (scientists, engineers, users) in which everyone has access to the knowledge of others, and they reproduce, improve, and transmit it. Hence, the attention paid in these communities to the creation of forms of systematic expression of knowledge (nomenclature, taxonomy, standardization of terminology), as well as to the mechanisms capable of reconciling the pooling of knowledge with encouragement and reward for individuals. In chapter 8 I study these communities in depth.

**Dynamic Loops**

For a long time the mediocre state of knowledge reproduction and transmission technologies, the small size of communities capable of absorbing that knowledge and, last, obscurantist attitudes, combined to impede the diffusion of knowledge. These obstacles reinforced one another, creating a world in which knowledge traveled badly. At the time of manual writing and copyist monks, pirating was certainly possible but nevertheless limited. In fact, this provided the main deterrent to the printing press, "which puts the fate of texts into mechanical hands and sells them to unknown agents." By means of manuscript copies, often autographs, addressed only to people close to them,

authors hoped to retain control of their work. These "scribal communities" greatly reduced the dimension of externalities (Love 1993).

But when technologies improve, communities grow and minds open,
the forces in favor of the free flow of knowledge multiply and progressively lay the foundations of knowledge-based economies.

## The Essence of the Knowledge Economy

Rachid and Joe are scientists and it was certainly within scientific communities that the knowledge economy (as defined here) flourished first.
This type of world—characterized by transmission and formatting
costs that are almost nil, and composed of sufficiently large communities of "intelligent" agents—can be seen emerging in many fields of
science. It is also in science that the norm of openness and knowledge
sharing initially emerged and is still being enforced through many
institutional mechanisms: "A simple HP 9000 has radically changed the
way scientists work today in the field of high-particle physics. Every
day almost 20,000 electronic messages send the abstracts of new academic papers across 60 countries. These messages can then be retrieved
by interested readers. Every day, close to 45,000 physicists explore electronic archives to find particular bits of old information" (Mulligan
1994).

However, the massive growth of externalities does not concern only
science and the very advanced knowledge associated with scientific
explorations. This phenomenon also concerns the very large sector of
science-based industries. In these kinds of industry a massive growth
of knowledge externalities is expected to take place. Members of the
industry share scientific and technological parameters, including
intellectual understandings concerning technical functions, use of
materials, performance characteristics, and so on. The increasing power
of absorptive capabilities of firms plays a critical role here. Thus, large
communities of "intelligent agents" combined with an intensive use of
new ICT are likely to make the marginal costs of reproducing, transmitting, and acquiring knowledge fall dramatically. This is also true for
basic knowledge and very large communities of people. In this case,
marginal costs of acquisition, codification, and transmission also fall,
such as new medical knowledge on the feeding of babies immediately
printed in all languages and disseminated by all possible media, or a
new pedagogical concept diffused through the traditional and modern
channels within the educational community (OECD 1999a).

If I relate the transformations in table 5.3 to the essential characteristics of knowledge-based economies (chapter 2), we see that the ICT
revolution causes knowledge reproduction and transmission costs to
drop, while the increase in learning-related investments (training and
education) leads to some decrease in acquisition costs. The knowledge-
based economy is therefore clearly an economy in which knowledge
externalities are more powerful than ever, consecutive to this double
trend of ICT development and increasing investments in education.

The significance of these transformations, including the new attitudes toward knowledge openness and diclosure as well as the increasing capabilities of agents for imitating, adapting, and reproducing
knowledge generated elsewhere (involuntary spillovers), is now easy
to grasp. All this progress allows more effective exploitation of the
properties of nonrivalry and cumulativeness of knowledge. In this
sense, it gives the knowledge-based economy a coherent physical and
social base but also compound problems of protection and compensation for the producers of new knowledge.

# 6

# Knowledge as a Public Good

In this chapter I explore various aspects of the main dilemma of the economics of knowledge, namely, the conflict between the social goal of efficient use of knowledge once it has been produced and the goal of providing ideal motivation to the private producer. The main part of this chapter is devoted to the analysis and comparison of the various institutional mechanisms, which provide different solutions to this dilemma. These mechanisms address the issues of funding and organizing activities which are specifically dedicated to the production of knowledge (essentially R&D). The learning-by-doing aspect of knowledge creation is not considered here, since being lodged in the process of other activities (manufacturing, using, consuming), it receives no direct expenditures.[8]

## Public Good and the Knowledge Dilemma

The main implication of the three properties studied in chapter 5 is the creation of a difference between the private and social return in the production of knowledge. Simply, the property of nonexcludability is sufficient to produce that difference. Assuming the production of knowledge generates profits, the recovery of all those profits is in itself a problem because of the difficulty of completely controlling knowledge. Some of the profits are harnessed by others; in other words, they are externalized. The other two properties (nonrivalry and cumulativeness) amplify the difference between private and social returns, opening the possibility of huge social returns.

It is basically the uncontrollability, nonrivalry, and cumulativeness threesome that accounts for the importance of social returns to research and innovation, and that makes these activities an essential basis for growth. Measurements of social returns to research generally give extremely good results.

Griliches (1995) conducted a survey of the econometric literature on this subject, showing that the social return varies between 20 and 100 percent (for one dollar spent). Mansfield (1977) examined in detail seventeen innovations and estimated an average social return of 56 percent compared to a 25 percent private return. Trajtenberg (1990) calculated a social return of 270 percent in the case of scanners. In a review of this literature, Mairesse (1998) recognizes the extreme sensitivity of the results to the choice of econometric methods and the quality of the data used. He concludes, however, that even though each of these studies seems fragile and open to criticism on many counts when taken on its own, the overall convergence of the results is quite convincing.

**Externalities and Lack of Incentives**
In the presence of externalities, inventors must expect to receive less than the social returns of their invention. Private agents therefore tend to "underinvest" in the production of knowledge since they cease their efforts devoted to innovation at the point where the marginal costs of those efforts (MOCi) meet the private marginal value of their investment (Mvi). From society's point of view, it would be preferable for them to cease their efforts only at the point where the marginal costs curve meets the curve representing the sum of marginal values (ΣMvi), that is, the social return. This is a typical situation of a lack of incentives, which leads to a level of insufficient private investments, for society (Xi* versus Xi**).

The problem thus formulated is qualified as a "public good problem." It is a general problem described by Pigou in 1932 and studied by Arrow (1962a) in the case of research and innovation. In Pigou's own terms, there is a large number of situations in which the net private marginal gain is less than the net social marginal gain because services are accidentally offered to a third party from whom it is technically difficult to obtain payment (Pigou cites scientific research as an example of this type of situation).

Not only is scientific or technological knowledge a good that is difficult to control, it is also a nonrival and cumulative good. These different characteristics enhance the strength of positive externalities and thus increase the difference between private and social returns. Thus, social returns may be so substantial that remunerating the inventor accordingly is unthinkable. What is the social return of Pythagoras's

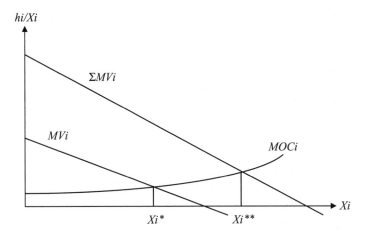

**Figure 6.1**
The public good effect
Xi: research effort of an individual $i$ ($i = 1, \ldots, N$); hi/xi: per unit product.
MOCi: marginal opportunity cost; Mvi: marginal value of ideas produced.

work and how can it be rewarded "fairly"? Of course it is only in an economy which is not reduced to monetary values alone and which also has, to use Montaigne's expression, "honorary rewards" that mechanisms for rewarding knowledge creation can be conceived.

**Redistributive Effects Reduce the Problem**  By suggesting other sources of profit for innovators, the analysis of redistribution effects tends to predict less of a problem of a lack of incentives (Hirshleifer 1971). By definition, innovators are the only ones to have information on future changes in the price of certain inputs that their innovation is likely to cause. Before revealing their innovation, they are therefore in a position to speculate on these factors. It is the inventor of a watermill who will buy cheaply all land through which a river runs; it is the agent who discovers the use of oil who pays next-to-nothing for the waste-land polluted by the oil fields. In all these cases, the question of maintaining control over innovation is no longer relevant. On the contrary, externality (diffusion) is not only tolerable, but it becomes highly desirable. Thus, this mechanism makes it possible to reconcile in the best possible way the preservation of private interests and the maximization of social returns (distribution of knowledge). This solution shifts the source of private profits and, as a result, does not affect positive externalities. Better still, by playing on effects that depend on the diffusion of the innovation, it forces the creator to disclose the new knowledge freely.

The limits of this solution are of course in the nature of the new knowledge. Only radical knowledge and inventions are able to change the prices of factors significantly. However, this very radicalness probably makes the condition of being the only one to have information on future price changes unrealistic (see chapter 8 for an analysis of this class of knowledge as a possible source of the tragedy of the commons).

**The Knowledge Dilemma**

Since the marginal cost of use of knowledge is nil, maximum efficiency in its use implies that there is no restriction to access and that the price of use is equal to zero. Knowledge should be a "free" good; that is the condition for optimum use of a nonrival good. There is no need to ration ideas by price since they already exist and cost nothing to replicate. In this case, if charging for access excludes some would-be consumers, the result is waste. Wants go unsatisfied that could have been satisfied at no cost.

But whereas maximum efficiency in the use of knowledge supposes rapid and complete distribution and hence requires that its price be nil, the same does not apply to its production. Producing knowledge is costly, very much so in some cases. As a result, maximum efficiency in the use of resources to create new knowledge requires that the costs of all necessary resources be covered by the economic value of the knowledge created.

That is the dilemma: Only the anticipation of a positive price on use will guarantee the allocation of resources for creation, but only a price that is nil will guarantee efficient use of knowledge, once it has been produced. It is a dilemma between the social objective of ensuring efficient use of knowledge once it has been produced, and the objective of providing ideal motivation to the private producer. There is no simple solution to that problem (or dilemma). The answer will differ from case to case.

While any kind of knowledge and information is characterized by this dilemma, only the cumulative nature of knowledge makes this dilemma a serious issue. In this sense it is not possible to consider and treat in similar terms knowledge as a consumption good—or, in Fritz Machlup's terminology, as "consumption capital"—and knowledge as an investment good likely to spawn new (knowledge) goods. The more knowledge is cumulative, the more wasteful is the effect of rationing it by price. In the field of scientific and technological knowledge, it is not only the individual enjoyment of a few consumers that is curbed by limiting the use of knowledge but, accumulation and collective progress are also limited—namely, the thousand opportunities afforded by new combinations between diverse elements of knowledge.

There is thus a danger of overgeneralization from both sides: on the one hand, in pursuing the public good analysis and deliberating on its welfare economic aspect, we are in danger of overgeneralizing a problem which is limited to scientific and technological knowledge (and even to a part of that domain). On the other hand, in seeking the best methods to support e-business—of, say, the entertainment sector—we are in danger of overgeneralizing methods such as Electronic Copyright Management Systems (ECMS) methods, that could generate huge social losses if applied to the part of the scientific and technological domain in which knowledge is highly cumulative.

Thus, by moving on from the property of externality to those of nonrivalry and cumulativeness, the contradiction worsens between the aim of increasing the private value of knowledge (implying restrictions on its use) and that of preserving its social value (implying free use). The more cumulative the use, the more control mechanisms—locks, tickets and patents—will tend to generate social losses. The dilemma imposes itself only with the notion of cumulativeness of knowledge which shifts it from the world of consumer goods to that of production.

The dilemma indicates that a positive externality, produced by a nonrival and cumulative good, cannot be corrected like a negative externality (or, more precisely, actions aimed at correcting a positive externality cannot be the exact opposite of those aimed at reducing a negative externality). In the case of negative externalities (noise, pollution) the problem is relatively simple: it is necessary to act on the source of the emission, either by demanding correction at the source or by taxing it. In the case of a positive externality the problem is not reducing it, because it is positive. The matter is more complex and the line is thin between the goal of protecting the creator's interests and that of maintaining benefits for society. Another difference is that monitoring and preventing opportunistic behavior is likely to be much more difficult in the case of positive externalities. For instance, it is easy to provide "too much" subsidy, encouraging those with a small chance of finding the invention to engage in the search. It is hard to know "how much is too much"; such an invention may not exist, but if it did it would have very high social value.

### The Collective Production of Knowledge as a Local and Temporary Solution to the Dilemma

According to Coase (1960), the problem of externality is not a unilateral one (that could be reduced by acting on the beneficiary) but a bilateral problem between transmitter and receiver. In the domain of knowledge production, the creation of collective entities (R&D agreements, technical centers, high-technology consortiums) makes it possible to "internalize externalities" and thus to reduce the problem (see chapter 3, on R&D collaboration). The idea is not to act on the controllability of knowledge but to reduce the size of externalities by expanding the area in which knowledge is voluntarily shared. In other words, this solution reduces the problem posed by externalities (by reducing their dimension) without affecting their positive impact on the economy, namely, the sharing of knowledge.

The limits of this solution soon appear, however. While coordination and organization costs increase with the number of participants, thus precluding agreements among "a very large number" of partners, the externalities derived from the production of basic knowledge are by definition very broad and always extend beyond the local perimeter of the collective institution.

### Three Institutional Mechanisms for the Provision of a Public Good

#### Is Knowledge Really a Public Good?

Saying that knowledge is a public good, when we are living in a historical period of accelerated privatization of knowledge bases (chapters 7 and 11), can be a source of misunderstanding. It is an interesting subject for debate and even controversy with those who maintain that no good is essentially public and who inappropriately illustrate their argument with Coase's famous article on lighthouses (Coase 1974), a service that was once provided by the private sector in the United Kingdom. It therefore seems relevant to recall that, saying a good (e.g., knowledge) is a public good, on the basis of the properties of nonexcludability and nonrivalry, does not mean that this good must necessarily be produced by the state, that markets for it do not exist, or that its private production is impossible. It simply means that, considering the properties of the good, it is not possible to rely exclusively on a system of competitive markets to guarantee production efficiently (David 1998c). Indeed, the example of the lighthouse shows that the private market functions because an agent is granted local monopoly on the right to collect a tax in exchange for the service provided. In the same way, the creation of a private monopoly on new knowledge (a patent) enables the market to produce that good. But in both cases the remedy is imperfect, for the owner of the monopoly will not supply the "light" (of the lighthouse or knowledge) at a price (harbor tax or royalties) equivalent to the negligible cost of making these goods available to additional users (the marginal cost of use of existing knowledge is nil, as it is in the case of using the harbor's lighthouse).

**The Importance of Institutional Diversity**

Pigou (1932) identified three institutional mechanisms for providing public goods (at the time he focused on the provision of public utilities): subsidies, direct governmental production, and regulated monopoly. These three mechanisms have a clear application in the domain of knowledge production and R&D.

• "Subsidies" support the constitution of a system of providing funding to individuals and organizations engaged in intellectual discovery and invention, in exchange for full public disclosure of the knowledge produced.

• "Direct government production" is the system of mission-oriented agencies and laboratories funded by the government. Public disclosure of knowledge is in principle secured with few (but important) exceptions such as the agencies dealing with military and national security issues.

• "Market for knowledge" is the system in which the stimulation of private initiatives is based on intellectual property rights which make it possible to grant temporary exclusive rights to new knowledge and innovation.

David (1993) refers to these three mechanisms as the three P's, because they can be described in highly idealized forms as patronage, procurement, and property, respectively. Each of those mechanisms provides a particular solution to the knowledge dilemma.

The first consists in financing knowledge production from public (or private) funds while at the same time identifying mechanisms aimed at providing forms of self-discipline, evaluation, and competition within the beneficiary community. In return for aid received, the beneficiary is expected not so much to pursue objectives set by the financier, but rather to relinquish exclusive rights on knowledge produced. In concrete terms, society is responsible for covering the costs of resources needed to produce knowledge. This means, however, that anything produced is the property of society as a whole and cannot be privately controlled. Rapid communication and sharing of knowledge are the norm, facilitating the creation of cooperation networks.[9] In chapter 8 I explore the ingenious "collegial reputation reward system" which creates contexts of races and competition, compatible with the disclosure of knowledge. I explain why such a reward system is a highly effective device that offers nonmarket incentives to the production of public goods (Dasgupta and David 1994). It is important to clearly understand that the existence of these cooperative norms does not run counter to the existence of competitive mechanisms. Yet the competitions which take place there do not usually result in apparatus to maintain secrets and restrict access to new knowledge. This "open knowledge" mechanism characterizes research undertaken in public institutions such as universities where in most cases exclusive rights cannot be granted on knowledge and where salaries and equipment are paid from public funds.

The second mechanism is suited to a few large-scale projects, when there is a need for a high level of concentration of resources and centralization of decision making. The monitoring of performance relies primarily on administrative processes. By minimizing the use of markets, this solution makes the greatest demand on administrative capabilities. In this system there are no predetermined rules in terms of knowledge access and disclosure. The rules depend on the kind of activities developed (military or civilian, strategic or nonstrategic).

The third mechanism is based on devices that remedy the public good problem at its source. These devices are intended primarily to facilitate the creation of a market to stimulate private initiative. Basically, this amounts to restricting access to knowledge by granting temporary exclusive rights to new knowledge and thus enabling the inventor to set a price for its use. Patents, copyright, and registered designs are the main intellectual property rights used to guarantee a degree of exclusive rights to knowledge. Creation and use of intellectual property rights are frequently combined with systems of public grants, such as tax credits for research or innovation subsidies, with a view to covering innovation costs. All these mechanisms are specifically characteristic of private R&D, carried out in companies' research laboratories.

The first two mechanisms form what is commonly known as public sector research. Yet it is important to maintain the distinction between the two forms of public research insofar as economic incentives are fundamentally different. In the former system, individuals are "free" to do the research they wish to (although the system of grants determines a few main research thrusts). In return for financing, individuals and institutions must provide teaching. Modern scientists receive a fixed salary for their lecturing and related tasks, in addition to other rewards (e.g., promotions and increased reputation) for successful research. By contrast, in the latter system research is organized by the state in relation to targeted objectives. Individuals are not "free" in the sense of the former system; they have to follow a certain research direction. It follows that they do not have to provide a service in return, such as lecturing, in order to create a fair balance of advantages and constraints. In short, there is a significant difference between university research and research carried out in a national laboratory.

**Shortcomings Associated with Each Mechanism**   The three main mechanisms composing the institutional architecture of knowledge production systems have significant shortcomings as a method of resource allocation.

• In the public (or private) patronage system, mechanisms of allocating research grants to individuals and teams rarely defy hysteresis effects (reputation increases the probability of receiving a new grant which, in turn, has the effect of increasing reputation even more); this diminishes the system's capacity to identify and maintain the "best" researchers (David 1994).

• In the public production system, many problems of asymmetry of information make it difficult for research administrators to manage the activity. Moreover, the state replaces the market to select the "best"; government failures (instead of market failures) are likely to occur; such projects are high-risk ventures (a few large bets are placed on a small number of races); and, lastly, they create distortions in industrial competitiveness of the main industrial suppliers (Ergas 1992).

• In the private property system, intellectual property rights determine monopoly prices that create distortions in the market. They can also generate excessive investments, while grants and tax incentives produce deadweights.

**Different Objectives and Modes of Managing Externalities** It is important to note that the three mechanisms have specific functionalities and are therefore complementary. In the patronage system the goal is to increase the stock of "reliable" knowledge. In the public production system the goal is to achieve a given technological (or scientific) objective. Finally, in the private property system the aim is to maximize profits derived from innovation.

These differences in objectives mean differences in the mode of managing externalities and solving the public good problem.

• Maximizing knowledge externalities is the raison d'être of the patronage system (for instance, of an open science system). This is based on a set of consistent institutions: weak intellectual property protection; funding largely from government or private foundations; and a reward system (based on priority) compatible with the fast and broad dissemination of knowledge. Moreover, management of externalities, namely, the organization of access to and integration of knowledge, is accomplished through norms and institutions. For example, it is usual for researchers to write and share "surveys" aimed at making the state of the art of a particular domain available to the rest of the community. Nothing like that exists in the private property system.

• Externalities are contingent in the public production system. They can be massive or they can be very weak. It cannot be taken as a rationale for public funding (see the debate on defense R&D expenditures and dual technology) (Cowan and Foray 1995).

• Minimizing externalities is an important objective of the private property system and most spillovers will be involuntary. Here the set of institutional mechanisms includes strong intellectual property protection. The production of further knowledge is funded by sale of commercialized results.

**Institutional Architecture**
These three mechanisms form the institutional architecture of any knowledge production system, defined as a public good. It is never-

theless useful to refine the analysis somewhat by considering the two dimensions of a knowledge production activity: financing and access. The perimeters of an activity defined by our three mechanisms vary, depending on the dimension. There is certainly a sort of general "public" versus "private" logic: public financing is usually associated with a rule of complete diffusion of knowledge, while private financing is based on the possibility of maintaining private control over the knowledge produced. In reality, beyond this general logic there is a multitude of possible combinations of financing and diffusion practices. This multiplicity of practices stems from a certain degree of independence between the question of financing and that of diffusion and access. We witness more private control of knowledge and limits to access in the public patronage domain: Universities patent their results and grant exclusive licenses. On the other hand, in certain sectors private firms produce scientific publications and thus diffuse some of their knowledge freely, to attract academic partners (Hicks 1995). There is a multitude of possible combinations of the practices and logic characteristic of each sector. In the table 6.1, the six quadrants correspond to particular combinations of a dominant form of funding arrangement and a knowledge disclosure regime.

Apart from "pure" forms characterized by some coherence between financing and access, there are two hybrid situations, which have recently occupied a lot of space on the institutional scene. Basic research campuses of private firms refer to the new organizational practices of major pharmaceutical (and ICT) firms which import modes of organization and academic research incentive mechanisms to maintain and reinforce linkages between their researchers and outside

**Table 6.1**
The Six Institutional Figures for the Formal Production of Knowledge

| | Dominant form of funding arrangement | | |
|---|---|---|---|
| Information disclosure regime | Public and private patronage | Public contracting and expenditures | Private business contracting and direct expenditures |
| Public access | Universities and nonprofit institutions | Government civilian labs and institutes | Corporate basic research "campuses" |
| Private access | University-industry research centres contract | Government defense labs | Corporate R&D organizations |

*Source:* David (2000b).

networks of expertise (Cockburn, Henderson, and Stern 1999). University-industry research centers account for all the situations in which universities compromise on the "rules" of free access in order to develop strong ties with industrial research and even to engage in their own commercialization activities (Cohen et al. 1998).

## From Public Sector to Public Property

It is important not to have a narrow view of what corresponds to public organization in this institutional architecture. There is obviously the public sector controlled by the government (represented mainly by the middle column in table 6.1). But there are also other forms of organization which are neither private nor controlled by the government, and are described by Rose (1986) as "inherently public." Some examples include the communities of users described in chapter 3 and other forms of collective actions that determine collective spaces of knowledge sharing. What Arrow (1969b) refers to as "collective action" and Hayek (1945) as "the third sector" corresponds more or less to this set of organizations characterized by a type of property that is "inherently public."

### Public and Private Property

I now simplify the analysis and move on to a more systematic study of relations between the public and private property.

### Functional Complementarities

The two spheres maintain close complementary relations and the prosperity of one depends on that of the others.

Consider the three main modes of knowledge production today (chapter 3). In each of the forms described (science-based, user-based, and coordination-oriented), the existence of a freely accessible stock of knowledge is crucial. The efficiency of innovation processes is fundamentally dependent on this domain of "public" knowledge and information. By public domain I do not necessarily mean the public sector "controlled by the state." I am referring more generally to areas in which knowledge is shielded from mechanisms of private appropriation and in which knowledge and information are revealed and shared.

**Public Knowledge in the Science-Based Innovation Model**  The public dimension of the first source of innovation is very clear. Knowledge resulting from basic research is generic and fundamental.

Accordingly, its "social returns" will be far higher if it can be used by a multiplicity of innovators. The free circulation of this knowledge facilitates cumulative research, increases opportunities for innovation, and enhances the quality of results (since everyone can examine them and try to reproduce them). This free circulation is at the heart of the organization model of science, which historically has proven its efficiency. In this model, the public sector of scientific research produces public knowledge, which can be used freely by industry. This pool of knowledge is an extremely important input for private R&D. It is generally considered that the existence of public knowledge generates (at least in the immediate vicinity) an increase in private returns to investments in R&D. Jaffe (1989) estimated the elasticity of the performance of industrial R&D in relation to the increase in university research investments. He revealed a strong positive relation between the increase in university research and the productivity of industrial research. Mansfield (1995) used a sample of seventy-six U.S. corporations to estimate the economic value of "new products" and "new processes" that would not have existed without the contribution of university research. By calculating sales derived from these new products and the economies of costs of the new processes, he estimated a social return of 28%. All the cited econometric studies show that these externalities are very real.

The public sector also generates training and screening externalities: disclosure and peer evaluation mechanisms afford R&D managers with a great deal of information, at a very low cost, on the qualities of scientists and engineers whom they might wish to recruit (Dasgupta and David 1994).

On the other hand, the private sector introduces and promotes cost-effective methods for technological development and commercialization of innovation, including, in particular, much attention to the time-to-market problem. Public research needs the market system because it is not a closed loop and could not survive on its own.

All in all, the prosperity of one sector seems to sustain that of the other and vice versa. Thus, the diversity of institutional arrangements matters. This mutual reinforcement and dependence between the two worlds is clearly illustrated in numerous empirical studies, for example, on the pharmaceutical industry. The study by Cockburn and Henderson (1997) of twenty-one cases of discovery and development of drugs shows the essential role of public knowledge produced and made available by public research institutions and subsequently exploited and commercialized by private firms.

**Public Knowledge in the User-Based Innovation Model**   The public dimension is a necessary condition for the functioning of communities of users. In these communities multiple potential sources of innovation are activated and each member of the community can benefit from them. If this condition were not met, each user would be obliged to make all the adjustments he/she desired him/herself, which would substantially increase the overall cost of the system. It would consequently have no chance of competing with "average" solutions (more or less suited to everyone) at a lower cost, proposed by commercial systems. The sharing and circulation of innovation is therefore essential to ensure a minimum of efficiency (see chapter 8).

**Public Knowledge in the Industrial Coordination-Oriented Innovation Model**   The public dimension of the third source of innovation is less known but equally evident. It results from the collective creation of quasipublic goods in private markets. It is crucial to preserve public access and the sharing of "essential" technological or informational elements composing the norm, standard, or infratechnology of an industry. As in the preceding cases, this poses thorny problems of compromise between the collective aspect of innovation and the safeguarding of private interests.

**Asymmetric Instability**   These three cases thus clearly illustrate the importance of a shared collection of basic knowledge that provides the building blocks for new inventions. It is nevertheless difficult to keep a good balance between the two sectors because of asymmetric instability. This means that the public domain is inherently fragile, as any cooperative system in the absence of third party enforcement (including the provision of penalties for defectors). Many historical cases as well as the present situation characterizing the involvement of universities in the commercialization of science are good examples of this inherent fragility. It is thus an important policy objective to maintain a productive tension between the public domain and the private sector.

**A Simple Model of Sharing between Private and Public Funding**
Figure 6.2 shows simply how knowledge production activities are spread out in the public and private sectors.

The private sector does research when the expected returns exceed a certain minimum level (quadrants A and B in the table). Commercial prospects, fixed costs of research, and the possibility of having exclu-

Expected profitability for firms

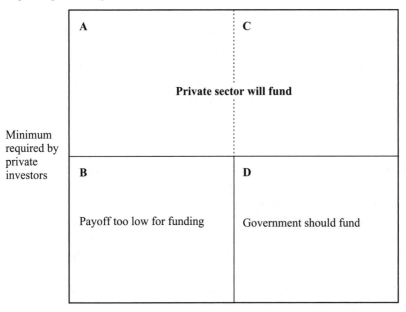

|  | Cost of public funding | Expected social benefits |

**Figure 6.2**
Private and social benefits from R&D. *Source:* Brown (1998).

sive rights to the new knowledge are essential factors governing expected private returns. The public sector takes charge of research with high social returns but with private returns that are below the minimum threshold. Science often corresponds to this situation; it involves an exploratory research activity that produces basic knowledge (high social returns) of which the possibility of commercial application is at best delayed in time and most often uncertain or even unknown (low private returns).

But public funding also has a cost. Depending on that cost, some research with low expected social benefits will not be supported (quadrant C). Moreover, the cost of taxes is usually added to the cost of public funding, that is, the disincentive effects of increased tax pressure. The expected social returns usually have to be at least 20 percent for the activity to be funded by the public sector.

This sharing of roles tends nevertheless to become less clear-cut near the boundaries. The area around the boundary between B and D is characterized by a certain type of scientific research that is different from pure science insofar as it is "oriented toward an application" (chapter 3). Institutional arrangements are less stable in such cases. Basic research oriented toward industrial application can have a multitude of forms, and it is in this respect that specific national characteristics are most marked. For example, in the United States large private laboratories have played a decisive part in the development of applied basic research, while in France this activity has most often remained in the public domain, as part of major national programs (nuclear, aerospace, aeronautics, electronics).

Thus, the two types of funding do not apply equally to different areas of knowledge (Zucker and Darby 1998). In some cases, the benefits related to use of the knowledge *cannot* be harnessed by a private agent, even if property rights have been granted, because the knowledge is too far removed from commercial use and/or is impossible to control. In such cases, public funding has to be provided. Moreover, in certain cases, gains related to the new knowledge *should not* be captured by a private entity, for the knowledge is so fundamental and so many socially useful applications could be derived from it that it would be dangerous to leave it to a private agent. Hence, there is a problem, located on the far right-hand side of quadrant B. A recent World Bank report (1998), for example, denounces the proliferation of private property rights in many areas of health and medicine, in which social returns are very high.

Boundaries between the market and the public domain are not set once and for all; they vary widely. In the diagram we see how the private sector can expand if the minimum threshold of expected returns is lowered. This can be done by reinforcing exclusivity on certain goods that were formerly "free" (see chapter 7). In general, the creation of new property rights combined with public R&D grants will substantially reduce the minimum return threshold and allow many activities to be taken care of by the private sector. That is typically the case today in many areas of the life sciences. Yet serious doubts remain as to the possibility of competitive private markets functioning in the domain of basic knowledge production. The mediocre economic performance of most biotechnology firms reinforce those doubts. The reason for these difficulties have already been discussed: knowledge is difficult to control and too many market failures (uncertainty, bad appropriability of knowledge despite the establishment of property rights) make these markets inefficient.

Boundaries also move upwards, for example, when commercial prospects disappear. A good example is that of pharmaceutical firms abandoning malaria research. Understandably, without a solvent market possible private returns are extremely uncertain, and, in any case, far more uncertain than those derived from the development of an AIDs vaccination or any pain-relieving drug. The fact nevertheless remains that the social benefits expected from malaria research are huge. These questions pose not only a problem of positive externalities but also one of equity between generations and between populations (an issue that I raise in the last chapter).

**The Importance of Institutional Diversity**

The conclusion to this chapter highlights the richness of institutional diversity in the production and diffusion of knowledge. The three mechanisms discussed each have specific functions and are, to a large extent, nonsubstitutable for one another; they differ in respect of both their "organizational virtues" and the criteria against which their performance is measured. An essential goal of public policies might therefore be to guarantee the balanced application of these three systems (with *balanced* obviously not meaning *equivalent*). I also noted that it is important not to have a narrow view of the "public sector" in the economics of knowledge. Government-controlled property (such as national R&D laboratories) and inherently public property (such as collective actions giving rise to horizontal systems of innovation where knowledge is shared and reused among users) are the two pillars of the public sphere.

# 7       Intellectual Property Rights in the Knowledge Economy

Intellectual property rights are the rights granted to the creators of intellectual products. Ideas are, of course, recognized as being part of humanity's common base and therefore not appropriable by a private person. In this respect, they are outside the law. A literary subject, an artistic principle, a political idea, or a scientific vision, for example, cannot be monopolized. What can, however, tilt over into private property is the concretization of the idea, theme, or principle. Only then may it be the object of a private right.[10]

## Definitions

Traditionally, a distinction is made among literary, artistic, and industrial property rights. In this vast domain, copyright and patents have become predominant in regards to scientific and technological knowledge. Surprisingly, these two categories have moved closer together. Initially, they were far apart, independently covering literary and artistic property rights and industrial property rights, respectively. The boundary was then somewhere between the beautiful and the useful. But with the development of scientific and technological knowledge these different rights now serve the same purpose. Their merger is due essentially to the fact that copyright has conquered new ground. By becoming the right most frequently used by the information technology, culture, and multimedia industries, copyright has "entered the corporate world."

Industrial property rights include patents, plant variety protection, industrial design, and integrated circuit design. Patents and related rights are based on the principle of disclosure of the invention by description or application, thus guaranteeing intellectual access to all in exchange for private ownership of its commercial use.

Industrial property rights also encompass other sets of items which, strictly speaking, do not fall under industrial property, such as trademarks and all contractual clauses granting exclusivity.

The patent ensures innovators the right to a temporary monopoly on a technical device or an engineering method. It is a property title that is valid in time (duration), geographic space (range), and the world of objects (scope of the patent). Filing a patent application means defining a set of claims concerning the concretization or application of an idea. After an investigation into anteriority and in some cases a study of patentability (see discussion on the criteria), the patent authority may grant or refuse property rights for a particular geographical area specified in the application. In exchange for patent rights the inventor must publicly divulge technical details on the new knowledge. Technical description is an essential act. It is the basis of the balance between the inventor's interests and those of society.

Unlike the patent process, the only condition governing copyright is "originality." Copyright protects the expression of an idea and not the idea itself. There is no inventive step or threshold of novelty. This protection acts with regard to patrimonial rights (protection against reproduction or representation) and moral rights (protection of the integrity of expression). But with copyright, parts of a protected work can be extracted and recombined to produce an original work. Copyright, unlike patents, gives the creator immediate, free protection without involving a lot of red tape.

Commercial secrecy is a different way for a company to appropriate the benefit of an innovation. As long as the secret is kept, profits from the new knowledge can be reserved. The most significant premodern incentive for invention was the capacity to capture the rents provided by a technical secret, and the most effective source of these rents was the craft guild (Epstein 1998). But the secret does not create a property right; by definition a secret cannot be revealed and therefore cannot be described sufficiently to make it possible to identify its nature or determine its owner. It therefore offers no protection against the risk of concurrent inventions. In 1990 Professor Maurice Escande registered a sealed envelope at the Académie des Sciences (a long-standing method in France to guarantee paternity of an invention without patenting). This secret document, filed under the number 16,933, sets out the principles of an innovative method in the therapeutic treatment of cancer. During the same period, the team of Dr. Judah Folkman at the Harvard Medical School and the Children's Hospital tested this method completely independently and obtained patents on the new molecules discovered by means of the approach. Professor Escande was suddenly deprived of all possibility of exploiting his invention. This episode clearly shows the bad appropriation strategy of the French team. It also illustrates the danger of trusting in secrecy. Moreover, recent measures by the World Intellectual Property Organization (WIPO) have weakened this means of protection even further. Since 1995 the onus of proof has been reversed: It is now the party accused of infringement of a patent to prove its innocence.

Finally, if the fact of keeping a process or formula secret is a strategy that can pay, the secret has little sense since it concerns knowledge destined to be exposed to everyone (e.g., knowledge incorporated in a new product).

## The Economics of Patent

### Economic and Legal Issues
Economic constraints exist to limit the use of patents. Any patent application involves payment of a fee in direct proportion to the size of the geographic area covered. The maintenance of huge patent portfolios consequently has high direct costs. Of course those costs are more than offset by exclusive exploitation of the invention by income generated by selling the rights and by effects of reputation and barriers to rivals.

Certain legal limits ensure that not all the knowledge produced by an economic agent is patented. Patentability of knowledge depends on conditions of absolute novelty of the invention, nonobviousness for a person of ordinary skill in the art, and the possibility of industrial application (utility). Theoretically, the condition of nonobviousness (or inventive activity) is intended to distinguish between that which is essentially the product of creative human work and that which is primarily the work of nature (chapter 1). The interpretation of this criterion is of course at the heart of discussions on the patentability of genetic creations.

The condition of industrial application is also important. The aim of this criterion was originally to exclude scientific knowledge from patentability.

Yet these criteria, which patent offices and law courts have to appreciate, are sufficiently flexible and even ambiguous to allow certain excesses in contexts of innovation races and striving for competitiveness through intellectual investment. Therefore, they no longer act as regulators. This is typically the case today with the patentability of genetic inventions. The tendency is to attach deciphered genetic sequences to the domain of invention and industrial application. The very specific nature of genetic creations is such that many of them would not enjoy private protection if the patent system were not gradually twisted to incorporate these new objects (Clavier 1998). The European directive[11] on the patentability of living organisms is totally ambiguous: Paragraph 1, Article 5 establishes that the human body and the discovery of one of its elements, including a gene sequence, cannot be considered as patentable inventions. But the following paragraph states that an isolated element of the human body, including a gene sequence, can constitute a patentable invention even if the structure of that element is identical to that of a natural element. What was an unpatentable discovery in the first paragraph becomes a patentable invention in the second.

These criteria are so unstable that institutions that assess the compliance of inventions with them, decide on patentatibility of an object, and sometimes solve conflicts wield a lot of power.

**Patent Institutions**
Two basic functions must be fulfilled by intellectual property institutions. The first function is to draw up a precise definition of rights and the objects to which exclusivity is guaranteed. The second is to make those rights enforceable and effectively to exclude all unauthorized agents from use of the relevant resources. These functions must be fulfilled in such a way that legal uncertainty is reduced, both in the definition of rights and in their enforcement. An intellectual property system qualified as "strong" is one that reduces legal uncertainty and increases the level of agents' confidence in its ability to defend their rights. One factor of surprise is the high level of institutional heterogeneity across countries, when more homogeneity and consistency would be expected, at least in patent offices' practices (legal systems are strongly influenced by national traditions and cultures).

Considerable differences in application procedures and modes of attribution of intellectual property rights can be observed in different countries:

1. National legal systems are grounded either in the principle of the first inventor (the United States) or in that of the first applicant (Europe and Japan). The latter principle forces the creator to go to the patent

office as soon as possible, even before initiating cooperation and trading knowledge. Although unfair in a sense, it has the advantage of providing an unambiguous criterion for the attribution of property rights. The U.S. principle, on the other hand, creates a degree of legal uncertainty insofar as conflicts between inventors are always possible and often lead to court action.

2. Certain systems provide for the possibility of opposing the application before the rights have been granted. This is possible provided the information concerning the application is published early enough (within 18 months of the application). Such mechanisms can avoid potential conflict, a source of high legal costs. In the U.S., where publication has until recently come in at a later stage,[12] once the property rights have been granted, this possibility of preempting conflict has not been used. Late publication of information creates legal uncertainty.

3. Some systems provide for an observation procedure. This is not an act of opposition; it simply consists of signaling existing similar knowledge. The aim is to complete the information available to the examiners and patent authorities. It is a very useful mechanism, for example, for limiting the scope of a patent.

4. Finally, the practices of patent offices are very dissimilar regarding their examination and search for anteriority, costs, and processing time. Basically, there are two extreme cases.

In the first approach, the examination is reduced to a minimum in order to minimize waiting time and costs. The result is an easy process, designed to favor the innovator (and the foreign investor) but it creates fragile rights. This is the somewhat caricatural case of the Australian office which recently accepted a patent for "a circular transportation facilitation device," that is, the wheel! The patent office works here as a simple registration agency. The fact of being indulgent with inventors by granting them everything they apply for creates fragile rights and increases the likelihood of conflict.

The other approach, clearly illustrated in Germany, advocates rigorous examination, with higher costs and longer waiting periods, but sounder patents and, consequently, less need for lawsuits.

## Advantages and Shortcomings

**Private Advantages**   The patent system has many virtues for the private innovator.

1. The patent provides an obvious solution to the public good problem. By increasing the expected private return of an innovation, it acts as an incentive mechanism to private investments in knowledge production.

2. Patents facilitate the market test of new inventions because they allow disclosure of related information while (in principle) protecting against imitation. The patent is thus a mechanism facilitating access to knowledge. Before its invention, inventors were hostile to the idea of revealing new knowledge. Brunelleschi warned the renaissance engineer Taccola to conceal his inventions from the public (qtd. in Eamon 1985, 327): "Do not share your inventions with many, share them only with few who understand and love science. To disclose too much of one's invention and achievement is one and the same thing as to give up the fruits of one's ingenuity. Many are ready, when listening to the inventor, to belittle and deny his achievements, so that he will no longer be heard in honourable places, but after some months or a year they use the inventor's words, in speech or writing or design. They boldly call themselves the inventors of the things that they first condemned, and attribute the glory of another to themselves." Thus, in the absence of effective provisions for intellectual property rights, Renaissance engineers were justifiably reluctant to publish their discoveries.

3. Patents create transferable rights (by granting a license, the owner of the knowledge allows it to be exploited by other agents) and can therefore help to structure a complex transaction that also concerns unpatented knowledge. This "virtue" is becoming very important at the time of the expansion of markets for knowledge and technologies.

4. Patents are a means to signal and assess the future value of the technological effort of the companies that own them (which is particularly useful in cases of new or young companies for which other classes of "intangibles," such as reputation or consumer loyalty, cannot be used for proper evaluation).

**The Patent: A Remarkable Mechanism that Is Not Highly Considered as a Protection and Information Mechanism**   Although there are a number of private advantages of patents, the mechanism is infrequently used. In Europe only 44 percent of product innovations (52 percent in the United States) and 26 percent of process innovations (44 percent in the United States) are patented (Arundel and Kabla 1998). Firms often prefer to keep their new knowledge secret or "simply" ensure that they are always one step ahead. The Yale survey on "appropriability mechanisms" (Cohen, Nelson, and Walsh 1997) confirms that in most industries patents are considered a less effective way to protect innovation than secrecy, lead time, or the use of complementary assets.

I can suggest three reasons for the weak propensity to patents.

1. The system provides a uniform right for very different sectors. Since it is not possible to create a level of variety of intellectual property right mechanisms equivalent to the variety of sectors, inconsistencies and inappropriateness inevitably emerge. It is very difficult to imagine a system adapted to all situations. In fact, the system is ill-suited to many industries, despite the creation of particular mechanisms and ad hoc procedures. Take the following two examples. In some industries, such as sports equipment, the innovation cycle is very short (one season is the period of market power for one innovation), given the extensive visibility of a new idea and the relatively easy imitation and improvement. In such circumstances, the delay in getting a patent granted is far too long, and accelerated procedures have been designed for these industries, while patent managers in private companies argue for the use of weaker individual property rights (IPR) (like registered design) granted through a faster and easier process. The other case describes the opposite situation. In some industries the duration of monopoly (20 years from the application) is clearly too short given the extremely long interval required for getting the product on the market. This is typically the case of drugs where the time span between drug approval and the termination of its patent protection has decreased by about three years every ten years, leading to an average effective period of patent use of seven years. There is clearly a need for some ad hoc mechanisms to extend the monopoly period.

Although such ad hoc amendments to the system can always be designed and implemented without altering the nature of the system, there is a potential risk of unsuitability between a uniform framework and a great variety of situations.

2. The protection afforded by a property right is neither automatic nor free. The onus is on the patent owner to identify the counterfeiter and take the matter to court, where it will be assessed and interpreted. The effectiveness of property rights is therefore inseparable from the creators' capacity to watch over them. These capacities depend, in turn, on legal facilities (can someone be sued for counterfeit?), technical capacities (microscopic analysis) and organizational capacities (infor-

mation networks). Moreover, globalization of markets clearly affects these surveillance capacities negatively. Yet there are systems, especially for copyright, in which these functions are fulfilled by an intermediate agency to which the owners of rights delegate a part of their management. That is typically the case of composers' societies that control the use of rights, collect subscriptions, and redistribute profits. In the case of universities, license offices have the same function.

3. The effectiveness of the system depends strongly on the quality of the legal environment, which varies widely from one country to the next. This quality increased in the United States after the Court of Appeals for the Federal Circuit was set up for the purpose of unifying the basis of interpretation and enhancing firms' confidence by reducing legal uncertainty (Jaffe 2000). In Europe, although procedures for applying for and granting patents are the same all over, these rights have to be defended in each individual country. As a result, there are no truly European patents yet. However, recent decisions by the European Commission make the creation of a real "Euro-patent" likely. At the level of the world economy, the Trade-Related Aspects of Intellectual Property Rights agreements oblige all members of the World Trade Organization (WTO) to establish a minimum level of legislation in favor of intellectual property rights. But the costs of upgrading the intellectual property system and increasing its quality (including, e.g., the training of patent personnel and the improvement of facilities in the intellectual property administration) are so high that a transition period has been organized for many developing countries (UNCTAD 1996).

**Social Advantages**   A first host of social advantages deals with the property of patents as a medium for the dissemination of knowledge. Although patents are primarily used to create excludable goods and increase the expected private profitability of R&D and innovation, they also support access to knowledge. Different devices exist for deliberately organizing the circulation of knowledge in a patent system.

1. The granting of a property right is accompanied by public disclosure of the protected technique. There is thus dissemination of knowledge owing to the patent. Albeit partial (only the codified and explicit dimensions of the new knowledge are described), this dissemination is particularly important in certain industries. It is a sort of instruction

manual for the invention, which should allow its reproduction. If this disclosure is carried out "in time," and insofar as the information thus constituted is available at a low cost, it allows for a better allocation of resources, reduces the risk of duplication, and facilitates the trading of information. It is therefore a useful means of coordination, fully exploited in the Japanese system, for instance (Ordover 1991). The case of pharmaceuticals clearly illustrates the use of patents as a means of information and coordination. Patent data bases are a unique medium for knowledge externalities. Each firm uses them to evaluate its own strategies and identify opportunities for cooperation or transactions concerning knowledge. Data on patents can be used as a tool for knowledge management (R&D teams look carefully at the patents of rival companies as a way to propel creativity).

2. Patents create transferable rights. This has already been listed as a private advantage: by granting a license, the owner of the knowledge allows it to be exploited by other agents and, in return, receives income. There are various levels of licenses: exclusive licenses limit diffusion to a single additional agent and may even be combined with territorial clauses, while nonexclusive licenses allow for far wider diffusion. In some sectors, such as computing and telecommunications, where it is important for a technology to spread so that it becomes the industry "standard," nonexclusive license policies are granted on a large scale. Yet the granting of licenses transfers knowledge only partially. It is often essential to draw up contracts in which sale of the technology is accompanied by the assistance and expertise needed to develop practical know-how (Arora 1995; Bessy and Brousseau 1999).

3. Patent systems may be effective as a signaling mechanism supporting collective invention (Ordover 1991). In Europe (and now in the United States), information is disclosed in the eighteenth month after the patent application, which is a way to send signals and improve ex ante coordination among R&D projects. (There is legal protection after the patent is disclosed, so that an applicant has the right to demand compensation if someone uses the disclosed information before the patent is granted). However, in Japan the information disclosure principle is implemented in the most fascinating way. As in Europe, the Japanese Patent Office discloses all patent applications eighteen months after the applications are filed. But the most striking feature is that in Japan only 17 percent of all patent applications are approved, so that the vast majority are disclosed with no ultimate benefit of

intellectual property protection. Quite paradoxically, the patent system becomes a mechanism for generating public information! Moreover, in Japan patents tend to be applied far earlier in the innovation process due to the "first to file" rule of priority, as opposed to the "first-to-invent" rule of priority that applies in the United States. Both automatic publication after eighteen months and the first-to-file rule of priority could contribute to Japanese companies' earlier awareness of what major R&D projects their rivals are working on. The Japanese system is an effective apparatus for sending signals and placing a large amount of information in the public domain, and thus contributing to the essential objective of "collective invention."

"Minor" institutional differences matter in explaining disparities in the value of patents as a source of information and thus as a mechanism for efficient coordination. When information is properly disseminated (as in the Japanese system) and the nature of the protection granted is specified in ways that encourage patentees to make their innovations available for use by others at reasonably modest costs (narrow patents as well as low degrees of novelty are crucial in this respect), the patent system becomes a vehicle for increasing information spillovers, rather than for capturing monopoly rents.

A second class of social advantage deals with the method of invention valuation that is enabled by the patent system. Patents leave the valuation of the intellectual production to be determined ex post, by the willingness of users to pay. It thereby avoids society having to place a value on creative work ex ante, as would be required under alternative incentive schemes, such as offering prospective authors and inventors prizes, or awarding individual procurement contracts for specified works. And the costs of the patent system are mainly borne by consumers instead of taxpayers.

**A Generic Shortcoming**   But the solution of establishing a monopoly right to exploit that "first copy"—the idea protected by the patent (or the text protected by copyright)—alas, turns out not to be a perfect one. The monopolist will raise the price of every copy above the negligible costs of its reproduction and, as a result, some potential users of the information good will be excluded from enjoying it. This represents a waste of resources, referred to by economists as the *deadweight burden of monopoly*: Some people's desires will remain unsatisfied even though they could have been fulfilled at virtually no additional cost.

Thus, there is a basic trade-off. By increasing the expected private return of an innovation, the patent acts as an incentive mechanism to private investments in knowledge production. The problem is that by imposing exclusive rights, the patent restricts de facto the use of knowledge and its exploitation by those who might have benefited from it had it been free. Many historical examples illustrate situations of deadlock caused by measures relating to intellectual property rights that leaned too far in favor of the inventor: "When in 1775 Parliament extended the patent granted to him in 1769, for 25 years, it gave extensive powers to a man whose ideas had long since become rigid. Watt refused to grant licences; he discouraged Murdoch's experiments on locomotives; he was hostile to the use of high-pressure steam; and the authority he enjoyed was such that he impeded the growth of the mechanics industry for more than a generation. If his monopoly had expired in 1783, England would have had railways earlier" (Caron 1997, 56).

These situations of deadlock occur because the person who has the knowledge is not necessarily in the best position to use it efficiently. As I argue in the next chapter, the more distributed knowledge is, passing "from hand-to-hand," the greater the probability of it being efficiently exploited. It is therefore important to find some balance between the right to exclusivity and the distribution of knowledge.

**Specific Classes of Shortcomings** Most of the shortcomings are caused simply by inappropriate modes of use of patents, from a social point of view. As in any private property system, it is less the concept of property that poses practical problems than the way in which the system is used. In this respect many shortcomings in the patent system are not inevitable, for they are not intrinsically associated with the concept of intellectual property but result from a mode of use that leads to blockages or slows down innovation. Basically, such situations stem from the fact that patents do not really create "a market for ideas" but "a market for rights to exclude." When too many (or too broad) rights to exclude are granted, blockages and drawbacks may occur. A "too many rights" (or "too broad rights") situation is caused by the fact that patents and innovations are two different realities that do not coincide. In some cases a single patent covers many innovations, especially when the field is too large or when the patent protects generic knowledge. In others a single innovation is covered by many patents. This case is the anti-commons regime.

**When a Single Patent Covers Many Innovations: Weakening of the
Cumulativeness of Knowledge**   The scope of a patent is a variable
that can be the object of strategic choices by private agents, and that
the legal authorities concerned will assess very differently, depending
on the case. It is at the heart of the dilemma between protecting the
first innovator and encouraging subsequent innovations (which is a
form of the classic knowledge dilemma) (Scotchmer 1991).

By staking a set of claims, inventors delimit the territory they want
to have recognized as their property (the same principle as fencing off
a field). If the field more than covers the territory of the innovation,
subsequent innovations by other inventors, based on the first one, will
be blocked. Moreover, legal uncertainty is increased, for risks of dispute
are greater. But if the field is too narrow the pioneer's efforts may not
be rewarded at their full value. Note that a large field is not a major
problem in the case of a discrete innovation. The metaphor of mineral
prospection is useful here. In a given territory where there is only one
deposit surrounded by nothing else, whether the prospector closes off
the territory very close to the deposit or far from it, creating a vast field,
makes no difference since the additional space appropriated is of no
value.

The problem is different in the case of interdependent and cumulative innovations. If an initial patent is too broad and generously
rewards the pioneer inventor, it blocks possibilities for subsequent
research by others. It thus reduces the diversity of innovative agents in
the domain and the probability of cumulative developments taking
place.

The case of a patent protecting a general result rather than the particular method used to obtain the result is a good example of a patent
that is too broad. In this case, all subsequent research aimed at exploring other methods of obtaining the same result will be blocked. Patents
on knowledge high upstream in the innovation process, particularly on
research tools, can also hinder the cumulative dynamics of knowledge
(Walsh, Arora, and Cohen 2000; Thomas 1999).

A related case is the patent that covers all elements relating to the
innovation and all imaginable applications, thus favoring the creation
of extensive monopolies on exploitation.

After studying numerous cases, Merges and Nelson (1994, 20)
suggest that, in a context of interdependent innovations, an intellectual
property policy that allows very broad patents leads to a number of
deadlocks that impact the general dynamics of innovation in the sector:

"In the cumulative systems technology cases, broad, prospect claiming, pioneer patents, when their holders tried to uphold them, caused nothing but trouble. . . . Nor is there reason to believe that more narrowly drawn patents would have damped the incentives of the pioneers and other early comers to the field."

**When an Innovation Is Covered by Many Patents: Anti-Commons Regime and Tragedy** The second type of problem is called "anti-commons" to indicate that its "structure" is the exact inverse of the common resources' problem (see chapter 8). It is a legal regime that has produced parcels of private property rights on "indivisible" goods (Heller 1998) so that each party, being the owner of a portion of the indivisible good, has the right to exclude others from its share and no one has the effective privilege of use. The distinction between the private property regime and the anti-commons regime is represented in figure 7.1 where goods 1, 2, and 3 are represented by cells, and the initial property rights of individuals A, B, and C are represented by lines in bold type.

The private property regime structures the material world vertically because A, B, and C each own exclusive rights 1, 2, and 3 to an entire good (e.g., a piece of land). In other words, this regime does not prohibit exploitation of the resource. In the anticommons regime the lines are horizontal since private rights fragment the goods.

Tragedy results from the fact that multiple owners of "parcels" or "fragments" of a good each have the right to exclude others from their parcel, so that nobody can exploit the good in its entirety. This property regime thus breaks down and fragments objects. If too many owners have such exclusive rights (i.e., if there is too much

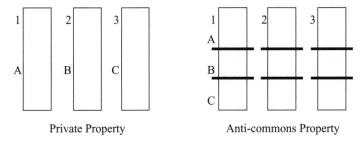

| Private Property | Anti-commons Property |

**Figure 7.1**
The distinction between private and anticommons property. *Source:* Heller (1998).

fragmentation), there is a chance that the good will be underutilized. The tragedy may then lead to exacerbated forms of nondistribution and underutilization of the resource, due to the fact that rights on fragments or parcels are solely rights to exclude and can no longer be rights to exploit. As in the case of common resources, the anticommons regime does not necessarily lead to tragedy. First, the problem of underutilization of resources can be solved through the trading of rights. In a world without transaction costs, owners can reorganize initial endowments through ex post exchanges, by gathering anticommon rights into property rights, that is, by recomposing the goods. Of course, the real world is one in which transactions are costly, but some problems of anticommons, particularly those concerning a small number of agents, may nevertheless be reduced through transactions aimed at recomposing the goods. Another solution is similar to the one used for the problem of common resources: the adoption of informal norms for managing ownership. Finally, to avoid the tragedy, it is logical to try to eliminate the regime itself by endowing those concerned with more coherent initial rights.

How does this regime apply in the knowledge economy? It corresponds to excessive fragmentation of the knowledge base, due to intellectual property rights on parcels and fragments of knowledge that do not correspond to an industrial application. The result is a proliferation of blockages.

### A Necessary Ill?

The patent system involves a trade-off: Weak patents lead to underprovision; strong patents create monopoly distortion. Not surprisingly, then, the subject of intellectual property policies has proven vexatious for the economics profession, because it presents numerous situations in which the effort to limit unfair competition and preserve incentives for innovation demonstrably results in a socially inefficient allocation of resources. Penrose (1951) expressed the difficulty of arriving at a "scientific closure" on such matters: "If national patent laws did not exist, it would be difficult to make a conclusive case for introducing them, but the fact that they do exist shifts the burden of the proof and it is equally difficult to make a really conclusive case for abolishing them."[13] This citation is important in so far as it provides a framework for the evaluation of intellectual property systems. I revert to it later on.

**Consensus Lost**   Nevertheless, economists reached some kind of consensus about twenty years ago: The patent system was a good thing for innovation and growth, provided its negative effects on the economy were reduced. In this respect three simple rules need to be applied: (1) the requirement of a technical description of the invention to maintain a balance between the inventor's private interests and the interests of society; (2) exclusion of science from the domain of patentability through criteria of industrial application; and (3) application of the criterion of inventive activity to clearly delimit the area of human activity that can be appropriated by a patent.

However, this consensus has collapsed for four reasons:

• There is abuse of how patents are used: a massive quantitative jump in the number of patents filed (topping the 300,000 applications per year mark in the United States); patents that are "moving up" to domains of scientific research; and amendment of the rule of technical description because it cannot be complied with in the case of certain new objects even though they are considered patentable (e.g., genetic creations). The rules mentioned to limit negative effects are not properly observed and consequently fail to do their job of regulating the system.

• Economists are realizing that other incentive mechanisms can efficiently support innovation without creating effects of exclusivity and monopoly power. A case in point is open source. This example can be used to verify and control real processes of support for innovation, based on open knowledge (see chapter 8).

From these first two reasons I infer that the expression *necessary evil* is probably inappropriate. The evil is greater than is generally believed and it may not be necessary!

• Patents now affect vital activities, including health and education. Hundreds of patents have already been granted in the U.S. Patent and Trademark Office (USPTO) category 434 concerning education and training methods.[14] While a patent on a new type of ball bearing shocks no one, the same cannot be said for a new patent on a drug, diagnostic test, or educational method.

• Finally, recent theoretical work challenges the very idea that special intellectual property laws are needed to support the production of ideas as opposed to the production of things. In other words, competitive markets for ideas succeed and exhibit optimal allocation properties. This is related to the fact that the property of nonrivalry (discussed in chapter 5) is an abstract property that does not prevent the first inventor from generating a sufficient competitive advantage (the supply of copies of the invention is not immediate; hence the fact of being first is an asset which can be converted into positive prices, even in a private competitive market). Boldrin and Levine (2002) conclude that intellectual property (IP) has two components: One is the essential right to own and sell ideas. The other is the economically dangerous right to control the use of those ideas after sale.

Economists' uncertainty is thus greater than ever. Should sectoral contexts not be taken into account to weigh the pros and cons?

**Economic Efficiency of Patents as Influenced by Sectoral Patterns of Innovation**
Patents are most likely to foster innovations when the following conditions converge: high R&D costs; reverse engineering and other means of knowledge absorption that allow competitors for rapid and inexpensive imitations; and low costs of manufacturing the final product.

In these circumstances, the establishment of IPRs strengthens private incentives, allows the commitment of substantial private resources, and thereby improves the conditions of commercialization of inventions. These conditions are, for instance, typical of the pharmaceutical industry where patents prove to have a tremendously positive effect on innovation. Mansfield (1995) estimates that 60 percent of pharmaceutical innovations would not have been developed in the absence of patents.

IPRs are most likely to retard rather than stimulate innovations when at least one of the four following circumstances is present:

1. Some other appropriability mechanisms work well and are considered more effective for protecting inventors while not imposing high social costs on the system. This is the case, for instance, of the advantages of first-movers who reap the benefits of the new knowledge, or the role of complementary assets (market access or manufacturing capabilities), which are effective appropriation mechanisms in several sectors.

2. Innovation is cumulative. This property has been reviewed in chapter 5. The more knowledge is cumulative, the more wasteful is the effect of granting property rights. This is why there is a particular concern when exclusive rights are assigned to data bases, research

tools, and other kinds of generic knowledge. For example, a data base can be defined as an information space constituting a dynamic collective research tool. According to the director of the European Bioinformatic Institute, discoveries in many domains are made in the course of *unplanned journeys through such information space*. If that space is restricted by a host of property rights, the journey will become expensive (if not impossible) and the knowledge base itself will suddenly be found to be shrinking. Therefore, seeking to apply the rights granted by the European Community's (EC's) directive for the legal protection of data bases[15] and to partition the information space so as to extract licensing fees from users would reduce the probabilities of unexpected discoveries. Targeted searches may be quite affordable, but wholesale extraction of the data spaces' content to permit exploratory search activities is especially likely to be curtailed (David 2000b). Scientific software is another case in point. The cumulative nature of innovation in this field is well known: Software programmers tend to rely heavily on the work of their predecessors. It is usual for programmers, when confronting problems that have been addressed before, not merely to learn from the solutions developed by their predecessors, but to copy those solutions verbatim. Recent trends in copyright and patent law threaten that socially efficient practice. Moreover, the current development of the voluntary open source model provides counterfactual evidence that other appropriability mechanisms can sustain innovation and growth in this sector. The provision of economic incentives that encourage people to reveal their knowledge freely, seems to be more consistent with the cumulative nature of knowledge in that field (see chapter 8).

3. Researchers in the field are motivated primarily by nonmonetary incentives. Obviously, the scientific research community has evolved a rather different approach to rewards for and spillovers from knowledge production than that suggested by a conventional economic property right analysis (one based on rapid publication and dissemination in order to achieve a prior claim as the inventor) (see chapter 8). This is the "open science model," creating an "IPR-free zone." It has proven to be extremely socially efficient (positive externalities are maximized while private incentives to "win the race" can be strong) but must rely on public funding. This "IPR-free model" is vulnerable to the expansion of intellectual property rights and can be threatened when one or some of the participants use the public knowledge and convert it into private domain information, leading to a one-way "IPR route." Once

intellectual property ownership and control are introduced, it is almost impossible to return to an open science model. Public disclosure as practiced in open science is complementary to the proprietary IPR regime of R&D in promoting high rates of innovation in the long run. Both parts of the system must be kept in balance.

4. The field is characterized by strong network externalities: In the new knowledge economy, network externalities—the more customers you have, the more valuable your product becomes—play a major role in shaping the nature of competition and creating strong forces toward standardization, both informal (monopolistic competition) and formal (cooperation) (Shapiro and Varian 1998). Network effects are strong in telecommunications and more broadly in industries (such as multimedia) where interoperability and interface standards are important. In some cases, a combination of network externalities and supply-side economies of scale can generate huge, positive feedbacks, which create tipping markets and winner-take-all (WTA) competition. Positive feedbacks cause the strongest to get stronger and the weakest to get weaker. In WTA markets the very best performers in their fields—even if just marginally better than their competitors—are enjoying a huge and widening gap in financial rewards. Across a variety of markets, the best player reaps hugely disproportionate returns in stock market valuation. At this stage costly battles of standards can occur. This is competition for the market (instead of in the market) among various technological designs; each competitor tries to push its own design to become the standard (the particular design that wins the allegiance of the marketplace, the one that competitors and innovators must adhere to). Network effects challenge conventional intellectual property policy. The informal emergence of a standard (or the formal and "official" adoption of a norm) suddenly adds immense value to those technologies which correspond to it, and hence to the intellectual property rights that are gatekeepers to it. Faced with this problem of sudden overvaluation of an IPR, related simply to the fact that the technology concerned is a gateway in the standardization process, economists traditionally argue for a weakening of IPRs (Farrell 1989).

The last three circumstances were all present during the development of the technical infrastructure of the Internet and are features of innovations in the new knowledge-based economy. Hence, there is a need for a "fine tuning" intellectual property system. Depending on the circumstances, patents and other IPRs prove to be either economically efficient or nondesireable.

**Lawyers and Economists Facing Sectoral Patterns**   To be sure, this sectoral analysis is not an issue for lawyers, for even if economists showed that patents work differently among industries, the fact remains that the TRIPS agreement includes no discriminatory principle. There is no room to adapt the patent system to sectoral particularities. For an economist, however, sectoral analysis raises important policy issues: Highlighting sectoral particularities in terms of patent efficiency makes a case for policies to increase the attractiveness or diffusion of other incentive mechanisms in sectors where patents cannot be considered as a "good solution." A public policy that opted for open source to equip government administrations or the education or health system is a good example in this respect.

## Current Trends

### Facts

The economic importance of intellectual property is rising. Its value is increasing as a share of average total firm value. The number of patent applications is growing at double-digit rates in the major patent offices, and licensing and cross-licensing are being employed with greater frequency than ever before, particularly so in high-tech industries. The greater intensity of innovation, characteristic of the knowledge-based economy, and the increase in the propensity to patent (i.e., the elevation of the ratio number of patents per number of innovations or number of patents per real R&D spending), which indicates the emergence of new research and innovation management techniques, are the main factors of this quantitative evolution (Kortum and Lerner 1997).

In 1998, 147,000 U.S. utility patents were granted, corresponding to an increase of 32 percent compared to 1997. Over the past ten years both patent applications and patent grants in the United States have increased at a rate of about 6 percent per annum, compared to about 1 percent per annum in the preceding forty years.

In Europe, similar effects are observed, with applications to the European Patent Office (EPO) rising at an annual rate of 10 percent per annum over the past five years. Interestingly, the response of the EPO, unlike the USPTO, has been to hold the grant rate steady, which means the application-grant lag has risen (see figures 7.2 and 7.3).[16]

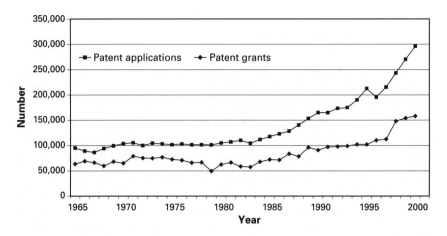

**Figure 7.2**
USPTO Utility Patents 1965–2000

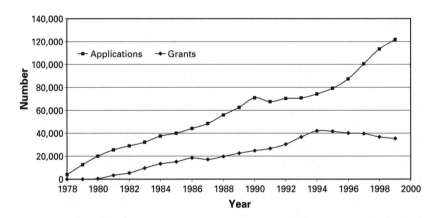

**Figure 7.3**
EPO and EPO/PCT Patents 1978–1999

The evolution is also qualitative. Patents are being registered on new types of objects such as software (17,000 patents last year, compared to 1,600 in 1992), genetic creations and research tools (see figure 7.4) and devices for electronic trade over the Internet, and by new actors (universities, researchers in the public sector). All this contributes to the unprecedented expansion of the knowledge market and the proliferation of exclusive rights on whole areas of intellectual creation (Arora, Fosfuri, and Gambardella 2001).

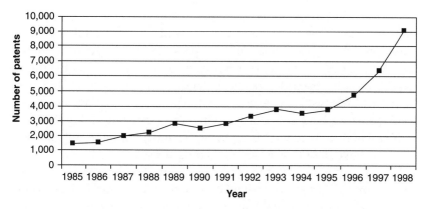

**Figure 7.4**
Number of patents in biotechnology. (*Source:* U.S. Patent and Trademark Office, Technology Profile Report, Patent Examining Technology Center, Groups 1630–1650, Biotechnology 1/1977—1/1998, April 1999).

This evolution creates a paradox, for patents are generally not considered a good mechanism to protect innovation.

**Reasons**
Three main factors explain such trends.

1. The first deals with changes in patenting policy in the United States and Europe. The main aspect of changes concerns the fact that patent offices have completely given up their regulatory role, as the amusing example of the Australian office shows. Until the 1970s, the general view of patent offices was that patents were anticompetitive and not good for the economy. Patent offices were more often considered "rejection offices" than institutions for supporting innovators. They therefore played a significant regulatory role, blocking or slowing down private appropriation in certain fields. For example, the patentability criteria of "industrial application" (utility) were very effective in blocking patenting of the first genetic inventions in the late 1980s. For several reasons patent offices have become extremely propatent since the late *1980s.* The new view is that innovation must be helped and foreign investors attracted. The applicant, formerly considered with suspicion, has become a "client" whose needs must be satisfied, owing to quick, cheap procedures. The result is a total deterioration of examination procedures, for the office's role is confined to that of a registry office and a statistics bureau.

Thus, the pendulum started swinging away from rigorous examination, toward a cheap, fast process. Nowadays, patentability criteria have ceased to play their role of preserving the public domain. Propatenting policies of patent offices mean that patentability criteria have gradually been eased and extended to new subject domains. Many research results have now become patentable, as a result of both legal (court) and patent office decisions. The increasing ability to patent fundamental knowledge, research tools, and data bases is part of a broader movement toward strengthening IPRs.

The consequence of this evolution is a sort of transfer of the responsibility for regulation from patent offices to the law courts. Since everything has become patentable and acceptable, most patents are legally fragile and therefore likely to be challenged by rivals. I clearly see this twofold tendency of deterioration of the patent offices' work, along with an increase in the efficiency of the legal system, especially in the United States.

A range of other factors in the institutional environment is reinforcing this trend in favor of the applicant, for example, the evolution of the judicial institution and jurisprudence which are increasingly favorable toward the patent holder as opposed to a party suspected of infringement. In the United States, whereas only 62 percent of holders of valid patents won their appeal case before 1980, this figure has risen to 90 percent (cf. Jaffe 2000). Finally, international legislation is creating new incentives to patent rather than relying on other mechanisms for appropriating the benefits of invention (secrecy, first-mover advantage, complementary assets, brands). For example, I have already mentioned that the WIPO recently decided to switch the onus of proof in infringement cases onto the accused. This is a fundamental change from the preceding period.

2. The second reason concerns the current context of technological revolution. The new emerging fields, such as information and communication technologies, nanotechnologies, biotechnologies, and so on, are providing numerous opportunities for innovation, which automatically generate an increase in patenting activities.

3. A third reason relates to the new methods of R&D management that make patents intangible assets of increasing importance. The creation of intellectual property becomes a central goal of the global strategy. For a long time, the belief about intellectual property was that patents were for defensive purposes only, and that patents and related know-

how should not be sold. Licensing was a drain on internal resources. Now patents are considered a unique means to generate value from intangible assets, and companies are starting to exploit this through aggressive licensing programs (Teece 1998). Thus, Arora, Fosfuri, and Gambardella (2001, 234) note, with regard to DuPont: "Reversing its tradition of treating in-house technology as the jewel of the crown, DuPont has started to exploit it through an aggressive licensing program." With the current (or expected) strengthening of national and regional legal systems of intellectual property, the expected benefits of amassing portfolios of legal rights to exclude began to outweigh their costs. Hall and Ziedonis (2001) explain the patent paradox in the semiconductor industry (i.e., the gap between the relative effectiveness of patents and their widespread use) with the fact that large companies amass vast patent portfolios simply as "bargaining chips" to allow them to sort out conflicting and overlapping claims to intellectual property.

Statistical analysis carried out by Kortum and Lerner (1997) tries to estimate the importance of each of those factors. They start with the friendly-court hypothesis: the increasing efficiency of the U.S. legal system makes patents more valuable and increases the propensity to patent. It cannot, however, explain a great deal of the patent upsurge because U.S. inventors have also increased their rates of patenting in other countries (where legal systems remain inefficient).

They also deal with the fertile technology hypothesis: new fields are full of innovation opportunities and thus automatically increase the number of patents. But approximately 70 percent of all patent classes (including very mature technologies) have exhibited an increased rate of patenting.

Proceeding thus by elimination, the authors argue that the most important reason concerns the diffusion of new R&D management practices, including the various aspects we listed. There are, in particular, some kinds of positive feedback and snowball effects between two phenomena: first the use of patents not so much for protecting as for generating value from assets; and, second, the creation of huge patent portfolios as bargaining chips.

4. There is, finally, a fourth reason to the upsurge in patenting. This reason is important to consider, for it points out some important qualitative changes in the knowledge system. However, it can explain only a very small fraction of the global increase. This reason concerns the entry of new players into "knowledge markets." It includes:

• Powerful commitments to basic research by private firms in certain sectors. This is, for instance, the case in the genomics area where economists observe the emergence of a new generation of firms which are highly specialized in fundamental research and are, therefore, in direct competition with the public research institutions. These new and/or small companies consider patents as the only reliable way to signal their value to the market (chapter 11).

• Changes in the behavior of open science institutions, which are increasingly oriented toward the promotion of their commercial interests (Henderson, Jaffe, and Trajtenberg 1998).

• Privatization of some of the activities of governmental civilian agencies, which become major players in the contractual research market (Jaffe and Lerner 1999).

**Problems**
These trends do not necessarily lead to an excess of privatization of knowledge. In many cases the establishment of intellectual property rights strengthens private incentives, allows the commitment of substantial private resources, and thereby improves the conditions of commercialization of inventions. Moreover, the establishment of private rights does not totally prevent the diffusion of knowledge, even if it limits it. Finally, a large proportion of private knowledge is disseminated outside the market system, either within consortiums or by means of networks of trading and sharing of knowledge, the foundation of intentional spillovers discussed by several authors (see chapter 8).

However, there is some concern when all these trends create a system with high transaction costs and some risks of blockage in knowledge exploitation and cumulativeness.

**Transaction Costs**   A large set of implications of this view involves various phenomena that can be grouped, for the sake of convenience, under the heading "transaction cost increases." Both qualitative trends (increasing fragility of patents) and quantitative changes (increase in numbers of patent applications and grants) are likely to increase transaction costs. Efforts and costs devoted to sorting out conflicting and overlapping claims to IPR will increase, as will uncertainty about the nature and extent of legal liability in using knowledge inputs. Policy makers and academics are concerned with the increase of litigation costs, including indirect costs, which may distort the innovative behavior of small companies (Lerner 1994). As John Barton (2000) put it, there is a problem when "the number of intellectual property lawyers is growing faster than the number of researchers." And this is exactly what has happened in the United States, while similar trends in Europe show that it is no longer a purely American problem.

Of course this problem is not new, as the following comment by a concerned industrialist, R. A. Macfie, shows: "In the manufacture with which I am connected—the sugar trade—there are somewhere like 300 or 400 patents. Now, how are we to know all these 400 patents? How are we to manage continually, in the natural process of making improvements in manufacture, to know which of these patents we are at any time conflicting with? So far as I know, we are not violating any patent; but really, if we are to be exceedingly earnest in the question, probably we would require to have a highly paid clerk in London continually analysing the various patents; and every year, by the multiplication of patents, this difficulty is becoming more formidable" (qtd. in Hastings 1865). One can, however, consider that the extent of the problem has grown substantially in recent years.

**Blockage and the Anti-Commons Trap**  It is possible that intellectual property-related transaction costs may increase so much that the result can be the deadlock in knowledge exploitation and accumulation. The following two cases are particularly indicative of the problem of anti-commons as it might happen in the knowledge economy (Heller and Eisenberg 1998).[17]

The first blockage results from the fact that knowledge is fragmented and rights are granted to portions of knowledge before the corresponding product is identified (whereas previously the genes corresponded to products that were patented, such as therapeutic proteins and diagnostic tests). The proliferation of patents on fragments of genes owned by different agents hugely complicates the coordination required by an agent wanting to develop a product. In particular, if the acquisition of all necessary licenses were too complicated or expensive, the product would never materialize.

A second blockage results from procedures known as *reachthrough license agreements*, which give the patent holder rights over future discoveries. These rights may consist of the payment of royalties on sales, licenses on future discoveries, or a priority option for obtaining licenses. The system was initially designed to enable researchers with few financial resources to use a patented discovery and pay only if the research produced results. But in the end, this kind of system gives the owners of first patents the right to be present at all stages of subsequent developments, even if they did not contribute to them. Once again, there is a risk of underutilization of certain discoveries because of situations in which the rights of those concerned are entangled.

Certain situations in the domain of information technology also pose this type of problem. Is the anti-commons regime described a transition or does it signal a tragedy? Theoretically, we can hope for the creation of appropriate institutions to help agents coordinate the trading of licenses (see Grindley and Teece 1997, for numerous examples). Also theoretically, collective learning can lead to real decreases in transaction costs. In practice, however, it is difficult to see how mechanisms of natural correction could appear and put an end to these situations of deadlock. There is a huge degree of heterogeneity between actors, and transaction costs are enormous for those wanting to group together rights to recompose fragmented knowledge. To make it worse, cognitive biases cause everyone to overestimate the probability of their own patent being a miracle patent, which leads everyone to want more than the probable value of that asset (Heller and Eisenberg 1998).

**Distortion**   Finally, introduction of new types of objects into the patent system can introduce imbalances, for example, by breaking the link between granting of exclusivity rights and the requirement of public description of the invention—a requirement that guarantees a balance between the general interest and that of the patentee. The requirement of a literal description of biotechnological invention harms the interests of applicants who cannot meet that condition. In order to bypass the obstacle, the requirement is relaxed somewhat. In other words, a description that fails to allow reproduction of the invention will be tolerated, contrary to normal requirements in general. A whole series of distortions result. For example, exemption in favor of research (which allows use of the invention for research purposes) is no longer valid since an inadequate description no longer allows access to it. In short, there is a shift from a literal description to a deposit procedure so that third parties can obtain a sample of the invention (i.e., of the microorganism). This accentuates the distortion of the system. While the literal description is independent of the actual realization of the invention, a deposit procedure necessitates effective realization of the invention. Description is a "direction for use" that allows effective reproduction of the invention, whereas deposit is a copy of a given state of living matter which has evolving properties, implying that the following state will not be accessible to the third party. The balance observed in patent common law between different interests is upset here. (This point is brilliantly discussed by Clavier 1998, 145–178.) Thus, the system's adaptation to new objects can be obtained only by moving away from certain guiding principles in patent law.

### Solutions
Penrose (1951) and Machlup (1958) offer insight on how to classify and develop appropriate solutions to the problems mentioned, with the latter noting, "If we did not have a patent system, it would be irresponsible on the basis of our present knowledge of its economic consequences, to recommend instituting one."

Certain sectors of the knowledge economy are still excluded from the mechanisms of private appropriation of knowledge through patents. In the education sector, for example, even if hundreds of patents have been registered, the patent does not exist in the sense that it does not constitute a fundamental reason for economic agents' entry into the market. In other words, it is not a decisive element shaping agents' expectations of possible private gains from innovation in this sector. In this case, I agree with the first part of the quotation: "It would be irresponsible to recommend instituting [a patent system]." "But since we have had a patent system for a long time, it would be irresponsible, on the basis of our present knowledge, to recommend abolishing it" (Machlup 1958).

Of course, in sectors in which the patent system has been working for centuries, the issue is to make corrections and improvements at the margin, which can bring about a certain equilibrium in some instances.

**Facilitate Access to Private Knowledge**   Mechanisms are devised to support the fast dissemination and free exploitation of private knowledge, in certain circumstances or for certain classes of economic agents. There are three main mechanisms:

• Compulsory licensing (compulsory diffusion of private knowledge in the general interest): While the very idea of a compulsory license was considered an insult to the notion of property (since a basic right—

that of not selling—is alienated), this practice is taking over and spreading to unexceptional circumstances. While most compulsory licenses are applied for in the general interest (cf. the struggle between South Africa and the major pharmaceutical multinationals), it tends to become a last resort in the field of competition policy when the refusal to grant a license can be interpreted as abuse of a dominant position.

• Patent buy-out: The state or an international foundation buys patents to put them back in the public domain (Kremer 1997). To illustrate this mechanism Kremer uses the historical case of Daguerre, the inventor of photography who neither exploited his invention nor sold it for the price he wanted. In 1839 the French government purchased the patent and put the rights to Daguerre's invention in the public domain. The invention was developed very fast!

• Price discrimination: Ramsey's pricing rule suggests price discrimination between users whose demands are inelastic and those for whom the quantity purchased is extremely price-sensitive. The former category of buyer will therefore bear high prices without curtailing the quantity of goods purchased, whereas the low prices offered to those in the second category (e.g., scholars and university-based researchers) will spare them the burden of economic welfare reducing cutbacks in their use of the good (David 2000b). The clause of fair use for research or educational purposes is an interpretation of this rule.

Of course, the well-known problem involved in compulsory licensing and patent buy-out schemes has to do with valuation of the invention and the likelihood of burdensome legal and administrative expenses that makes these schemes second-best solutions.

One should also observe that the basic mechanisms aimed at maintaining free access to patented knowledge for research or educational goals (research exemption) or for national security reasons (compulsory licensing) only provide a fragile legal basis. The recent case of *Madey v Duke University* in the United States shows that research exemption might be no longer a reliable device in the future: because basic research and higher education might be considered the core business of a university, the criteria of an activity undertaken for "amusement, to satisfy idle curiosity or for strictly philosophical inquiry" (which is at the base of the exception) might not apply here. Thus, the Federal Circuit Court of Appeals case of *Madey v Duke University* emphasizes that most basic science and higher education conducted in U.S. universities is ineligible for this exception.

**Navigating the Patent Thicket**  A classical solution to the anticommons trap is offered by cross-licensing mechanisms (Grindley and Teece 1997; Shapiro 2000). Processes of learning on the trading of rights and systems of mutual concession can occur, for example, within a consortium. This may keep transaction costs at tolerable levels and thus favor regulation of the anticommon regime to a certain extent. But it is a solution that can work only with a small number of companies. In that respect, the rapid growth of new kinds of firms cautions against overconfidence that anticommons problems can be overcome. For example, the computer hardware industry had few problems with its cross-licensing arrangements until new kinds of semiconductor companies emerged.

**Creating Incentives for Companies to Clear Up Their Patent Portfolio**  Patent fees should reflect the cost of patents to society, rather than patent office examination costs and patent fees being used to encourage patent applicants to screen their applications: For instance, a tax could be established on some quantitative measure of patent scope, such as the number of claims. Renewal fees should be made steeper so that they play a role of self-selection mechanism to encourage high valuable inventions to be patented and discourage the least valuable ones (Encaoua, Guellec and Martinez 2003).

**Actions Directed at Patent Office Practices**  A great deal of action needs to be taken if patent requirements are to be strictly enforced (utility requirement, nonobviousness, patent scope). Policymakers should launch programs to convince patent officers of the critical need to create initial endowments of property rights which are more coherent insofar as they respect the indivisibility of goods (avoiding the anticommons trap).

One should note, however, that hybrid and complex objects, such as genes, DNA sequences, software, and data bases, generate a lot of uncertainties about the appropriate intellectual property policy related to them, making the tasks of patent offices very difficult. It is difficult to provide nonambiguous and clear answers to the question of whether these new objects should be privately appropriated and, if so, what class of IPR should be used. We now live in a period in which these new objects are being put to the test.

This brings to mind a novel by the French writer Vercors, *Les animaux dénaturés*. In the late nineteenth century, a new species, called the

Tropis, was discovered by English anthropologists. Nobody in Victorian England, neither the scientific academy nor the church, could decide whether Tropises were humans or apes. The main theme of the novel is the search for legal truth. In the story a journalist kills a Tropis, simply to force the judicial system to qualify this act as murder or not. This is a good metaphor (developed by Clavier 1998) to illustrate the perpetual necessity—in the presence of a new "object"—to proceed to a classification in order to infer a particular regime.

Under this circumstance of great uncertainty, it might be useful to think about the creation of new categories of intellectual property such as the "common good," a category which would match those situations in which "we don't know," meaning that society needs time to think about the legal status of the new object while the economy needs some legal certainty to go ahead with R&D investments. In this respect, lawyers think that certain new complex and hybrid objects (like genes) do not fit in the usual categories of private-public goods, and propose to work on a new category: the common good. Under a common good regime, innovation defies patrimonial and commercial appropriation. The private company that is in possession of it for industrial exploitation is not the owner of the good but serves as a sort of manager. Such a regime would allow for the emergence of an industry while avoiding private and exclusive rights.

**Beyond Intellectual Property**   In contexts in which reliance upon these mitigating devices is not feasible or very effective, the alternative mechanisms for solving the public good problem based on public property may be superior to intellectual property rights as ways of stimulating innovation. I discuss these mechanisms in chapter 8.

**Understanding What a "Strong" Patent Systems Actually Means**
The arguments developed here may suggest for a shift toward a weaker patent system. Before saying that, I would like to offer a more precise definition of what a strong (and a weak) patent system is. The idea of strong does not necessarily have to be related to the exclusionary value of the patent. In fact, many of the solutions proposed (compulsory licensing, the Ramsey pricing rule, narrower patents, the new common good regime) are actually means to diminish the private value of individual increments to the privately owned knowledge base, even though they may raise its social value. But the conditions that make a patent system "strong" concern a different set of issue: enforcement,

minimum level of legal uncertainty, minimal probability of litigations, and so on. That means that the system as it stands now is not "strong" at all; it is weak and making it stronger does not mean just making the life of patent applicants easier—on the contrary.

Reinforcing the protection of intellectual property, which is a matter of institutional and legal adjustments (in the sense of unifying patent doctrine for minimizing ambiguities and uncertainties in patent suits, or decreasing the cost of patent application or improving enforcement conditions), *does not mean* reinforcing the exclusivity value of patents, which impedes knowledge dissemination and the collective progress of industries. And actions and policy recommendations aimed at reducing the exclusion value of patents are compatible with this "version" of what makes a strong system of IPRs.

**The New ICT Destabilize Enforcement Conditions**   Current techno-logical developments pose new problems concerning the exercise of property rights and especially control over the use of works. In chapter 5 I noted that ICT creates favorable conditions for knowledge exter-nalities. Not only are the costs of reproduction and transmission of digital works collapsing, but reproduction and transmission are carried out without any loss of quality. The idea of an original work thus dis-appears. The most recent developments in the multimedia domain reveal the full intensity of the problem. The Internet offers one free access to cultural and musical programs that can be downloaded and copied onto any medium. Problems concern not only patrimonial rights but also moral rights: The integrity of the work is threatened when, to use Roger Chartier's expression, the reader writes not in the margins but in the text itself, which is exactly what the electronic book allows (Chartier 2000). Faced with these threats, the major multimedia product distributors are trying to adopt classic solutions, such as the creation of new property rights to protect digital intellectual creation. New rights on data bases and the protection of digital information push the pendulum very far toward private protection. It is as if the intel-lectual property system were swinging from a logic aimed at protect-ing invention toward one aimed at encouraging investment and commercialization of information products and services on a global scale (Mansell and Wehn 1998). Similar mechanisms include sales tax on blank disks, electronic marking and coding devices to prevent copying of programs, and access rates to the sites that present those programs. But this type of solution reflects the powerlessness of copyright faced with these new situations. A "more intelligent" answer would probably be a change of behavior in order to free access to programs and draw revenue from derived products. This is a strategy familiar to firms wanting to impose their standard in the network industry.

Hence, there are two alternatives. Either derived products are totally foreign to the core trade and are essentially a form of advertising for revenue, as in the case of the Encyclopaedia Britannica, or they are specific charged services, complementary to the information delivered free-of-charge. That is notably the case of many statistics organizations that allow free access to information but charge for knowledge (specific work on a particular type of data).

**The Necessary Adaptation of an Old Institution**

Intellectual property rights seem to be reinforced everywhere, from both a microeconomic point of view (they are more and more essential to firms' strategies, used intensely, and entering areas formerly prohibited) and a macroeconomic one (see the TRIPS agreements already discussed). Moreover, the patent system that was assumed to be devoted solely to the protection of innovation is now fulfilling other functions of increasing importance in knowledge-based economies. As patents are used to draw attention to resources and establish a reputation, patent portfolios are becoming an essential element in the evaluation of intangible assets by financial markets. The paradox is that intellectual property rights are simultaneously threatened more and more by current technological changes leading to massive reductions in the costs of formatting and transmitting knowledge.

Thus, at the turn of the new century, IP institutions are being put to the test. The important challenges to the system are the following:

• Its ability to extend to new subject areas (software, data bases, genetic creations) without being distorted too much. This challenge also involves the ability of the existing classes of IPR to provide social and economic regulations for the production and distribution of knowledge in cyberspace.

• Its ability to create new regulatory mechanisms (such as compulsory licensing, licenses with minimal diligence, patent buy-out, fair use) to reduce those economic side effects of patents that are likely to make the system less efficient.

• Its ability to provide a framework to facilitate international regulation in the domain of the production and exploitation of knowledge as an international public good.

To address these issues, the intellectual property institution is changing. It is shifting away from a system preserving the right of the inventor to "say no" (to refuse access and to keep the knowledge unexploited) to a system promoting systematic access rights while preserving a right for the inventor to be remunerated. The increasing importance in policy discussion of compulsory licensing (beginning to be used not only in areas of public health and security but also for competition policy reasons), the new policy interest in price discrimination schemes, as well as the abundant literature on various ways to obtain a "freedom to operate" by bypassing or ignoring intellectual property, are signals of such an evolution (Nottenburg, Pardey, and Wright 2001). How far can the system go, and to what extent can the provision of this kind of tool help to solve the problems of knowledge access? Are these mechanisms sufficiently strong and enforced in domains where "essential human rights" are at stake (health, education, food)? Is, for instance, a system of compulsory licensing the solution to the problem raised by the broad patents covering diagnostic tests for breast cancer, as well as other similar problems in the health care and pharmaceutical area (see chapter 11)?

There are some doubts about the fact that in the age of the knowledge economy, the new equilibrium (with intensive patenting activities, large amounts of cross-licensing, aggressive patent enforcement strategies, and privatization of some basic research activities) is better than the preceding one that was characterized by a moderate level of patenting activities, firms allowing diffusion of their own knowledge in return for low-cost absorbtion of other's knowledge, and a large public research domain. The latter seems to be a system with lower transaction costs, while the former does not seem distinctly superior in terms of knowledge production.

# 8           Knowledge Openness and Economic Incentives

What I call "knowledge openness" is a system in which the principles of rapid disclosure of new knowledge are predominant, and in which a number of procedures facilitate and reinforce the circulation not only of codified knowledge but also of practical knowledge and research tools. It is not pure chance that in this context new knowledge is codified and carefully systematized in order to facilitate its transmission and discussion. But particular attention is also paid to the reproduction of knowledge, that is, to learning. It is not because knowledge flows freely—in the form of manuals and codified instructions—that it is necessarily reproduced from one place to the next. It is also necessary to create and maintain relationships between "masters and apprentices," either in the context of work communities or in formal processes of teaching practical knowledge. The significance of knowledge openness is particularly important for knowledge, which is an input for further cognitive works. In this case the principle of openness allows external users of that knowledge to reproduce it for investigation, modification, and improvement.[18]

Systems of knowledge openness relate to public (or semipublic) spaces in which knowledge circulates. Such spaces can include areas in which exclusive property rights cannot be granted, either constitutionally (as in the case of open science) or within the framework of organizations specially designed for the purpose (research networks where partners share their knowledge) and markets whose modi operandi are conducive to efficient knowledge dissemination. In such circumstances, a fundamental economic issue is the design of private incentives (to give credit to the knowledge producer) without creating exclusivity rights (as in the private property system described in chapter 7).

## Virtues and Vices of Knowledge Openness

### Virtues

Knowledge openness and sharing behaviors do not only express some kind of ethics or moral attitude (although ethical conviction certainly plays a role). Knowledge openness is viewed, above all, as a mechanism generating economic efficiency that people in certain circumstances are willing to implement and maintain in order to be players in a positive sum game (David and Foray 1995). In fact, knowledge openness that entails rapid and complete distribution, facilitates coordination between agents, reduces risks of duplication between research projects, and functions as a sort of "quality assurance." Above all, by disseminating knowledge within a heterogeneous population of researchers and entrepreneurs, it increases the probability of later discoveries and inventions and decreases the risk of this knowledge falling into the hands of agents incapable of exploiting its potential.

**Open Knowledge and Cognitive Performance**   These "good properties" have recently been modelled by David (1998b), who shows how the disclosure norm positively influences the cognitive performance of the system under consideration. David models stochastic interactions in a group of rational researchers individually engaged in a continuous process of experimental observation, information exchange, and revision of choices in relation to locally constituted majorities. This modelling is then used to link microbehaviors (being open, being closed) and macroperformances. Simulations suggest that the social norm of openness, which influences microbehaviors, favors free entry into knowledge networks and, in so doing, prevents researchers from closing in on themselves too quickly and excluding different opinions. David shows that a system situated beyond the critical openness threshold ensures confrontation of ideas and provides a mechanism that guarantees the production of consensus and preserves the diversity of opinions. The capacity to produce scientific statements collectively while preserving a degree of diversity of opinions and arguments is thus an important feature in an open research network, and standards of disclosure and openness appear to be decisive in the cognitive performances of the network. The advantage of such an approach is that it produces formal results, derived from the mathematical theory of percolation, on the basis of which more political reflection can be envisaged:

• The size of the network is important. The smaller the network, the greater the risk of it rapidly becoming trapped in one of those "absorbing states," namely, in a situation of complete agreement of all agents, from which it is difficult to withdraw collectively;

• The network can tolerate certain shortcomings and divergence from the openness norm. In other words, the same cognitive performance is guaranteed as long as the network is above a certain critical threshold. Cooperative behavior can emerge and be maintained without everyone complying perfectly with the openness standard.

Apart from this first aspect of cognitive performance, David defines creativity as a function of the size of the network and the propensity to share information (which makes it possible to recombine it). Creativity then becomes an emergent property of social networks possessing certain characteristics of size and openness.

### Vices: "The Tragedy of the Commons"

The discovery of a gold mine or a rich fishing zone can lead to excessive allocation of resources to exploration and discovery in the relevant area. This is likely to reduce substantially the private and social returns of the research and exploration activity. Under certain conditions this problem applies to the economics of knowledge, when private property rights are established on research results, whereas the right to research is free (the research domain is a common resource).

**Introduction to the Commons Regime** In this regime everyone has the privilege of using the resource and nobody can exclude anyone else from that use. Everyone has one right only: that of not being excluded. In this regime tragedy may result from overexploitation of the resource. This case characterizes shared ownership (impossibility of private control) of exhaustible resources for which users compete. Examples include public hunting areas, fishing zones, or communal grazing ground where entry is free. There is no fee for hunting, fishing or grazing; the rule of capture applies (whoever captures the resource owns it) and agents compete to consume the good. When too many people have these rights the resource is likely to be overused. The example used by Hardin (1968, 1244) is that of the pasture open to all herdsmen:

As a rational being, each herdsman seeks to maximize his gain. Explicitly or implicitly, more or less consciously, he asks 'What is the utility to me of adding one more animal to my herd?' This utility has one negative and one positive component:

1) The positive component is a function of the increment of one animal. Since the herdsman receives all the proceeds from the sale of the additional animal, the positive utility is nearly +1.

2) The negative component is a function of the additional overgrazing created by one more animal. Since, however, the effects of overgrazing are shared by all herdmen, the negative utility for any particular decision making herdsman is only a fraction of −1.

Adding together the component partial utilities, the rational herdsman concludes that the only sensible course for him to pursue is to add another animal to his herd. And another; and another. But this is the conclusion reached by each and every rational hersdman sharing a commons. Therein is the tragedy.

An in-depth analysis of the structure of the problem shows that the tragedy is possible only when exploitation of the common resource allows the production of private goods (livestock, in Hardin's example) and when a market for those private goods exists. In a regime of common resources in which the livestock is subject to other usage rights, no tragedy of overutilization is likely to occur. Thus, the tragedy of the commons is a problem only in a context of the market economy.

Of course, the potential problem does not necessarily lead to tragedy. Collective adoption and compliance with informal norms aimed at regulating access to the resource are possible solutions (Ostrom 1990). Moreover, the creation of property rights represents a form of solution to this problem, as Karl Polanyi (2001) clearly shows in his study of the enclosures movement in seventeenth-century England.

**The Tragedy of the Commons and the Economics of Knowledge**
How is this tragedy reflected in the economics of knowledge? There are four basic cases depending on the nature of the knowledge.

1. Knowledge is a consumer good. Free access and the absence of methods of exclusion can result in the disappearance of the market and thus of the industry producing those goods. Thus, the Napster affair, concerning a principle of free access to possibilities of music consumption, typically poses a problem of tragedy of the commons, a potential threat to the activity of music production. Those who believe in such a threat say that a new enclosures movement is necessary, similar to the initiative taken by major music producing and publishing companies, to educate students regarding copyright laws (Sherman 2001, 36): "In response, the record industry launched an educational

initiative aimed particularly at universities, where Internet access was greatest to educate a new generation of students (and administrators) about copyright law and the rights and wrongs of music online." Critical arguments against this position are given in this chapter.

2. Knowledge is a production good (an input making it possible to produce a commercializable good as, for instance, a method of production). In this case, free access to the new methods of production may create disincentives for potential innovators: given immediate imitation, any advantage in the market would not last for any time at all. Free access can, thus, reduce commercial opportunities and the entry of new firms into the domain concerned.

3. Knowledge is a research tool or a research field (an input making it possible to produce further knowledge). The tragedy can be seen, then, in an excess of incentives to carry out the same type of work, leading to wastage and duplication. This excess is the result of a lack of coordination between independent agents working in the same research field. From a theoretical point of view, this type of situation is produced by the combination of a shared resource—the research field—and the existence of property rights on the results. Like the fishing zone, the research field is a shared resource to which the rule of capture applies. It is necessary here to distinguish clearly between property rights on discoveries and the right to discover (just as there is a distinction between rights to fish caught and fishing rights). In this case, the tragedy of the commons can be expressed by two types of phenomenon (David 1998c):

• Common pool problems arise because individual competitors may try to challenge a dominant position by exploring the same field of research without taking into account the effect of their entry on expected returns on the investments that others are making. The result can be duplicative investments in areas in which the anticipated prizes are big, in other words, an excess of investment in research by rivals.

• Racing behavior can also lead to a tragedy of commons: The value of being a week earlier at the patent office, or six months in advance to launch a new software application, can be very large in comparison with the incremental social value of letting the consumers use the innovation that much sooner. Firms then have an incentive to structure their R&D programs for speed, rather than quality or cost minimization. Here economists encounter the problem of premature applications. As in the classic tragedy of the commons, too many little fish are captured:

"Since the basic knowledge is costless to the innovator, he introduces a discovery when it first become profitable instead of waiting until profits are maximized. Basic knowledge is thus overexploited comparably to public roads, fisheries, and oil and water pools, although in this case the excessive use of resources takes the form of their premature application" (Barzel 1968, 348).

A solution to these problems of common pool and racing behavior, similar to classic solutions, might consist in auctioning research rights. However, uncertainty on the value of the right (due to uncertainty on the importance of discoveries not yet disclosed) makes this difficult.

The solution referred to most often in the literature consists in granting a property right not only on a new idea but also on all subsequent "hoped for" developments. This amounts to delimiting a "hunting ground" and avoiding overinvestment in the area. Thus, the regime that associates a common resource with private rights provides an argument for broad patents. The broad patent aims not only at reinforcing private initiative in the context of the public goods problem, it also concerns the need to avoid tragedies of common resources. When patents are delimited "far afield," a vast domain is created in which risks of excessive research no longer exist. This solution has been argued by Kitch (1977) who used it to show the validity of very broad patents. But by creating exclusive rights to a large domain, one is eliminating the advantage of research carried out by multiple agents (multiplicity determines a diversity of "talents"), as opposed to research monopolized by a single agent. The knowledge dilemma resurfaces here. Broad patents provide a solution to the problem of an excess of incentives, but at the same time exploration of the field by a diversity of actors with multiple talents is precluded. The same dilemma is found in the utilization of very large scientific facilities (accelerator, synchrotron, giant telescope, space base), a common resource which can lead to a tragedy of commons. To avoid this tragedy, should a mechanism of marginal cost pricing be adopted to limit access, or is it better to optimize exploitation of the resource by offering everyone free use of the facility? This is a trade-off between setting a price for access, which could result in underutilization of the resource, and maximization of the social benefits by allowing free access, which could result in a problem of too many incentives (David 1997).

4. Knowledge corresponds to what Hirshleifer (1971) calls *aforeknowledge*. What Hirshleifer means is knowledge that is at first restricted to

the single individual and relates to facts which, if they become generally known, will influence the overall price structure. In some circumstances, the knowledge of such facts may be without any great social value. Yet as a foreknowledge it may possess considerable private value because it permits profitable speculation. For example, a person who knows before others that an incurable epidemic is about to annihilate most of the bee population can speculate in honey, whose price will rise sharply as soon as the imminence of the epidemic becomes generally known. (In chapter 6, I analyzed the use of aforeknowledge as a solution to the incentive problem posed by the production of a public good.)

**Tragedy or Comedy?** I would like to examine in more detail the conditions which make it possible for a tragedy to occur in "innovation races" when several firms compete for the same invention. The research field must be free (this is the common resource), the rule of capture must apply (full property rights on the new knowledge), there must be only one element of knowledge to discover—for which everyone is competing—and, finally, there must be no knowledge externalities between rival agents (e.g., in the form of scientific publications). Cockburn and Henderson (1995) note that these hypotheses are strong. In their empirical work on twenty-one discoveries of drugs in the United States, they show that, even in cases of innovation races, there are often knowledge externalities between rival agents (who carry on publishing) and that, in the end, the agents still discover different knowledge (that is, drugs of the same type with varied therapeutic effects). Another argument against the likelihood of a tragedy of commons is that a research domain is not necessarily a common resource, even if it is not formally private. The identification and definition of the domain is usually a function of the agents' scientific capacities and previous work. Not everyone has access to it.

The tragedy of commons situation is therefore rare, although contexts of innovation races in a well-defined field where the object of the search is known or predictable (e.g., the race between the Pasteur Institute and the U.S. firm Abbot to develop an HIV test) can correspond to this situation. The international breast cancer consortium offers another example, examined by Cassier and Foray (2000). The race to publish first on the location and identification of the gene, as well as the race to patent resulted in imperfect coordination among groups working on the subject. But more generally, situations are less "tragic" in the knowledge economy than in the economy of exhaustible resources. As noted several times, the knowledge commons is not only inexhaustible, it is also enriched by intensive exploitation by a diversity of agents. Hence, there is no phenomenon of overgrazing. Faced with the virtues of the system of knowledge openness, the risks of tragedy of the commons seem minimal and correspond to very particular situations, as Cockburn and Henderson (1995) show empirically.

Recent theoretical works also make the point that there is no tragedy of commons in the world of intangibles and knowledge. According to Boldrin and Levine (2003), "Napster is right" because, first, the downloading of copyrighted music is not a theft at all since it does not deprive the owner of use of the object; and, second, there is no risk that treating the stock of products (musical recordings) as a common resource might generate a tragedy of commons since a lack of copyright protection would never prevent artists from creating music. In a situation in which original producers compete directly with the buyers of their own product (the latter having the "right" to reproduce and sell it), early purchasers (those who want to do business with the product by reproducing and selling it) will pay a high price, higher than the one they will be able to charge subsequent consumers. Thus, it is the temporal dimension of the competitive process that creates the incentive mechanism. The first creator (the author) will by nature be better rewarded than the second creator (the copier). Competitive markets for this kind of digital product do not fail, and they exhibit optimal allocation properties.

The knowledge commons is less tragic than comedic!

**Institutions Supporting Knowledge Openness**

**From Open Science to Open Technology**
The economic analysis of open knowledge has been developed extensively in the field of scientific research owing to the seminal work of Dasgupta and David (1994). The approach of the "new economics of science" develops two important arguments for theoretical analysis as well as policy implication in the field of the economics of knowledge:

• First, as already mentionned, knowledge openness is viewed as a mechanism generating economic efficiency.

• Second, open knowledge does not mean the absence of individual incentives. There is a need for individual rewards, which are compatible with the complete disclosure norm.

These two features apply in the world of open science as well as in local systems of open technology.

**Open Science**   As noted in chapter 6, private markets based on a system of intellectual property rights, are ill-suited to the production of certain forms of knowledge. It is then up to the public authorities to take care of those activities by providing the necessary funding. This public funding is granted in exchange for complete and immediate disclosure of the results and knowledge produced. It is a sort of contract between society and the institutions and researchers it finances. Public production of knowledge is thus organized according to very specific norms that can be referred to as "open knowledge." Knowledge is often disclosed through scientific publication, and since anything published can no longer be patented, it definitively becomes public knowledge. (In the U.S. system the grace period mechanism allows patenting in the year following publication.)

In many countries public funding of a large part of this system is facilitated by the close ties that exist between research and higher education. As Arrow (1962a) points out, the fact that research and teaching activities are two sides of the same profession is a *lucky accident* since it ensures that researchers are remunerated not on the basis of what they find (their income in that case would be highly irregular, and only the best would survive) but on that of regular teaching. It is because this public system produces both knowledge and human capital that it easily harnesses a large proportion of public resources. The paradigmatic institution of this dual activity is the university. Note that the union between research and teaching is not always maintained, which is what determines the partition of the public research system between universities and national (or regional) laboratories (chapter 6).

Yet there is still a piece missing in this system. How can people be encouraged to be efficient and effective researchers if their work is immediately disclosed, without any possibility of private appropriation, and their salaries guaranteed? An ingenious mechanism comes into play here, consisting of the granting of moral property rights that are not concretized in exclusivity rights (in other words, they are compatible with the complete disclosure norm). It is the priority rule which identifies the author of the discovery as soon as he or she publishes and which thus determines the constitution of "reputation capital," a decisive element when it comes to obtaining grants. "The norm of openness is incentive-compatible with a collegiate reputational reward system based upon accepted claims to priority" (David 1998a, 17). The priority rule creates contexts of races (or tournaments), while ensuring that results are disclosed. It is a remarkable device since it allows for the creation of private assets, a form of intellectual property, resulting from the very act of foregoing exclusive ownership of the knowledge concerned. Here the need to be identified and recognized as the one who discovered forces people to release new knowledge quickly and completely. In this sense, the priority rule is a highly effective device that offers nonmarket incentives to the production of public goods (Dasgupta and David 1994; Callon and Foray 1997).

This form of organization is particularly efficient, for it ensures the rapid and complete diffusion of new knowledge while preserving a certain level of incentive. Moreover, complete disclosure functions as a sort of "quality assurance" insofar as published results can be reproduced and verified by other members of the community. They are thus peer-evaluated.

Of course, the ideal world of openness described here does not exclude the possibility of bending or departing from the rules. On the contrary, the tournament contexts created by the priority rule, as well as the size of related rewards, tend to encourage bad conduct. The notion of "open science" is therefore based on an ideal never achieved (in other words, there will always be many cases of various degrees of retention). It is nevertheless still part of the "scientific culture" (an ethos) and as such influences researchers' behavior. It is a type of prescriptive norm that, all things considered, facilitates the formation of cooperative networks.

**The "Grande fabrique lyonnaise": Knowledge Openness Outside the Scientific Field**   I have discussed "open science" because it is probably the organization of science that is closest to this standard of openness. Yet in the past there have been numerous cases of "open technology," albeit limited in time and space. Historically, most situations of openness were linked to a specific territory: Lyons in the case of the circulation of techniques and inventions relating to the silk

industry (Hilaire Perez 2000); Lancashire in the case of collective invention in the metallurgical industry (Allen 1983); the Clyde area in the
case of collective invention in shipbuilding (Schwerin 2000); and the
Cornish mining district in the case of collective invention related to
pumping engine technology (Nuvolari 2002).

The historical analysis of open technology, and the particular case of
the *fabrique lyonnaise*, allows us to draw a parallel with the economics
of open science:

1. First, in both systems some kind of collective ethos is present,
generating a sort of "natural" inclination of inventors to diffuse their
knowledge. Such an ethos can be seen both at the policy level and the
individual inventor level. At the policy level, the municipality, following the Ancien Régime tradition, kept on rewarding inventions to put
them into the public domain; then, in Lyons, great technical innovations were treated as true common goods. At the individual level,
some inventors were emblematic of this natural inclination to reveal
knowledge freely. The best example is Philippe de Lasalle's career
path (1723–1804). According to him, artistic creativity, technical
invention, and transmitting knowledge were closely connected.
Collaborating and imitating were the main principles everywhere and
the only ways to progress. Art and invention rested on a cumulative
process, methods, rules, devices, lines, and colors to be learned side by
side with the master, teacher, contriver, or nature itself. De Lasalle had
created a garden in the South of France where he sent his best students
to train in drawing flowers. For him, there was no genius without
copying:

You are not unaware that art is learned through emulation and great examples.
Work and my observations of the works of those who have distinguished themselves in the career that I follow have shaped my talents. Even more ardour
to warrant the protection that you grant them can afford them one day that
celebrity which offers models to imitate and stimulates other geniuses to outdo
it. Thus, amongst us, as soon as a striking piece has left the hand of a skilled
artist, it is lifted up to be seen by all rivals seeking the means to acquire it, and
often provides, by its character, either the season's fashion or the example of a
beautiful subject. When in 1756 I treated a tiger skin worked with a touch of art
on a golden background, one witnessed budding in each workshop tasteful
drawings representing diverse furs. The same happened on other occasions
when I introduced landscapes, birds and people. (qtd. in Hilaire Perez 2000, 76)

De Lasalle would not condemn the theft of patterns or inventions; his
aim was the circulation of knowledge and the progress of qualifications

which could result. He was even pleased when his printed silk cloth was copied and his workers seduced by rivals. All means were good if diffusion were at stake: teaching, imitating, stealing, and, not least of all, deeds and free offers. Several times, de Lasalle gave away inventions and taught about his new device without asking for anything in return. In 1760 he was offered a 200 pound bonus for each student he taught, but he refused and preferred to offer all his knowledge freely. How such an ethos appears and becomes forceful is a broad question, addressed for instance by Hilaire Perez (2000) in the case of the *fabrique lyonnaise*.

2. The efficiency of systems of open technology is similar to the efficiency of open science: both are a way to increase the performance of a system of invention by making the existing stock of knowledge more socially useful, through improved transfer, transformation, and access to the existing innovations. In Lyons a good example is the diffusion of the Jacquard loom. The invention matched the needs of the Lyonnaise silk industry. The new loom immediately spread and the mental mobilization it entailed resulted in several useful improvements. Jacquard's invention could then be improved by other loom builders, who made hundreds of them, compared to Jacquard who built only fifty-seven. The establishment of technical standards provided another positive effect of this intense circulation of technical knowledge. The historian Cottereau (1997) found an essay written in 1863 describing the networks of newly invented looms in Lyons: "The most convincing proof that these successive inventions were borrowed from one another is that a Jacquard card in use today may be applied both to Vaucanson's planchette with needles and to Falcon's, and the match is so good that Falcon's initial matrix must have fixed dimensions." According to Cottereau, the effects "were comparable to what could easily have been the case today if computer systems had been standardized from the start and made cumulatively compatible as they progressed," even if contrived by several different firms.

3. Similar collective belief, in both cases, of being part of a positive sum game plays a key role as well. Such common knowledge that open technology is a positive sum game was particularly effective and "had force" in the case of Lyons since the city was engaged in international competition with London and the inventors knew full well that the prosperity of the local system to which they belonged directly influenced their own individual prosperity.

4. Both collective ethics and common knowledge about the efficiency of open technology are not enough to sustain a system based on the free dissemination of knowledge. A need for some kind of mechanism aimed at rewarding inventors without granting exclusive rights exists. Particular mechanisms were designed in Lyons to reward inventors who agreed to disclose their knowledge and actively to participate in the diffusion of that knowledge (teaching). The setting up of a reward fund, the process of examining inventions and the system of financial bonuses awarded to those who agreed not only to disclose but also to teach their knowledge were institutional mechanisms which made the system very effective. The system of bonuses shows how well the conditions for an efficient reproduction of the knowledge, once created, were understood: Michel Berthet received six hundred pounds for his invention plus four hundred pounds if he taught his knowledge and if four of his looms existed in various other places (Hilaire Perez 2000).

The "collective fabrique" appears very fragile, however, and somewhat vulnerable to individual claims, frustrations, and hopes. Jacquard agreed initially to give up his rights to patents and left the fruit of his art to the community. The invention became the property of the town and quickly spread. But later on, Jacquard started to complain that the Lyonnais administrators had not treated him well enough, considering the importance ("the social return") of his invention. A conflict arose between the great inventor and the municipality which compelled him to stay in Lyons, fearing that he would sell the invention to competitors. In 1814, after Jacquard had left Lyons, the police were urged to take him back and to check if he had transmitted his invention to rivals! There was thus a degree of fragility in these systems, especially when areas close by (Paris, in this case) offered inventors the possibility of obtaining a patent. It is the coexistence of different incentive systems that makes those not based on private property fragile.

This is probably the main argument to discuss: apart from the beauty of systems of collective invention and the fine economic performance such systems can produce, the individual incentive dimension remains decisive and calls for institutional mechanisms to give credit to inventors without granting them exclusivity. This is the kind of mechanism Dasgupta and David have explored in the case of open science and which remains uncertain in the case of open technology, although the case of the *fabrique lyonnaise* provides some ideas about it.

**Open Source Development**   Linux, like other open source software developments, is a recent example of a technological community based on openness, without being territorially limited. It is a computer operating system inspired by Unix, delivered free-of-charge with the source code (the series of instructions that forms the program before its compilation). The most important feature of Linux is not that it is free to buy but that it is free to modify and to improve. When users are given access to the source code, gigantic effects of learning-by-using can be generated; in other words, a fantastic amount of distributed intelligence can be fully exploited (see chapter 3). Thousands of users reveal problems and thousands of programmers find out how to eliminate them. According to the terms of the Free Software Foundation, everyone can use the code and amend it, provided they inform the organization of the change so that it can be checked and assessed. Linux clearly shows that open knowledge does not mean the absence of legal rules. The necessary "legal equipment" to protect the free nature of knowledge from private appropriation exists. In the case of Linux, this is general public licensing (GPL) which protects Linux from private appropriation. Another example is simply the scientific result that, once published, cannot be patented.

We have here the "good properties" of knowledge distribution and systems of open knowledge: only with the fast and large-scale circulation of knowledge can we benefit from the unique potential of a very large number of skilled individuals. In a way, the billions of dollars spent by Microsoft to maintain huge teams of researchers seems very expensive compared to Linux's capacity for "bringing together and exploiting the IQs of thousands of users in the four corners of the Internet" (Alper 1999, 28). I note that the "good properties" of openness are amplified in this case for various reasons relating to the peculiar features of software as a technology: First, software is a very complex system that generates unbounded learning processes, so that a system of thousands of developers working for a long time on the same software continues to show increasing returns; second, it is a technology that is highly codified, thus making it possible to increase the efficiency of the collective learning process by exploiting the potential of the new electronic infrastructure; third, software belongs to a certain class of technologies that have the particular property of bringing consumers and knowledge production closer together (Quah 1999). Thus, the innovation process that characterized the Linux enterprise stems from improvements and refinements put in place by a large world-wide base of users. Users are developers!

## "Common Knowledge" on Knowledge Openness

As is clearly shown in both cases of open science and open technology, a critical factor of the historical origin of open knowledge institutions is the emergence and reinforcement of a convention, that is to say, a way of aligning individual expectations. What matters above all is that the players somehow possess the same consistent expectations about the ruling convention and are mutually aware of that fact. Each player must know that the other players know that he or she knows that they know that, and so on, with the result being that he or she will disclose the knowledge, once discovered, without delay and in a well-documented form. This argument raises a question about the "causal-genetic" moment. How do such jointly held expectations become established? Where does such common knowledge come from, if not from shared history and fine institutional mechanisms elaborated in a given historical context (see chapter 5)? Thus, precedent emerges as an important factor allowing the players to align their individual expectations. The emergence of "open knowledge" institutions is always based on the historical emergence of structures of mutually consistent expectations, resulting in the creation of "common knowledge." It becomes common knowledge that openness increases the general performance of the system and that diffusing one's own knowledge contributes to a positive sum game. Such a collective belief is particularly strong in cases of localized systems of open knowledge that compete with other systems (e.g., Lyons against London).

## A Dual-Incentive Structure

However, this is not enough as Dasgupta and David (1994) clearly demonstrated in their analysis of open science. Any system promoting knowledge openness involves a dual-incentive structure: incentives that can motivate people to reveal their knowledge freely to others, and incentives that make it more profitable to be an innovator than a free-rider in a context of knowledge openness.

**Five Classes of Incentives to Freely Reveal Knowledge**   I propose five cases:

1. Voluntary spillovers are likely to occur *when reward systems specifically address the issue of knowledge diffusion and reproduction*. A mechanism is designed to give credit to inventors without creating exclusivity rights. This is the case of the ingenious mechanism of collegial reputation as reward working in open science: in this system the need to be

identified and recognized as "the one who discovered" forces people to release new knowledge quickly and completely (Dasgupta and David 1994). Benefits of reputational capital may then be, harnessed through grants and awards (as in the case of academic system) or on particular labor markets (as in the case of open source). In the case of the *fabrique lyonnaise*, a financial reward is attributed to inventors who agree to diffuse their knowledge and bonuses are given if the inventor actively takes part in the adoption of his technology by others (Hilaire Perez 2000).

An inventor prize is usually considered in the literature as an efficient mechanism because it creates incentives while keeping the knowledge in the public domain, if the amount of the reward is equal to the social surplus afforded by the invention. However, as the Jacquard case shows, the ex ante prediction of the social value of the invention is not a trivial condition.

In both cases—open science and open technology—the reward system introduces competition and increases the risk of conflict. That is where the force of ethics as well as the effectiveness of common knowledge about the efficiency of the system come into play to reduce individual misconduct and frustrations.

2. Voluntary spillovers are likely to occur *when agents or companies need to create "general reciprocity obligations" in order to capture external knowledge* (from a scientific network, from engineers or users working on similar problems) (Allen 1983; von Hippel 1988b; Schwerin 2000).

3. Voluntary spillovers are likely to occur *when a private agent freely reveals an innovation in order to benefit from its increased diffusion*. A direct result of free revealing is to increase the diffusion of that innovation relative to what it would be if the innovation were either licensed at a fee or kept secret. Increased diffusion of free knowledge may be beneficial to private agents when (1) they are interested *in setting a standard advantageous to them*, and thus freely reveal their innovation so that other agents (including rivals) can adopt it as well; and (2) they are interested *in inducing manufacturer improvements*. This last strategic use of spillovers is particularly important for users: by freely revealing an innovative product, a user makes it possible for manufacturers to adopt that innovation (Harhoff, Henkel, and von Hippel 2000; von Hippel 2001b).

4. Voluntary spillovers are likely to occur when firms are interested in the improvements of the average aggregate performance of the indus-

try. A clear case deals with safety issues: Individual failure (a technological accident) may imply a costly strengthening of regulation and safety standards for all. Therefore, knowledge is shared to increase average safety of the industry (Fauchart 2003). Allen (1983) describes another type of situation in the iron industry: Entrepreneurs who shared knowledge about technical advances of furnaces were also owners of the iron ore mines. Thus, improvements of efficiency of all furnaces led to a substantial increase in the value of the iron ore deposit.

5. Voluntary spillovers are likely to occur *when private agents play strategically with the public good nature of knowledge*: incumbents can pursue the so-called strategy of the commons to create market failures and eliminate the incentives for any firm to develop and commercialize an invention by creating an intellectual property commons (Agrawal and Garlappi 2001). For instance, large pharmaceutical companies have created the SNP Consortium, which is designed to speed up the development of new drugs and diagnostic tests and which aims at keeping the data produced in the public domain. On the one hand, such a mechanism will facilitate access to new knowledge and, thus, support cumulative research and sequential innovation. On the other hand, small biotechnology companies racing for the discovery of genetic data with huge commercial potential may fear a new kind of "tragedy of the commons." Once put into the public domain, the potential for commercial gains is simply suppressed, which can be detrimental to commercialization strategies of new biotechnology companies.

Finally, some market and technological conditions may play a role: *low rivalry conditions* as well as *low marginal cost of diffusion* are not so much incentives as an absence of disincentives.

Of course, any deliberate strategy to reveal knowledge freely has a cost for the private agent which is the partial loss (or at least the sharing) of the monopolistic rent potentially created by an innovation. Table 8.1 shows the costs and benefits of various options for knowledge sharing.

## The Private Benefits of Being a Knowledge Contributor (Rather than a Free-Rider) in an Open System

Now, might such cooperation encourage "free-riding" behavior (a large number of members of the system stop any creative effort because they can free-ride), undermining the whole innovative capability of the system? The answer is striking and counterintuitive: no, because the

**Table 8.1**
Options for Knowledge Sharing

| Option | Nature of access | Knowledge owner's reward |
|---|---|---|
| Trade secret | Exclusive use | Monopoly rents |
| Patent no license | Exclusive use | Monopoly rents |
| Patent and license | Bilateral | Duopoly rents and license fee |
| Know-how trading | Bilateral | Duopoly rents and knowledge |
| Collective invention | Network | Oligopoly rents and knowledge |
| Publications | Open use | Variable |

*Source:* Appleyard (1996).

private rewards to those who contribute to collective developments are much higher than those available to free-riders. Several such "selective incentives" for project participation have been identified in the case of open source projects (von Hippel and von Krogh 2003):

• Although a freely revealed code (in an open source development project) becomes a public good, its production also creates some *spin-off private benefits*, such as learning and enjoyment. In many open systems, the technical learning opportunities are enormous and are an important motivation for participation.

• Contributors to a project report valuing the *sense of control* over the direction of their work. In many cases, innovations are created by individuals for *private purpose* and are tailored to their individual needs. They are then openly revealed and contributed to the community as public goods for whatever general use there may be. To the extent that the conditions faced by the contributor differ from those faced by free-riders, the contributor is in a more favorable position than free-riders to gain private benefit from the code he or she contributes.

## A New Structure to Support Knowledge Openness: Knowledge Communities

In chapter 5 I underscored the growing awareness of the importance of the "community" as an organizational system allowing the exploitation of the virtuous properties of knowledge. Knowledge-based communities are networks of individuals striving, first and foremost, to produce and circulate new knowledge, and working for different, even rival, organizations. These communities are becoming an exemplary form of organization of knowledge-based economies. Although knowledge-driven communities are not the whole story of a knowledge society and a focus upon them will not uncover everything of interest concerning the economics of knowledge, their organizational forms and functions will become or have already become of wider relevance in a knowledge society. This is evident in the cases of scientific research communities and more recently open source software development communities. There is thus a high value to study them as new kinds of "machineries of knowing."

## Concepts

Knowledge communities are, as a rule, oriented toward the production and reproduction of knowledge through decentralized and cooperative processes. This definition is very broad and covers a variety of institutions and organizations of varying degrees of formality. Communities of this kind are hardly a new phenomenon, one familiar prototype being the communities of researchers in the sciences. Recently, however, some knowledge communities have acquired new characteristics partly related to their intensive use of new ICT. New ICT increase the power of individual and collective production and circulation of knowledge, while creating new tensions and difficulties. To overcome those conflicts and resolve tensions, new adaptations and innovations in other technological and social domains are necessary. Thus, a complex of interdependent changes supports the transition of these communities toward new forms of knowledge-driven activities.

Such a cluster of developments may dramatically alter the way in which other preexisting communities (including "communities of practice") have traditionally functioned. There is thus a potential for the emergence of new knowledge communities in areas where they do not yet exist. Four key domains of development (or constituents) are identified for analysis of this process:

• Adaptation and intensive use of new ICT as a tool for collective invention, codification, and transmission of knowledge.

• Increasing tendency toward the decentralization of knowledge production. There are two processes at work here (chapter 3): increasing importance of explicit cognitive learning at the production level, and increasing numbers of users and lay people involved in some kind of knowledge production processes.

• Social norms for knowledge sharing that create public (or collective) spaces for knowledge circulation.

• Trust formation. What is at stake here is the entire range of mechanisms that will facilitate interpersonal and interorganizational transactions, given the new conditions for knowledge transactions and exchanges (increasing specialization, ever greater anonymity among interlocutors, and so on).

This range of developments represents a broad framework in which a variety of trajectories is possible. In some cases, ICT create the initial opportunities for introducing changes, thereby generating the need for mutual adjustments and adaptation in other domains. In other cases, the increasing tendency toward the decentralization of knowledge creation acts as a trigger. The assumed requirement of complementarity among the several identified domains holds the potential for positive feedback to either drive the transformation process or, if changes in some domain become blocked, cause the dynamic movement to stall.

**Virtues and Vices**
The communities characterized by the four components mentioned—multiple capacities for creation and reproduction of knowledge, mechanisms for the exchange and circulation of knowledge created, intensive use of new communication technologies, and norms and mechanisms for the establishment of trust—will rapidly shift toward knowledge-driven activities. This will tend to be manifested in increasing innovation rates (due to the possibilities of recombination, synergies, and cumulativeness of knowledge), increasing reliability of knowledge (insofar as it is diffused, the new knowledge can be reproduced and scrutinized by other members), increasing static efficiency (the wheel is not reinvented and each "great" invention will benefit from a strong collective focus on it), and increasing productivity of learning (people "learn to learn" the kind of knowledge that is circulating within the community). A knowledge-driven economic activity can be caricatured as possessing these four "virtues," and may therefore be conceptualized as the emergent property of the array of concurrent, mutually reinforcing technological and social transformations. Knowledge-driven communities also involve potential risks for knowledge creation.

First, there is the classic problem of the "tragedy of the commons": The public space for the circulation of knowledge creates opportunities for sequential innovation. But it can simultaneously create various problems that I have already discussed. I nevertheless concluded that in the knowledge-based economy these problems are neither as big nor as serious as those concerning the economy of exhaustible resources. Some theoreticians even think that they do not exist.

Second, there are questions of "technological lock-in." The capacity of a strongly decentralized community to extract itself from the situation of decreasing returns and technological lock-in is weaker than that of an R&D laboratory with centralized coordination.

**Examples**
The communities most deeply engaged in the knowledge-based economy are scientific communities. They are indeed communities: where, by definition, most members are producers of knowedge; in which specific institutions push everyone to "free" and share their knowledge (Dasgupta and David 1994); which historically have always been pioneers in the use of new information technologies; and which benefit from tried and tested mechanisms of certification of knowledge (trust).

Open software networks provide good examples of communities embracing the knowledge economy. There is, for instance, a very interesting result produced by Lakhani and von Hippel (2003), showing that the success of any system of "free" user-to-user assistance in open-source software communities is based: First, on the skills and competencies of a critical mass of users (the low-cost provision of solutions only works because some users know the solution); second, on some kind of incentive structures to share knowledge (including reputational reward systems); and third, on the very low marginal cost for writing and transmitting the information (the willingness of information providers to contribute what they know is related to the cost to them of doing so). Such systems illustrate an increasing shift of innovation toward users. Other examples, especially well-documented by von Hippel (2001b), concern particular cases of "sophisticated users." If this is so, the emergence and multiplication of "user-only innovation systems" represents an important, possibly signal development in the historical emergence of the knowledge-driven economy (see chapter 3).

Another interesting example of a community beginning to migrate to the knowledge economy is provided by the health care system, in which general practitioners are contributing to the production and codification of "evidence-based medicines," that are stored in electronic databases and shared among the community. Here again, all four key domains of development are involved. By contrast, an illustrative example of a community still lagging behind may be drawn from the education sector. There is, in this sector, a massive innovative activity in the "tinkering" of teachers in their classrooms, finding new solutions to pedagogical problems. However, the greater portion of those innovations are neither articulated and documented, nor horizontally diffused, with the result that this activity has not acquired a transformative cumulative momentum. The basic norms and institutions of the teaching profession, and the mechanisms of trust in the expertise of teachers, the integrity of the examination and evaluation process for students, and the design of curricula are essentially undisturbed (see chapter 9).

### The Penetration of Knowledge Communities into More Conventional Organizations

These "knowledge communities" are not independent of the rest of the economy. They are strongly connected to other activities, due to the fact that their members are specialized and must obtain needed resources through exchanges of goods and services, or otherwise derive sponsorship from more conventional organizations such as business firms, research institutes, and public agencies. Some of the members of the knowledge communities may also have important roles in the work of those other entities. Thus, knowledge communities may be interconnecting individuals who are members of different, and sometimes rival, organizations. One important manifestation of the new knowledge-driven economy is these organizations' integration and assimilation of individuals who, in order to be of value to their employers and clients, must maintain connections and access to quite differently organized, external knowledge communities. In this sense, knowledge-driven communities may act as the transformative agents in the emergence of "knowledge societies."

However, conflicts may emerge between some of the mechanisms used by profit-oriented companies (and by public agencies) to keep knowledge privately controlled (through trade secrecy and information restriction policies), and the ethos of knowledge communities that are more oriented toward cooperation, through open circulation of information, and active sharing of knowledge. These conflicts may result in an adaptive evolution of the organizational practices within private companies, pushing them to formalize policies that permit employees to publish openly (a good example is the pharmaceutical industry; Cockburn, Henderson, and Stern 1999). In some other cases, the participation of employees in reciprocal exchanges of information with correspondents outside the firm, even those in rival companies, may be tolerated without becoming institutionalized (as in the cases of engineers "trading trade secrets"; von Hippel 1988b). Elsewhere, some of the basic features of a knowledge community may undergo alteration because its members enter work environments where they lose the freedom (or willingness) to follow the rules of knowledge disclosure and sharing (the absorption of specialized academic researchers into classified defense work is an obvious example). All these tendencies cause the boundaries between the open, public domain and the closed, private domains of knowledge to become blurred.

## Knowledge Openness Appears at the Heart of the Knowledge-Based Economy

One of the most interesting challenges to the knowledge-based economy has been discussed in this chapter, namely, how to encourage individuals to freely reveal their knowledge, without discouraging the inventor? What incentive mechanisms are compatible with the circulation and free access of knowledge? I have identified and analyzed these mechanisms. Some have been historically tried and tested and are robust, such as open science; others depend on "almost nothing": A series of positive attitudes toward cooperation, which are gradually reinforced as trust grows and general rules of reciprocity are affirmed. These mechanisms are at the base of new knowledge communities, an organizational form, which places knowledge openness at the heart of the economy. Yet the modernity of these communities stems not only from the norms of knowledge sharing that they institute. It also derives from an intensive use of information technologies which strongly reduce the marginal cost of copying, transmitting, and sharing knowledge (cf. chapters 2, 4, and 5), from the highly decentralized nature of knowledge production (chapter 3) and the invention of original mechanisms for creating trust in new situations spawned by electronic transactions among a large number of individuals.

# 9             On the Uneven Development of Knowledge across Sectors

This chapter applies the concepts and tools developed in chapters 3, 4, and 5, on the ways in which knowledge is created and codified, and on the factors determining spillovers, with a view to elucidating the question of uneven development of knowledge across sectors. To illustrate the challenges and problems posed by this uneven development, I analyze the fields of education and health. This means that the methods and problems of the knowledge-based economy apply not only to the sectors of science and technology but to all human activity based on processes of creation and exchange of knowledge.[19]

### Framing the Problem

A strongly unbalanced and uneven development of knowledge across sectors and fields can be observed (Malerba and Orsenigo 1996). These advances have been spectacular in some sectors such as ICT, and remarkable in dealing with some kinds of human illness, but have been very limited in other areas, for example education, managerial know-how, avoiding wars, or developing cities (Nelson 1999). A major policy concern is to understand the factors at the origin of such uneven development, and to implement a proper strategy in order to fill the gap between sectors with fast knowledge accumulation processes and those in which these processes remain weak. The kind of question I ask opens the door to comparisons among extremely different and heterogeneous social and economic institutions. Is it fair to compare the process of knowledge creation between sectors allocating billions of dollars to R&D and sectors which exhibit far less generosity for their knowledge creation tasks? Is it acceptable to compare industrial activities based on a sound and rich scientific knowledge corpus with people-centered professions in which the creation of scientific knowledge, the generalization of rules and hypotheses, and the construction of predictive models are all tasks which are by nature very difficult to achieve? In making that kind of comparison there is certainly a risk of neglecting the very specific nature of both cognitive processes and socioeconomic institutions operating in each particular sectoral case.

I think, however, that sectoral comparison remains a promising avenue of research if the framework used captures enough regularities and constants (some kind of "laws") on which the comparative work can be based. And this is what the economics of knowledge, as a framework, is able to provide. By carrying out empirical investigations on sectors as diverse as the pharmaceutical industry, financial services, health, or education, I would find some strong regularities and constants in terms of the properties of knowledge and the kind of socioeconomic institutions that can be relied upon to create and exploit knowledge efficiently.

The fact that knowledge has several properties which economists identify as those characterizing the general class of "public goods" is a good illustration of the regularity that outweighs sectoral particularities.

There are only two modes of knowledge creation (chapter 3), irrespective of the sector: formal R&D and learning-by-doing. Moreover, in all sectors the organization and management of these modes of production are based on the same problems.

A last example of a common feature is the fact that knowledge is "sticky," namely, costly to transfer from one site to another. This is another general issue prevailing over sectoral attributes.

These few examples show that the economics of knowledge provides a generic framework for the elaboration of common problems and issues across sectors and the development of cross-sectoral comparisons.

### Why Is There Unbalanced Development of Knowledge across Sectors and Fields?

In this section I draw on chapters 3, 4, and 5 to identify two factors that seem to be of critical importance in shaping the way knowledge is created and accumulated. I thus build a model, which may be viewed as a heuristic device to help understand how some sectors might be transformed in order to obtain a more rapid and effective trajectory of knowledge development.

## On the "Epistemic" Mode of Knowledge Creation

A first set of factors concern the cognitive dimension: how is knowledge created and advanced from a cognitive point of view; what is the cognitive method for determining the best practices? I propose to differentiate two "models" that I refer to as the "science model" and the "learning-by-doing model," respectively. They have been explored in depth in chapters 3 and 4.

The first is based on robust and systematic relations between science and technology. Nelson (1999) calls it "a strong science that illuminates technology." This means that the creation of scientific knowledge is directly valuable in developing process and product innovations. As such, this model enables rapid knowledge creation and accumulation in a particular field. It is characterized by the following: experimentation in the development of science; strong linkages and feedback loops between the development of science and the advance of technology; most of the inventing taking place offline (in R&D labs); and a large part of the knowledge base codified in instructional guides and documents, providing an effective way for transferring knowledge from science to technology and practices. In this model there are also feedback loops from advances in technology (instruments), which open new fields in basic research and reduce costs. It is thus a complex of interdependent dynamics—with science illuminating technology and technology equipping science—which is at the origin of a rapid accumulation of knowledge in some sectors. However, such a model may not work in all sectors, so there is the question of what alternative model may be needed to support rapid knowledge creation in other sectors.

In some sectors the main source of knowledge is related to some kind of learning-by-doing effects, where individuals learn as they go along and, as a rule, can assess what they learn and hone their practices for what follows next. This model is based on learning processes occurring on-line (in the plant, on the site of use, in the classroom). In this context R&D, as usually defined, is not of immediate value for developing applications and practical knowledge. Advances in know-how are not dependent on scientific progress but on the ability to fully exploit the opportunities offered by learning-by-doing. Some kind of R&D may play a role in this process, in order to develop methods and techniques for assessing and promoting the innovations emerging from the learning-by-doing process. This does not mean, however, that learning-by-doing is a scientific experiment; it is not, for the reasons discussed in chapter 3. In cases in which the learning-by-doing opportunities are well exploited, this model can be an extremely potent form of knowledge creation. However, in most cases know-how advances are slower than in the "science illuminating technology" model.

I have just characterized two models that are different from the point of view of the nature of the knowledge base. The two models differ not only in terms of the way knowledge is created, but also in the way it is diffused. Scientific knowledge can quite easily be made explicit and codified, and can thus be transmitted via books and journals.[20] Much knowledge generated "by doing" is tacit and so requires interpersonal interactions, such as coaching and mentoring, if it is to be transferred.

I do not believe that in practice any sector relies on a single model. Even the most "science-based sectors" (e.g., transport technology, biotechnology, and new materials) have some new knowledge deriving from learning-by-doing processes. In the same way, people-centred professions which strongly rely on learning-by-doing may also benefit from scientific knowledge: Doctors build up their expertise through a combination of science-generated, explicit knowledge with their own learning-by-doing expertise from work with their own patients. Of course, there are strong variations across sectors in the relative weight of the two models.

## Knowledge Spillovers

The second factor governing the speed and rate of knowledge development has to do with the importance and magnitude of knowledge spillovers. The existence of knowledge spillovers is a sine qua non condition for increasing the amount of innovative opportunities. Thus knowledge spillovers (voluntary and involuntary) are crucial issues when one looks at the determinants of the evolution of knowledge at the sectoral level (chapter 5).

Factors that may influence the importance of knowledge spillovers in an industry have been explored in chapters 5 and 8. Sectors in which both voluntary and involuntary spillovers are high are sectors in which massive innovative opportunities are constantly created. The importance of voluntary spillovers is contingent on the existence of incentive structures which encourage people to freely reveal their knowledge (chapter 8) while involuntary spillovers are dependent on the absorptive capacities developed by organizations in competitive markets.

## A Matrix to Identify Four Types of Knowledge Base

I thus have a model describing various contexts for knowledge creation and advances in know-how. The two parameters can be combined to yield four cases illustrating various modes of knowledge production and accumulation.

In contrast to a detailed representation of a sectoral knowledge base, such a representation does not claim to describe in exhaustive detail those institutions and practices supporting the production and distribution of knowledge. The aim is rather to suggest the existence of some kinds of "dominant" characteristics in the knowledge base of a certain sector.

The top row of table 9.1 describes cases in which R&D is a key pillar of the knowledge system. Deliberate, formal efforts to produce knowledge are taken seriously by entrepreneurs and decision makers, since such efforts are a considerable part of overall innovation efforts. In these situations, companies and other kinds of institution are eager to link themselves to scientific networks. These scientific networks are themselves powerful mechanisms for maximizing knowledge spillovers (which is, in a sense, the raison d'être of an open science community; see chapter 6).

The bottom row of table 9.1 describes cases in which the relation between research and the production of goods and services is of

Table 9.1
A Matrix to Identify Four Types of Knowledge Base

| Knowledge spillovers (intentional and nonintentional)<br><br>Science and technology interface | *Strong* (incentives to freely reveal/to capture) | *Weak* |
|---|---|---|
| *Science model* (Science is in a predictive stage, formal R&D is crucial and knowledge is highly codified) | Biotechnology, transport technology, new materials, chemicals and pharmaceuticals | Defense equipment |
| *Leaning-by-doing model* (Learning-by-doing is the key process, formal R&D is of secondary importance and knowledge is poorly articulated) | Financial services Consulting activity | Education (primary school) Early nineteenth-century medicine |

secondary importance and in which the lack of codification can impede the diffusion and reuse of knowledge. Column 1 of table 9.1 involves areas where knowledge spillovers are important and determine the existence and growth of a "knowledge infrastructure." In these sectors, the absorptive capacities of firms are key factors in the diffusion of knowledge. Column 2 of table 9.1 covers the opposite case.

A sector in which the science illuminating technology (S-i-T) model works well, which is characterized by a high degree of spillover, is a sector where an extremely rapid rate of innovation and a spectacular advance of human know-how can be expected. The northwest cell of table 9.1 describes a combination of a scientific model of knowledge creation and economic incentives that strongly support knowledge circulation and informational spillovers (incentives to reveal freely and incentives to capture).

In the pharmaceutical sector, for instance, the connection between private enterprise and public research is a key factor in innovative performance. But this connection has a cost. Establishing and maintaining it require private firms to contribute to basic research and to adhere to prevailing norms of publication and disclosure in the sector. This is a "model" consisting of equilibrium and compromise: equilibrium between the two spheres whose roles are relatively well-defined in relation to our definitions of objectives, and compromise by private firms which, even in the last stages of the innovation process, keep on publishing and disclosing information in order to maintain the rule of exchange and reciprocity. The model thus allows many powerful externalities between the public and private sectors and, even within the private sector itself, between rival firms (Cockburn and Henderson 1997). By contrast, sectors in which the science-technology interface does not work properly and knowledge spillovers are weak is a sector where a slower process of knowledge accumulation may be predicted. In other words, these sectors (located in the southeast cell of table 9.1) are not necessarily those with the slowest knowledge development (as already noted, a system of learning-by-doing characterized by proper mechanisms to exploit learning opportunities fully and maximize knowledge externalities can be as powerful as a model based on "science illuminating technology"). Rather, they are those whose performance is the most dependent on effective organizational structures and knowledge management practices in order to compensate for the absence of the classical incentives that maximize information spillovers and knowledge diffusion. And where organizational structures and knowledge management practices fail, one can predict a slower process of knowledge development.

### Variations and Divergencies within Sectors Regarding "Epistemic Cultures"

It cannot be assumed that there is consensus in a sector about the nature of its knowledge base. At any one point a sector may contain competing knowledge bases, though one of them may eventually become dominant and displace the others.

A sector may be taken to constitute a *community of practice* (Wenger 1998), that is, a set of practitioners who participate in a system about which they share understandings concerning what they know and what they do, and what that means in their lives and for their communities.The community has a domain-specific knowledge base that both guides practice and makes sense of the community's heritage. Medical doctors, schoolteachers, aeronautical engineers, and any other kind of professional community may be treated as examples of communities of practice.

Within such professional communities of practice there will be sub-communities, characterized by variations and divergences from the community of practice as a whole. Such variations reflect what Knorr-Cetina (1999) calls *epistemic cultures*, which are cultures that create and certify knowledge. All communities of practice have a positive orientation to "best practice," which may be something preserved in the community's traditions as a standard to which practitioners aspire, or something yet to be identified within the community and disseminated to members. The methodology a community adopts to determine "best practice" within its domain will reflect the dominant epistemic culture within the community. An epistemic culture can thus be defined as a means of identifying "best practice."

A prime example of an epistemic culture is science. Different communities of practice—physicists, chemists, biologists—may nevertheless subscribe to the shared epistemic culture of science. Other professional communities of practice may be differentiated into sub-communities that subscribe to different epistemic cultures. Most industrial sectors are shifting quite rapidly toward the scientific epistemic culture, which is displacing others. This is also the case of medicine which is now dominated by the epistemic culture of science, with a smaller alternative community that adheres to the culture of human-ism. It is not the case of education that is a divided community, not one dominated by the epistemic culture of science.

## Why Is the Education Sector Traditionally Characterized by a Slow Development of Knowledge?

Consider the efforts to develop more effective educational practices in schools. Nelson (1999, 121) has argued that this is clearly a sector characterized by a slow process of knowledge creation about teaching: "This is not to say that there is no understanding about principles of good teaching. But these have been known for generations. And it is not clear that we know much more now than one hundred years ago. This clearly stands in sharp contrast with other arenas of human know-how, like information processing and communication, or trans-port." To put it in somewhat less dramatic terms, one can at least claim that even if society knows more about educational practices than we did, knowledge creation in this domain has indeed been very slow, and there have been severe difficulties in diffusing the "superior" knowledge.

A robust explanation is that knowledge creation in this sector is not based on the S-i-T model and that there are very few knowledge spillovers. Or, in other words, the epistemic culture of learning-by-doing is both persistent and very influential. In this section I provide a description of the structure and dynamics of the professional knowl-edge base within the education sector. This evidence is analyzed under three distinct headings:[21]

• Formal R&D is of secondary importance. The ability to conduct edu-cational experiments is limited, so that many benefits of research and learning are not exploited.

• Most of the practical knowledge remains tacit, so that an important contribution of knowledge codification to the rapid accumulation of human know-how remains at a low level.

• There is a great deal of innovation without R&D (learning-by-teaching). However, two factors limit the economic value of those innovations: (1) linkages and feedback between formal R&D and professional practices are weak, so that the practical knowledge of innovative practitioners is rarely drawn upon by professional researchers; and (2) due to the absence of proper incentive structures, information spillovers and diffusion of innovation remain at a low level: much innovation in education, unless it is mandated, does not get beyond the classroom where it has been generated.

### Weak Role for Science

Formal R&D is of secondary importance both for the training of people and for the generation of useful innovation. In the words of Murnane and Nelson (1984), R&D should not be viewed as creating "programs that work"; it only provides tidy new technologies to schools and teachers. It is, thus, certainly a mistake to think of educational R&D in the same way as industrial or biomedical R&D (i.e., generating knowledge of "immediate" value for solving problems and developing applications).[22]

As Nelson suggests (1999), an immediate explanation deals with the limited ability to conduct educational experiments, the results of which provide reliable guides as to how to improve teaching practices in real world settings: What is reported to work in a lab school or in another chosen testing locus has been hard to duplicate outside of the locus of the original research. Thus, one of the basic conditions of the model of "science illuminating technology" simply does not work here. However "limited ability" does not mean inability, and techniques are currently developed in some educational R&D labs to conduct randomized controlled trials (RCT) (Fitz-Gibbon 2001).

Finally, the modest scale of educational research has to be noted. For instance, in the United Kingdom, total expenditure on educational research is estimated at £50–60 million per year, while R&D expenditures in the pharmaceutical industry are about £2 billion. But the low level of investments in educational research cannot be taken as an explanation in itself. It "concludes" the sequence of cause and effect that traps the system in a low level equilibrium (low level of R&D): weak role of science attested by the specialists, hence low investments, hence role of science ever weaker.

### Low Codification of Knowledge Causing Weak Cumulativeness

The absence technical language has been well-stressed by Jackson (1968); "One of the most notable features of teacher talk is the absence of a technical vocabulary. Unlike professional encounters between doctors, lawyers, garage mechanics or astrophysicists, when teachers talk together any reasonably intelligent adult can listen in and comprehend what is being said . . . [and] . . . the uninitiated listener . . . is unlikely [to] encounter many words that he has never heard before or even any with a specialised meaning." This absence of technical language determining the absence of professional codebooks is certainly critical in explaining the lack of codification. The knowledge of the effective practitioner remains in its tacit state, and this is a critical element in explaining the difficulties and impediments to knowledge creation and diffusion in education (Hargreaves 1999). There is no equivalent for the field of pedagogical knowledge to the recording found in surgical cases, law cases, and physical models of engineering and architectural achievement. Such records, coupled with comments and critiques of highly trained professors, allow new generations to pick up where earlier ones left off. Thus "the beginner in teaching must start afresh, uninformed about prior solutions and alternative approaches to recurring practical problems. What student teachers learn about teaching, then, is intuitive and imitative rather than explicit and analytical; it is based on individual personalities rather than pedagogical principles" (Lortie 1975). Low levels of codification in the education sector makes it difficult to produce "learning programs" or codified instructions that can be commented on and added to by practitioners. Teachers in regular classrooms develop their own classification systems and rules of evidence.

### The Economic Value of Learning-By-Teaching Is Hampered by Two Factors

As very well-analyzed by Huberman (1992), primary education is a sector where forms of learning-by-doing are the main mechanism for generating knowledge: "Essentially teachers are artisans working primarily alone, with a variety of new and cobbled together materials, in a personally designed work environment. They gradually develop a repertoire of instructional skills and strategies, corresponding to a progressively denser, more differentiated and well-integrated set of mental schema; they come to read the instructional situation better and faster, and to respond with a greater variety of tools. They develop this repertoire through a somewhat haphazard process of trial and error . . . Teachers spontaneously go about tinkering with their classrooms." An interesting parallel with doctors can be considered. Primary education and health care are sectors where forms of "tinkering" are the main mechanism for generating knowledge. Whatever science might contribute to their practice, both doctors and teachers have to exercise considerable professional judgment in making their higher-level decisions;

they have to "read" both client and context and be prepared to adapt their treatment until they find something that "works" with the client, whether patient or pupil. In short, they learn to tinker, searching pragmatically for acceptable solutions to problems their clients present. However, the learning potential of those processes are not well exploited at the system level.

A first problem concerns the weak feedback from the production of practical knowledge to science. There are several impediments to the creation of more teacher-researchers and the full exploitation of the potential for experimental learning (Hargreaves 1999). As a consequence, the practical knowledge of the experienced practitioner is rarely drawn upon by professional researchers and very few innovations emerging in the field are evaluated and systematized as "best practices." For example, one should note the failure to reshape the profession so that teacher work in classrooms is set at a higher professional level. When teachers are asked to estimate the proportion of their time in school that is devoted to tasks that can be done efficiently and effectively only by a qualified and experienced teacher, the answer is usually under 50%. By contrast, doctors learn to delegate much of their work—the minor ailments that are easy to treat or some specialized tasks—to trainee doctors, nurses, or other paramedical staff. By delegating more to assistants, teachers could reserve the more important educational problems that require high level skills, experience, and professional judgment.

The second problem deals with the issue of horizontal diffusion. I started this section by showing that there is massive innovative activity and potential locked up in the "tinkering" of teachers in their classrooms, finding local solutions to pedagogic problems. The problem is that teachers have no natural incentive to diffuse their findings (and this stands clearly in contrast with, e.g., innovators in any supply industry). This is the result of these innovative activities which—if only codified—could provide the basis for strengthening a teacher's knowledge base (better than any new development in cognitive psychology). More and better studies of "what works" in schools and classrooms could provide a knowledge base. However, much innovation in education, unless it is mandated, is not diffused because insufficient attention is paid to the deep problems associated with collective adoption. There are, of course, some institutional channels that support knowledge flows. Some professional associations work as "epistemic communities." Professional journals also play a role in disseminating information about new innovative practices. However, in most countries, professional journals are more a newspaper than a scholarly journal, and thus do not play a significant role in mediating research evidence to strengthen the knowledge base of teachers.

In these conditions, innovations may occur but there is very little probability of exploiting them at the system level. If an agent who innovates does not share what he/she knows, the implication for the whole system is that any other agent facing the same problem must invest in developing a solution anew. As the number of agents that must duplicate answers goes up, clearly the system-level efficiency goes down.

## Trajectories of Knowledge Development: Health and Education

While different sectors in their current state may lie clearly in one of the four cells of our model (see table 9.1), this ignores the historical development of its knowledge base. It is possible that over time a particular sector has followed a complex trajectory that, in terms of our model, means that the sector should be placed in different cells as its knowledge base changes. When a community of practice changes its epistemic culture, its means of identifying "best practice" is also likely to change.[23]

Table 9.2 illustrates some trajectories. I have to put in a strong warning here to avoid any misinterpretation of this figure. Arrows indicate the direction of changes, not full migration. Thus, the representation of the trajectory of the education sector does not mean that this sector is becoming fully scientific, with a high degree of spillovers. It

**Table 9.2**
Examples of Developmental Trajectories

| Knowledge spillovers (intentional and nonintentional) Science and technology interface | High (incentives to freely reveal/to capture) | Low |
| --- | --- | --- |
| Science model (Science is in a predictive stage, formal R&D is crucial and knowledge is highly codified) | Biotechnology, transport technology, chemicals and pharmaceuticals | Defense equipment |
| Learning-by-doing model (Learning-by-doing is the key process, formal R&D is of secondary importance and knowledge is poorly articulated) | Financial services Consulting activity | Education (primary school) Early nineteenth-century medicine |

means that the knowledge base of this sector is in a process of transformation by mixing *some* features of the scientific model with the basic features of the learning-by-doing model, and by introducing some incentives to generate or exploit spillovers.

### Case Study in the United Kingdom
During the nineteenth century the medical profession changed its epistemic culture under the influence of modern science, and this led to the rapid growth and accumulation of medical knowledge that continues to this day. In modern medicine the various subcommunities that make up the medical specialties fall within the epistemic culture of science; those that do not are given the generic name of "alternative medicine," which demarcates (and perhaps stigmatizes) a starkly different epistemic community. It can be argued that some branches of psychiatry, under the influence of psychoanalysis and its subsequent development, also stand outside the epistemic community of science and fall within an epistemic community that might be called *humanistic* (as essentially covering learning-by-doing). It is possible for some members of a community to espouse two epistemic cultures, as when a medical practitioner subscribes to both conventional *and* alternative medicine, or a psychiatrist follower of R. D. Laing who also uses drugs as part of the therapy for a schizophrenic patient.

One of the most significant developments in modern medicine has been the RCT, the significance and use of which grew rapidly after its application to tuberculosis in the 1940s. Today the RCT is widely treated as the evidential "gold standard" for demonstrating "what works" and what is medical "best practice." In branches of medicine that adhere in whole or part to an epistemic culture of humanism, objections are often raised against the RCT, including ethical reasons.

The developmental trajectory of medicine may thus be described as a movement from a prescientific model in the nineteenth century into an S-i-T model that marked the transformation of the medical community of practice from a prescientific to a scientific epistemic community (see table 9.1). However, elements of the humanistic model persist, insofar as doctors, in applying science-based medical knowledge to the individual case, see their practice in more artistic and humanistic terms.

In more recent times, during the Thatcher years and subsequently, the national health service in Britain was pushed into a more competitive environment. The government encouraged competition within public sector medicine, as well as between the public and private medical sectors, in order to promote greater responsiveness to the consumer and so greater efficiency and effectiveness. In my model this policy change should be associated with an increase in involuntary spillovers given that people and organizations increase their capabilities for adapting and reproducing knowledge generated elsewhere.

Education is following a different developmental trajectory. Until the end of the nineteenth century it was in a noncompetitive, prescientific state. The application of science to educational problems was much slower than in the case of medicine. Compared to medicine, the results for education in the first half of the twentieth century were disappointing and, in some areas, led to an abandonment of the scientific model for educational research. Disputes in the social sciences as a whole, over whether they could or should be essentially science-based, are inevitably reflected in the study of education in universities. There is a deep rift between two fundamentally opposed epistemic cultures: on the one hand, those who believe that it is possible to treat medicine as a potential model for the advancement of knowledge in educational practices and who are thus currently inclined to support the application of the RCT to education problems; on the other, those who reject this totally and favor the epistemic culture of humanism that has deeply influenced work in the arts and humanities in universities. For this latter group, "best practice" consists in the judgment, based on depth and breadth of experience, of the individual practitioner as a unique case, and it is achieved through "reflective practice," a widely used term taken from Schön (1983).

In Britain during the Thatcher era, there was a policy of increasing competition among schools, through greater parental choice and information provided to parents about school performance based on the results of tests and examinations, published in "league tables." This approach has been maintained since 1997 by the Labor government, which has been highly favorable to evidence-based policy and practice in education and other areas, in parallel to developments in medicine, with an increased commitment to educational research and its direction. This combination is driving education to the same destination as medicine in my model, but the route differs, since in this case the introduction of competition and the growth of knowledge spillovers precede the stronger scientific base of R&D (see table 9.2). It is also more disputed within the educationists' community of practice. Many academic educationists are deeply hostile to the epistemic culture of science.

At present, it seems unlikely in Britain that one of the two epistemic cultures will prevail in university-based study of education. The teaching profession's community of practice will thus not subscribe to a dominant epistemic culture, as in the case of medicine, but will come to share elements of *both* epistemic cultures in a new synthesis of practice that selects and blends elements of both. Foray and Hargreaves (2003) predict that there will be pressures toward such a synthesis because of the current pressures in both cultures to disseminate "best practice." The methodology for determining "best practice" differs between the epistemic cultures of science and humanism. The scientific approach will stress the need for experiments to yield formal and explicit knowledge of "what works," the action involved being carefully specified and disseminated through written and visual media (articles, books, videos, etc.). The humanistic approach will identify "best practice" as embodied in outstanding practitioners who will disseminate their tacit knowledge and practice through modeling, mentoring, and coaching.

**International Comparisons**
All trajectories are possible for countries: changing dramatically (in both dimensions), moving along a little in one single dimension, or essentially not moving at all. While the United Kingdom is a good example of a country trying to change drastically the basic structure of the knowledge base (in both dimensions), some other national cases provide examples of a different kind of policy. In the French case, for instance, there is no explicit policy to change the parameters of the knowledge base of the education sector. Accordingly, the main policy target is the improvement of the existing system, traditionally shaped by a very weak competitive environment and a strong domination of the humanistic culture. At this historical moment, nothing can be said about the comparative advantages of those various national strategies. It can simply be said that keeping the sector in the southeast cell of table 9.1 makes its performance extremely sensitive to the design of proper organizational structures that can substitute for the classical incentives to innovate and absorb knowledge which are very strong in northwest cell of table 9.1.

## On the Nature of Scientific Knowledge and Knowledge Spillovers in the Educational Sector

After a journey through the abstract space of the economics of knowledge which stimulated our attempt to study the developmental trajectory of health and education sectors within a generic framework, it is perhaps useful to return to some of the specific characteristics of the education sector in order to discuss the particular nature of the two main directions of change in the knowledge base—the scientific model and the knowledge spillovers—as far as the education sector is concerned.

It is certainly important to define a notion of practicable scientific research and a notion of workable incentives to support knowledge spillover, in order to discuss policy implications and implementations for a sector in which processes of knowledge creation and diffusion remain weak.

**On Scientific Research**   The term *scientifically based research* means research that involves the application of rigorous, systematic, and objective procedures to obtain reliable and valid knowledge relevant to educational activities and programs. I already highlighted the potential of randomized controlled trial or randomized field trial to generate scientific knowledge and robust evidence in a sector like education (Fitz-Gibbon 2001) (see chapter 3). It is clear that such experiments have to be targeted toward precise and well-focused problems (for instance, what kind of software should be used for this kind of pupil). Is this not the first step toward the age-old dream of Robert Musil's *The Man without Quality*, who remarked that: "Scientists and engineers refuse to a large extent to see the scientific methods that they successfully use in their technical domains to be applied for addressing the most important issues for life and well-being, and they tend, as everybody, to rely on the most antiquated and classical conceptions" (qtd. in Bouveresse 1996, 28). Part of the answer to this problem lies in the establishment and efficient use of the new experimental protocols previously described.

**On Knowledge Spillovers**   Readers see how intensively the notion of network is used in policy discussion to solve the problem of insufficient spillovers in a sector such as education. Network is certainly a useful metaphor showing that the diffusion of knowledge requires some forms of organizational practices involving connectivities and communication. However, a metaphor is not the same thing as a well worked-out economic model involving the provision of incentives and the design of coordination mechanisms appropriate to the economic processes of knowledge creation and diffusion (David, Foray, and Steinmueller 1999). A range of incentives can be selected for prompting teachers to reveal and share their practical knowledge (see chapter 8), including:

• creating rewards for those who not only disclose their knowledge but also identify potential users;

• inducing trust-based deliberate knowledge exchange;

• supporting collective actions of teachers to create pedagogical "standards" or to induce pedagogical material improvements or to create intellectual property commons.

Increasing involuntary spillovers concerns an entirely different option, which is to introduce some degree of competition between schools or even teachers while training people to increase their capabilities to imitate and reproduce innovations generated elsewhere.

**There Is More than One Model of Knowledge Development**

The main question raised in this chapter is whether the model of knowledge development defined by the two parameters (a strong science illuminating technology and a high level of knowledge spillovers) is the best one that all sectors with weak performance in terms of knowledge development should adopt. The answer is probably neither a full yes nor a full no. Certainly, some convergence toward this model is desirable but this is only partial convergence (for instance, a simple transposition of the S-i-T mode of knowledge creation will not work in some sectors because science will never illuminate technology in the same way that it does in the case of biotechnology or transport technology). And the routes toward the destination (the northwest cell of table 9.1) will differ strongly and are very sector-specific as the examples of health and education show.

I believe that a relevant approach for sectors like education is to promote the two epistemic approaches in a consistent way: (1) carrying out some kind of experimental research (based, e.g., on randomized controlled trial); and (2) creating the right conditions to maximize the social benefits stemming from the development of learning-by-doing expertise. The latter option acknowledges the fact that each teacher can perform experiments while providing teaching services, and that there is a value to exploit those experiments at the system level (issue of creating the right incentive structures for freely revealing and for capturing and absorbing knowledge). Formal R&D may guide and inform the professional trial-and-error learning process; and the knowledge, which is generated as a by-product, must be carefully "managed."

# 10       A New Organizational Capability: Knowledge Management

Knowledge management covers any intentional and systematic process or practice of acquiring, capturing, sharing, and using productive knowledge, wherever it resides, to enhance learning and performance in organizations. These investments in the creation of "organizational capability" aim at supporting—through various tools and methods—the identification, documentation, memorization, and circulation of the cognitive resources, learning capacities, and competencies that individuals and communities generate and use in their professional contexts (Davenport and Prusak 1998). It is therefore a matter of processing a category of goods that have the peculiarity of being difficult to observe and manipulate and sometimes even being unknown to those who possess them. This is inevitably a challenge for firms, more familiar with the management and valorization of tangible capital. Anecdotal evidence as well as first systematic surveys show that this new organizational practice is massively diffused within the private sector and that the impact of knowledge management on innovative and economic performances is not negligible. In this chapter I explain why knowledge management emerges as a new organizational practice in the context of the knowledge-based economies, and identify a strong relation between knowledge management practices and the general economics of the firm (or organization) considered.[24]

**Knowledge Management: What Is New?**

In chapter 1 I highlighted the difference between knowledge and information. Thus, management of knowledge clearly can not be equated to that of information.

The crucial aspect of knowledge management is the "identification, description, and documentation" of that which is not directly observable. This constraint of collecting and recording knowledge is essential but also difficult because knowledge is tacit and produced unwittingly in the course of the action. The setting up of incentive mechanisms to encourage employees to express and share their skills and the creation of feedback loops between this learning and formal processes of knowledge production (R&D, design) are often mentioned in manuals. The ability to identify and record expertise is indispensable for the accomplishment of four currently essential functions:

• Making the best use of existing knowledge (Prusak 2001). This is a static efficiency principle aimed at "not reinventing the wheel," improving corporate memory and knowledge sharing, comparing and evaluating competences in order to create best practice, and capturing external knowledge;

• Increasing innovative opportunities through recombination and the exploitation of synergies and cross-sectional know-how;

• Solving coordination problems which arise because of the increasing complexity of products and systems (modular architecture, loosely coupled systems); and

• Generating economic value directly from knowledge assets. Intellectual property management is a part of knowledge management economics.

New organizational practices, grouped under the heading of "knowledge management," are emerging for the following historical reasons:

1. some of the older practices that helped in knowledge management no longer work;

2. some entirely new problems have emerged; and

3. the understanding of the phenomena pertaining to learning and the transmission of knowledge is increasing; this, in turn, provides an opportunity to forge new tools and techniques for knowledge management.

**Some Practices No Longer Work**
The memorization and transmission of tacit knowledge has always been ensured by internal institutions (the craft guild, see Epstein 1998; the internal labor market, see Lam 2000) and external organizations (professional networks), in which it was an essential function. The unobservable element, in this case knowledge, was handled in a con-

tingent manner in the context of employment and industrial relations policies which effectively ensured the memorization, circulation, and transmission of knowledge. However, these institutions have largely disappeared or find themselves in profound crisis. Communities no longer seem capable of "spontaneously" taking charge of the essential functions of knowledge memorization, transfer, and sharing. The principle of lifelong careers and very long-term attachment to the company led to a kind of common destiny between the employee and his or her company. From that point on, the individual's knowledge was an almost inseparable part of the company's intellectual heritage. Recent developments in terms of turnover, mobility, and flexibility make it necessary to invent new forms of knowledge retention and transmission. This implies a need for new types of incentives and the reconstruction of a rationale of knowledge sharing to replace the one that has disappeared. It also implies a greater role for knowledge codification. Recent knowledge management methods thus attempt to create new modalities for memorization and transfer (organizational memory) in order to encourage people to share their knowledge and reduce knowledge losses resulting from high rates of mobility among staff (Hatchuel, Masson, and Weil 2002).

**New Problems**
Relatively new problems have necessitated the introduction of explicit forms of knowledge management. These involve the increasingly central role of innovation as a condition of business survival and, consequently, the growing importance of what I refer to as the "capacity for innovation." They also involve a cluster of structural changes which can be grouped, for the sake of convenience, under the heading of "new economy." These changes concern the extension of the role of market transactions into the field of scientific and technological knowledge, the massive use of information and communication technologies, and the importance attached to "intangible" resources in the stock market valuation of companies. All of these changes require that companies invest in extensive formalization and systematization of procedures for the identification, storage, and evaluation of intangible resources.

**Managing Knowledge in Order to Increase the Capacity for Innovation**
In chapter 2 I argue that innovation is becoming a condition of wealth, if not survival. The cost of missing the boat on an innovation (bypassing and ignoring a "good idea") becomes so enormous that companies

can no longer afford to miss out on one or two innovations. Thus, it becomes essential to introduce planned strategies for the collection and documentation of ideas and suggestions by employees. In addition to this type of knowledge management, processes for stimulating creativity become essential.

As soon as innovation takes a central place in a business's strategy, its internal and external resources have to be controlled. This is the goal of new intra- and interorganizational learning systems, and the intention behind the development of efficient memorization and sharing procedures.

**Intraorganizational Learning**   The new intraorganizational learning systems are characterized by a wider distribution of the knowledge production function (see chapter 3 and Steinmueller 2000b). The previous period, referred to as that of mass production, was characterized by intense specialization in knowledge production or reproduction functions within the company and between sectors. Under the new systems, knowledge production is more inclined to be distributed throughout the community. This translates into the extension of experimental forms of learning in companies, which require employees to conduct experiments in the course of their everyday productive activities in order to select the best strategy for the future (chapter 3). It is not enough, however, to let people experiment. It is also necessary to establish mechanisms that will encourage these people to evaluate, document, and share their experiences. In this sense, the emergence of new learning systems in which knowledge production is more collectively distributed is inseparable from the management of knowledge.

Linkages and feedback between the various loci of knowledge production have to be recognized and supported. We can observe a potential failure of this feedback stemming from the nature of knowledge produced in the two locations. It is relatively tacit knowledge that is generated on-line, and this sort of knowledge is difficult to incorporate into the process of formal research. Formal research tends to place more emphasis on codified (more visible) knowledge. There can be a sort of a vicious circle. The part of the knowledge stock that is produced "outside" (not in places dedicated to formal research) remains invisible or tacit. Its invisibility implies that when resources are being allocated among learning activities, this location is overlooked. Thus, it is "underfunded" and produces less than the optimal amount. This can generate a further decrease in the amount of learning that takes place "outside," and the cycle continues until "outside" locations are perceived as contributing nothing to the advancement of knowledge.

Such problems will also arise in sectoral cases, as my short presentation about the weak linkages and feedback between educational R&D and the professional practices of teachers showed in chapter 8.

Some firms manage to recognize the learning dimensions of each production process, to capture the knowledge thus produced, and to promote links and feedback between learning processes and formal processes of production and acquisition of knowledge. These firms are not necessarily recent. F. Caron (1997, 159) describes the organization of innovation at Saint Gobain in the 1920s: "Saint Gobain's success as regards mirrors and glazings was the result of close and well-organized cooperation between management, laboratories and factories. These were not just places of production; they can be considered as huge laboratories oriented towards R&D activities. New processes could be tried and tested. The dominant feature remained the absence of separation between research and production." It is nevertheless characteristic of knowledge-based economies to have a proliferation of such "learning" firms.

**Interorganizational Learning**   Von Hippel (1988a) documents many cases where users are the true innovators (see chapter 3) but where the knowledge produced is typically difficult to absorb by the manufacturer. This situation creates a strong rationale for knowledge management. Von Hippel refers to the field of medical instruments. Users perceive a need to improve an instrument, calibrate the improvement, produce a prototype, and disseminate information on the value of the improvement and how the prototype was made. In this example, the locus of innovation is transferred almost completely to the user level, yet the external link between the user and the instrument manufacturer is essential if the manufacturer is to exploit the user's creative effort and problem solving. Yet von Hippel brilliantly shows that this deposit of knowledge is almost invisible to the firm that supplies the equipment. It is very difficult for the firm to acknowledge that the user (who uses equipment or instruments manufactured by the firm) is a source not only of information but also of innovation. In practice, many experts within the firm producing the equipment, who are in contact with users, have no interest in finding a place in their own organization for users' suggestions. The employees in charge of maintaining the equipment at the client's site have to carry out standardized maintenance operations that match the standard equipment installed. These employees would therefore be very unhappy to discover that a user had done some tinkering and changed the equipment, which would definitely complicate the maintenance work. They therefore block any transfer of knowledge. In the same way, the sales manager is interested in obtaining orders for catalog products from the home plant; there is no interest in looking too closely at the prototypes users themselves may have developed. In this way, there are many obstacles to the firm's acceptance of these innovations.

Given these difficulties, the internalization of this external knowledge cannot rely on the spontaneous actions of people but requires, in many cases, explicit practices of knowledge management.

**Organizational Memory**   The issues linked to organizational memory and knowledge sharing are particularly important for a firm's innovative performance (Steinmueller 2000b). Not engaging in deliberate knowledge management strategies may result in significant losses, stemming in particular from redundancies, repetition of errors, and shortcomings in the accumulation of knowledge. If problem solving procedures and creative efforts are conducted exclusively at the local level, there will be some benefit from being in direct contact with the problem to resolve. From another angle, however, keeping problem solving and creativity at the local level increases the risk of producing specific solutions with no input from prior experience which could potentially have value in addressing the problem. Small organizations, characterized by some job stability, can overcome this problem by developing effective staff networks. But large organizations are confronted by particular difficulties when it comes to reusing existing knowledge to resolve previously encountered problems. Steinmueller (2000b) identifies three difficulties:

1. The organizations must identify the salient features of a given problem to see if it resembles problems encountered in the past.

2. They must locate the source of relevant information (i.e., the actors who were able to resolve this kind of problem).

3. Where it is impossible to locate the individual with the required knowledge, they must come up with the information through other means.

These three difficulties—being capable of discerning, in a "new" problem, what identifies it with previously encountered problems;

being able to find the individuals who resolved those problems; and being able to find the information in the absence of those individuals— are the most common problems of "organizational memory" that large organizations have to confront. Thus, the extension of the capacity for innovation essentially implies the management of knowledge, both at the level of internal learning and in the coordination of external resources.

**Managing Knowledge in Order to Enter into the New Economy**
The extension of knowledge markets, the dissemination of information technologies, and new methods for the evaluation of intangible assets are three characteristics of the new economy that require the introduction of explicit knowledge management methods.

1. Never before has there been such growth in market transactions in connection with knowledge. The increase in the rate of patent applications, the impressive growth in income derived from licenses, and the explosion of costs associated with intellectual property settlements are all indicators of the current development of the "knowledge-based market economy" (Arora, Fosfuri, and Gambardella 2001). Yet knowledge markets are, by definition, inefficient markets (Teece 1998). Buyers and sellers are not well informed about the commercial opportunities (no one knows who has what or who wants what). There are problems associated with revealing the characteristics of the product. Intellectual property rights, even though they can reduce the first two difficulties, are fragile, uncertain, and heterogeneous. The product (or consumption) unit is not clear; knowledge is sold neither by weight nor by size! Finally, the characteristic of this product that is hard to control generates massive externalities, continuously sapping the foundations of the market transaction which assumes that the product can be owned. At this stage, knowledge management can be interpreted as an effort to create less inefficient market conditions. From this point of view, intellectual property policies clearly form part of knowledge management. The issue is not only one of protecting innovations by applying for patents, even though this is a central element which, in itself, presents enormous problems; rather, it is one of ensuring preventive management, which is to say checking to be certain that the research and innovation areas that are being targeted remain free. Intellectual property also concerns trade secrets and legally protected codified know-how (often called *proprietary information*), such as technical drawings and training, and maintenance and operating manuals. It is difficult to

manage this aspect of intellectual property since this information has often not been collected or consolidated, and it remains poorly identified within the company. It then becomes evident that an effective intellectual property strategy involves codifying and organizing the company's knowledge. This goes well beyond the patented processes and products, which are merely the tip of the iceberg.

2. Before they can become solutions, the new information and communication technologies appear to be problems! The paradox of productivity can be expressed very simply as the delay between the appearance of new knowledge tools and instruments and the persistence of old forms of organization (chapter 2). Decentralization of the processes of knowledge creation, which are made possible by the new information technologies, requires the development of interorganizational interfaces in order to minimize the time required to establish and carry out a transaction. It then becomes a matter of moving to a higher level of systematizing organizational skills and procedures. The management of knowledge, particularly in terms of the codification of procedures, is central to these changes (Steinmueller 2000b).

3. The evaluation of intellectual capital becomes a decisive element in the evaluation of the company. Based on the observation that variations in its stock market values were not correlated in any significant way with variations in its accounting value, the Scandinavian firm Skandia deduced that measuring its intangible capital was extremely important, especially for its shareholders. The quantification of intangible assets is based first and foremost on their identification. Numerous methods exist today, each with its own structure. Theoretically, software developed in-house, employees' know-how, and intellectual property all form a whole. For example, it is common practice to consider software developed by the firm as an asset. But the rate of renewal of products, customer satisfaction, and organizational change can also be quantified to a greater or lesser degree. Here again, the management of knowledge involves techniques for the identification and quantification of intangibles in terms of the company's knowledge base.

### Managing Knowledge Means Negotiating between Conflicting Requirements

The requirements associated with intellectual property may conflict with those arising from the company's need to be open and to connect with external networks and sources of knowledge. In science-based sectors the connection to external networks is so essential that it impacts the internal organization of the firm: researchers in the firm have to publish in academic journals in order to have something to trade with university researchers. This requirement can go as far as the establishment of very open organizations, firmly oriented toward cooperation (Cockburn and Henderson 1997). Thus, the company is forced to negotiate and make compromises between openness and secrecy.

Managing knowledge increases a firm's risk of losing control over its intellectual capital. One of the benefits of a situation in which knowledge is not managed is that it remains shielded, invisible to others and, therefore, very difficult to imitate or reproduce. Defining knowledge, codifying it, providing incentives to encourage employees to describe and disseminate their skills are all high-risk activities from the point of view of the control that a business would like to exercise over its intellectual capital. Therefore, knowledge management involves accepting compromises and negotiating full control of the knowledge produced within the company. Diana Hicks (1995) illustrated this point perfectly with her explanation of how some companies publish (freely provide knowledge) to broadcast their skills and attract scientific partners.

**Toward an Increased Understanding of the World of the Intangible!**
The management of knowledge, as an activity, requires project engineering in the form of tried and tested tools and techniques that have themselves been buitt, on the basis of general advances in the economics and management of knowledge as a discipline. Yet since the work of Nonaka, Pavitt, Teece, von Hippel, and many others, there has been significant progress in this discipline, which has afforded an opportunity to understand the field better and, thereby, the possibility of new tools. I offer three examples of this improvement in understanding of the phenomena, which may open the door to improved knowledge management practices.

The works of von Hippel and associates are fine examples of advances in understanding the learning process. The development of a "situated perspective" highlights the importance of the physical context of learning, often ignored in analysis yet an essential component in the process. This perspective is based on the pragmatic argument that knowledge is not absolute, but must be defined in relation to a specific physical context. From a concrete point of view, Tyre and von Hippel (1997) review the reasons why an engineer will pay frequent visits to a user in order to settle a technical problem. The key reasons touch on the importance of the visual experience in understanding a situation (the engineer "sees" the problem, whereas the user does not), the importance of the context within which the machine is used, and the interaction between the user and the machine. In other words, solving a problem involves more than simply choosing a good representation of it and selecting a solution from an inventory (Simon 1982). Rather, it is a matter of drawing from the physical context in which the problem arose. Such an understanding of the situational nature of learning provides an opportunity to design principles of location and "optimal mobility" for experts as a function of the operational stages. In particular, it becomes evident that mobility must also concern the engineering consultant who has to visit the user and the doctor who has to make a house call in order to benefit from this essential component of learning, which manifests itself in the physical context.

The work of Thomke, von Hippel, and Franke (1998) provides another example of progress made in the level of understanding. The authors develop a framework to compare different experimentation strategies (experimental trial-and-error process in companies), including parallel experimentation and serial experimentation. Experiments conducted according to an established plan that is not modified as a result of the finding from other experiments are considered to have been conducted in parallel; while experiments which incorporate learning derived from other experiments in a set are considered to have been conducted in series. The relative efficiency of experimentation strategies can be estimated using what is known about the topography of the solution space, and what is known about the time and money costs associated with generating and testing alternatives in the solution space. For instance, a parallel experimentation strategy may be the fastest, although not necessarily the most efficient choice. This depends in particular of the value of information which is gained from each experiment in a serial process: when each failed trial provides very little information that would be of use in a serial experimentation strategy, parallel experimentation strategy is more efficient and vice versa.

Hansen (1999), who presents the problem of negotiation between the requirements of searching for information and transferring knowledge, provides a last example. In a large organization, a team may be faced with the problem of searching for information. From this point of view, there would be an advantage in building a system of weak ties (distant and infrequent connections). Maintaining a weak tie is inexpensive, which makes it possible to "keep an eye" on the entire organization. In addition, weak ties reduce the risk of redundancy in the collection of information. Transferring knowledge presents a different problem. It requires that strong ties be built, particularly when the knowledge is tacit and specific. The differentiation between information search and knowledge transfer issues leads to reconcile two types of literature which provide initially contradictory solutions (weak tie, strong tie). Therefore, this work provides an opportunity for fine management of these ties and, thereby, for successive improvements in information search and knowledge transfer.

Just as progress in scientific instrumentation makes it possible to observe phenomena that were previously invisible, so progress in the "scientific management of innovation" introduces a world that was previously ignored. The exploration of this universe makes it possible to improve the understanding of the process of knowledge production and use and, in the end, provides new operational opportunities.

**Summary**
There is rupture and discontinuity in current knowledge management practices because some of the older practices, buried in human resources and employment policies, no longer work. For this reason, it is becoming important to develop explicit and deliberate procedures for managing knowledge, which are detached from employment policies and connected to the institutional management of knowledge.

There is rupture and discontinuity because new problems arise, largely linked to the urgent need to master innovation and control the phenomena of the new economy. It therefore becomes important to implement explicit forms of knowledge management in innovation.

I believe in a certain degree of "scientific push" in the management and innovation sciences. As the understanding of the world of the intangible improves, tools and operating methods are introduced, tested, and improved, which encourages practitioners to develop knowledge management methods on the basis of scientific methods.

**Two Main Strategies**

As described by Hansen, Nohria, and Tierny (1999), there are two extreme knowledge management strategies:

• knowledge remains in its tacit form and is closely bound to the person who developed it; it is shared primarily through person-to-person contact;

• codification: knowledge is transformed so that it can be stored in databases and then easily accessed and used by anyone in the company; while codification involves high fixed costs, it enables agents to perform a number of operations at a very low marginal cost (chapter 4).

**Personalization and Codification**
Hansen, Nohria, and Tierny (1999) illustrate these two variants with the example of consulting companies.

Some kinds of consulting companies clearly select the codification strategy. They have developed ways to codify, store, and reuse knowledge using a "people-to-document" approach. Knowledge is obtained from the person who developed it, made independent of that person, and then reused. The company develops "knowledge objects" by taking key pieces of knowledge (such as interview guides, benchmark data, market segmentation analyses) from documents and storing them in an electronic repository for further use. As a result, many people can search for and retrieve that (codified) knowledge without contacting the original developer (the codification strategy provides an opportunity to achieve economics of scale in knowledge use).

This model is appropriate for firms or organizations that deal repeatedly with similar problems. For them, the efficient reuse of codified knowledge is essential, because their business model is based on fast and cost-effective service, which an efficient system of knowledge reuse provides. Firms or organizations that follow a codification strategy rely on this. Once a knowledge asset—software or manual—is developed and paid for, it can be used many times by many people at very low cost, provided it does not have to be substantially modified at each use. Reuse of knowledge saves work, reduces communication costs, and makes it possible to take on more projects.

The personalization strategy is implemented by a different kind of consulting company. Such companies focus on dialogue between individuals and do not produce codified knowledge objects. Knowledge is transferred in brainstorming sessions and one-to-one conversations. To make this strategy work, companies invest heavily in networks of people (mobility, culture of bilateral interaction). In a sense, this strategy is simply another form of the traditional "internal labor market" as a powerful mechanism for capitalizing on, transferring, and sharing knowledge. It relies on the logic of expert economics. Both the problem and the knowledge are unique, and the service is expensive and time-consuming.

**Table 10.1**
Two Strategies of Knowledge Management

| Codification | Personalization |
| --- | --- |
| Knowledge is put into a certain stage which makes it possible to store it in databases | Knowledge remains in its tacit stage. It is closely tied to the person who developed it and is hared mainly through direct person-to-person contact |
| "people-to-document approach" | "networks of people" |
| Efficient reuse of codified knowledge in companies where people are dealing with similar problems all the time | The problem is unique and the knowledge is also unique |
| Economies of scale | Unique expertise |

*Source:* Adapted from Hansen, Nohria, and Tierney (1999).

The same dichotomy applies in industry and public and private services. Hansen, Nohria, and Tierny (1999) use the healthcare system and computer manufacturing to illustrate the power of this framework.

The first case compares "access health" (a call-in medical center based on efficient reuse of codified knowledge—clinical decision architecture—to assess the caller's symptoms) and the Sloan-Kettering Cancer Center, which provides highly customized advice, with a variety of experts sharing tacit knowledge. The second case contrasts Dell (codification) and Hewlett-Packard (personalization).

Of course, all firms and organizations use both strategies, but the hypothesis is that those that excel focus on one and use the other in support. Hansen, Nohria, and Tierny see an 80-20 split: 80 percent of their knowledge management follows one strategy, 20 percent the other. Those that try to excel at both risk failing at both. The argument is that the selection of a particular knowledge management strategy must reflect the firm's or organization's business model, which relies either on knowledge reuse or on unique problems and expertise. Thus, firms that rely on codification can get into trouble by overinvesting in person-to-person systems because they undermine their business model—fast services at reasonable prices.

### Defining Sets of Consistent Practices for the Two Strategies

Clearly, various dimensions of knowledge management will differ, depending on the firm's main strategy. As long as knowledge remains tacit its management is part of the human resources management. The exchange and diffusion of tacit knowledge implies intentional action by individuals. Capitalization and learning require the maintenance of a teacher-learner relationship, and the acquisition of tacit knowledge necessarily involves recruitment. Only with codification can knowledge management be made autonomous by separating it from human resources management (although the two functions naturally remain closely related). Various dimensions can be identified, which may differ from one strategy to the next:

• Role of ICT: These are crucial in both cases, but for codification the focus is on the computer, while in personalization, computers are used to help people to communicate knowledge, not to store it.

• Incentives/rewards: The codification strategy needs incentives that encourage people to write down what they know and enter the documents into the electronic repository. Level and quality of employee contributions to the document database should be part of annual performance reviews. In the personalization strategy, rewards for sharing knowledge directly with others are crucial. How much help an employee has given directly to colleagues would be part of the performance review.

• Recruitment: The two kinds of strategy mean hiring different kinds of people and training them differently. In one case, new employees use the knowledge management repository to improve business processes and are trained to implement not to invent. In the other, new employees are trained to invent, using their analytic and creative skills on unique business problems.

• Critical tacit knowledge: In the codification strategy, some kinds of tacit knowledge are essential (knowing how to retrieve and reuse codified knowledge stored in the database). In the personalization strategy, "know-who" knowledge is essential and requires huge investments in building and developing internal social networks.

• Organizational memory: The codification strategy raises difficult memory issues. It requires recording and storing not documents but sets of instructions that have to be interpreted and managed by appropriate equipment and software before the information they contain can be used. Although short-term storage and retrieval costs are decreasing, long-term storage (i.e., archiving) and access to old documents present a problem. In the personalization strategy, memory performance is wholly dependent on human resources. That can be a source of problems: People leave and people forget.

• Knowledge integration: Knowledge is divided and dispersed (chapters 1 and 5). An increase in the division and dispersion of knowledge makes it more and more difficult for economic agents to locate and retrieve elements of knowledge that would be useful to them. The two kinds of knowledge management strategy mean developing different "integrative tools," either strongly based on ICT or investments in networks of people.

The final aspect of knowledge management is the assessment of intellectual capital, which is becoming a decisive element in corporate evaluation. Again, the differences between the two main knowledge management strategies should lead to different methods for increasing the economic value of intellectual capital.

### How to Choose the Right Strategy between Codification and Personalization?

Choosing the right strategy requires getting a clear view of a company's business model. Does it offer standardized or customized products? The degree of maturity (or novelty) of the product also matters. As Hansen, Nohria, and Tierny (1999) stress, it is important to know whether the knowledge strategy must change as new products or services mature. Take the example of "reengineering." This was a highly innovative service provided by consulting companies on the basis of a personalization strategy (at the beginning, each reengineering problem was unique and required a particular expertise). But then the service started to mature with the development of standardized procedures and "on-the-shelf solutions." The question is: Should the consulting company switch from a personalization to a codification strategy? Or might it be more profitable, as the basic service matures, to give up the strategy of providing it and to search for innovations and new services, so that the knowledge management strategy (that is to say, the incentive structures, corporate culture, mode of recruitment, ICT system, and so on) can be kept unchanged?

It is tempting to think that the two knowledge management strategies can coexist within big corporations. This is certainly the case for companies where business units are loosely integrated. But, as Hansen, Nohria, and Tierny (1999) suggest, companies with tightly integrated units should focus either on one knowledge management strategy or should spin off units that do not fit the main business model.

Knowledge Management, Innovation, and Productivity

At the start of the twenty-first century, there is, thus, a recognition of
the need to understand and to measure the activity of knowledge management (KM) so that organizations, and systems of organizations, can
do what they do better and so that governments can develop policies
to promote these benefits. Facing such new emerging practices, economists, management scientists, and statisticians have not yet collected
much systematic evidence. Among the various categories of knowledge-related investments (education, training, software, R&D, and so
on), KM is one of the less known, both from a quantitative and qualitative point of view, as well as in terms of costs and economic returns.
The OECD, in collaboration with Statistics Canada, took the initiative
of launching a series of pilot studies conducted in various countries by
their national statistics offices (Foray and Gault 2003). The questionnaire included a survey on the use of twenty-three KM practices and
was complemented with questions on incentives for using KM practices, results, responsibilities, and so on. The questionnaire included
many informal management practices in order to accommodate how
microfirms are managing knowledge. This activity provided a unique
opportunity offered by "official surveys" carried out at the national
level to link the KM data bases with data coming from other sources
(R&D, innovation, enterprise surveys).

Some of the most interesting findings to emerge from these pilot
studies are the following:

• KM practices diffuse massively across the economy, like technology
diffusion;

• KM practices are implemented to deal with a great variety of objectives (static efficiency, innovation, coordination);

• Size matters: firms manage their knowledge resources differently
upon their size with little regard to industrial classification;

• KM practices matters for innovation and productivity performances.

This last result is particularly important. It has been generated in the
French study (Kremp and Mairesse 2002), which covered a very large
number of firms (5,100 firms with a response rate of 85 percent): whatever company size, industry, or R&D effort, firms innovate more extensively and file more patents if they set up knowledge management

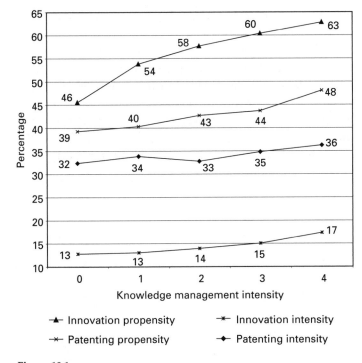

**Figure 10.1**
Knowledge management intensity and innovation performance. *Source:* Kremp and Mairesse (2003).
*Key:* All things being equal, the companies without any KM policy have a 46% propensity to innovate compared to the companies rolling out the four policies that have a 63% propensity to innovate.

policies (see figure 10.1). Knowledge management also has a positive effect on labor productivity.

## No Easy Task: Managing Knowledge on a Day-to-Day Basis

Some crises or catastrophes, whose solution entails coming up with new knowledge, lend themselves well to effective knowledge management. In many industries, effective procedures for accumulating knowledge on accidents and sharing it do very well (Cowan et al. 2002). What is probably more difficult is knowledge management on a day-to-day basis, in peaceful situations, when there are no crises. Everyone thinks that the fact of overlooking a knowledge-management activity will, after all, be of very little importance since it will not have a large impact on the immediate operations of the organization. Therein lies the main danger. While one cannot tolerate disorderliness in the equipment room and while one must not forget to put tools back where they belong, it is very easy to overlook putting one's ideas in order and to forget, for a day or two, to make a record of new knowledge. This is the major difficulty: "cleaning up the ideas room" is a daily activity that costs money and is difficult and unrewarding, for the outcomes are not spectacular. In fact, no one will notice for a long time if the "ideas room" is indescribably messy or, by contrast, properly arranged!

# 11 The Public Dimension of the Knowledge-Based Economy

In this chapter I briefly consider the following four subjects which constitute the challenges determining the evolution of knowledge-based economies: the question of privatization of knowledge; the questions of employment, exclusion, and public policy raised by the accelerating rate of knowledge creation and depreciation; the issues of memory, knowledge integration, information search, and trust in knowledge society; and, lastly, the new challenges facing economists and statisticians studying these economies. All these challenges have a strong public dimension.[25]

## Knowledge Creation: The Right Balance between the Public and Private Domains

I have emphasized the complementarity of different public and private institutions set up for the purpose of efficient resource allocation in the production and use of knowledge (chapter 6). A recent book reminds us that the basic rationale of intellectual property law depends on an independent public domain containing a stock of freely accessible information (McSherry 2001). That shared collection of basic knowledge provides the building blocks for new inventions.

That was how the system functioned until the early 1990s. There was a clear division of effort between upstream open science and downstream large, highly integrated companies that did market-oriented applied research. The structure of this division, discussed in chapter 6 (see figure 6.1), appears clearly in the case of the pharmaceutical industry (Cockburn 2002). The modern era shows a somewhat different model. By the mid-1990s several thousand biotechnology ventures had been launched. This evolution was facilitated by a number of reforms and changes in the legal intellectual property right system, which resulted in a proliferation of patents granted for basic knowledge. Obviously, without patent rights in inventions such as DNA sequences, gene expression systems, and other types of research tools, many biotechnology companies could not exist. Certain reforms to financial markets, especially in the United States, have also played a significant part by facilitating high-technology start-ups' access to venture capital.

**Unbridled Privatization of Scientific Knowledge and Research Tools**
The use of intellectual property is thus becoming increasingly important in the domain of basic research, and within that general domain use of the patent is growing rapidly. This general trend is also reflected in the increase in exclusivity rights over instruments, research materials, and data bases. The now classic example is that of exclusive rights to medical, genetic, and genealogical data on Iceland's population, granted to a U.S. company.

Many factors explain this trend (see chapter 7). They relate mainly to the emergence of a new generation of firms which are specialized in fundamental research and in the increasing orientation of public research institutions toward the promotion of their commercial interests. This double evolution shows a general tendency toward the privatization of basic knowledge, as a public good.

**The "Academic Capitalism" Model of the University**   I would like to trace back the "academic capitalism" model of university from a few historical transformations in the nineteenth and twentieth centuries. The Humboldt model of the university emphasized the university as a place linking education and research (Lenoir 1998). In this model, universities have two basic products, knowledge and talents, and enjoy economies of scope since higher education in science and engineering is a joint product with research. The MIT model emphasized universities as a place linking education, research, and innovation. The creation of a "permeable" engineering school was a clear manifestation of this model, involving a strong orientation toward the development of an instrument of research regarding the problems of industry (Lecuyer 1998). New mechanisms were set up to facilitate the transferability of knowledge to industry: industrial advisory committees, cooperating teaching programs, industry-supported laboratories. Two major structural transitions in the United States were critical to promote this model (Rosenberg and Nelson 1993): the rise and institutionalization of the engineering disciplines and applied science as accepted areas of academic teaching and research by the end of the nineteenth century; and, during the postwar period, the massive increase in federal funding of academic research. Although the MIT model was clearly addressing specific challenges for scientific and engineering disciplines, it was quite successful in managing the conflicting missions of education, research, and contribution to technical advances in industry. Indeed, the relation between university research and industry were mainly promoted through collaborative agreements (instead of patents and spin-offs).

The current evolution involves the development of a new model, called academic capitalism. This model strongly emphasizes the commercialization of some of the basic functions of universities. Its growth is thus conditional to the development and globalization of private markets for education and research. Innovation policy experts impute the development of this model in the United States to the evolution of laws and regulations authorizing universities to grant exclusive licenses (new knowledge is sold exclusively to one firm) on the results of research financed by public funds (especially the Bayh-Dole Act of 1980). These laws aim to solve the problem of "post-invention" costs and risks in taking a new invention out of the laboratory and developing it into a successful commercial product. Firms would be unwilling to support these costs without some assurance of protection from competition. Patents and exclusive licensing thus facilitate the transfer of new technology to the private sector by providing exclusive rights to preserve the profit incentives of innovating firms. As a consequence, two ways to transfer knowledge to the economy are getting more importance (as compared with the more traditional cooperative way):

• university patenting and granting exclusive licenses to industry

• startup based on a patent (research tools companies)

The direct effects of the Bayh-Dole Act and related legislations are striking (Lita 2001): The number of patents issued to U.S. universities more than doubled between 1979 and 1984, more than doubled again between 1984 and 1989, and more than doubled again over the 1990s. The number of universities with a Technology Transfer Office increased from 25 in 1980 to 200 in 1990. University licensing revenues have increased greatly, from $221 millions in 1991 to $698 million in 1997. A very large number of startups were established based on university research. The post Bayh-Dole Act university was a major actor in the new economy during the nineties. It contributed, together with the venture capital industry and the patent office, to the kind of high-tech exuberance that marked the economy during this short period. It is, however, useful, to bring some nuances to such a success story (Lita 2001, Nelson 2001).

First, imputing all these quantitative features to the Bay-Dole Act alone would be misleading. The commercialization of academic research started far before the 1980s, and the rise of academic capitalism has been caused by some other factors (e.g., the changes in intellectual property rights regime, the growth of the venture capital industry, and the ascension of the National Institute for Health and the biomedical sciences). Second, not all universities are winning at the patent lottery and many universities are paying more to run a Technological Transfer Office than they are bringing in license revenues. Finally, the most important nuance deals with the damages to research and educational missions caused by the post Bayh-Dole Act model of universities. Threats to educational missions are due to the increasing importance of secrecy and access restriction in research-based training programs (in chapter 7, I noted the fragile legal basis of the research exemption provision in the U.S. patent law); conflicts of interest; and decline in the quality and focus of education.

Mowery et al. (1998) study the impact of the Bayh-Dole Act on the research missions. They show that by focusing on exclusive licensing only, these laws are based on a narrow view of the channels through which public research interacts with industry. In reality these channels are multiple (publication, conferences, consultancy, training, expertise) and all contribute to the transfer of knowledge, while the incentives created by such laws promote only one channel (patenting and licenses), with the risk of blocking the others. The authors' conclusion is unambiguous: "The Bayh-Dole Act and the related activities of U.S. universities in seeking out industrial funding for collaborative R&D have considerable potential to increase the 'excludability' of academic research results and to reduce the 'knowledge distribution' capabilities of university research" (Mowery et al. 1998, 29). Most studies on these issues show that this evolution represents a real risk of irremediable alteration of modes of cooperation and sharing of knowledge in the domain of basic research. When there is nothing left but exclusive bilateral contracts between university laboratories and firms, there are forms of quasi-integration that undermine the domain of open knowledge.

**Another Type of Tragedy?**  The famous case of Myriad Genetics is a good illustration of how detrimental the extension of a very broad patent in a field like health care can be to Europe. This case concerns patents granted to a private company that "discovered" the genes predisposing individuals to breast cancer. The patents are very broad, covering not only the structure of the genes but also a large range of diagnostic and therapeutic tools (Cassier and Gaudillère 2001; Wadman 2001). The patent's extension to Europe may have the potential of seriously hampering the system of therapeutic and diagnostic services provided by public hospitals in European countries. Since the U.S. company has no intention of selling operating licenses, European hospitals will be forced to send samples for testing to the United States. The social cost imposed on the system would rise steeply and European researchers might be deprived of a powerful research tool (because a great deal of knowledge can be accumulated through tests). The prospect of such a transition is clearly explained by the company itself: "The Company believes that the industrialization of diagnostics R&D now being catalyzed by genomics will transform the diagnostic industry from its current dependance on non-patented products generated sporadically by academic researchers into a market characterized by a steady flow of novel, proprietary tests protected by strong IP positions thereby achieving premium pricing and margins similar to those enjoyed by drugs and vaccines . . . The Company believes the diagnostics market is poised for a comparable value transition as a result of genomics and patenting" (statement by Diadexus, a subsidiary of Incyte and SmithKline and Beecham 2000). This kind of transition toward a market for diagnostic tests seems at least highly disputable in countries in which those services are provided mainly by public hospitals (e.g., France, Canada, Germany, the United Kingdom, and the Netherlands).

**Institutional Diversity in Danger**  The diversity of institutional arrangements is threatened and therefore a cause for concern. Traditionally, IPRs are considered as one of the incentive structures society employs to encourage innovative effort. They coexist with other incentive structures, each of which has costs and benefits as well as a degree of complementarity. The new view is that IPRs are the only means to commodify the intangible capital represented by knowledge, and should therefore be a common currency or "yardstick" for measuring the output of activities devoted to knowledge generation and the basis for markets in knowledge exchange (Steinmueller 2002a).

In chapter 6 I analyze such diversity (the 3 P's) as being important because each institution fulfils specific functions and strong complementarities exist among them. But the space for public research (procurement and patronage) is shrinking and functions which were assumed by open science are no longer assumed at the same level. This is a problem not only for the survival of open science per se but also for the sustainability of the system as a whole. Excessive privatization may undermine the long-term interests of industry itself (which will benefit from less public knowledge, less training and screening externalities). Finally, the scenario of a pure functional substitution, where the private sector would simply carry out the functions which were formerly assumed by the public sector, is wrong. Private companies will never fund the same type of basic research that the public sector abandons (Brown 1998). Similarly, the need for scientific training could be satisfied only very partially by market-based institutions. As argued by Cohen, Florida, and Randazzese (1998), spillovers from the downstream R&D conducted by firms engaged in basic research are not likely to replace entirely the information flows initially blocked for several reasons. First, firms will try to restrict spillovers to retain proprietary advantage. Second, there will typically be considerable lags between the time when the firm receives the valuable information and the time when information spills over to the other firms.

Of course, we can also count on academic researchers who are learning to negotiate their industrial contracts more and more advantageously in order to preserve areas of public knowledge (provided that the researchers themselves are not caught up in a sort of money-making frenzy). Industrial firms are often aware of the advantages of not completely undermining open and independent academic research and try to establish "good practice" so that universities work with and not for industry.

The fact remains that economic studies on the U.S. model reveal a degree of concern. Cockburn and Henderson (1997, 30) conclude: "Policies which weaken these institutions (of open science), make public sector researchers more market-oriented, or redistribute rents through efforts to increase the appropriability of public research through restrictions in the ways in which public and private sectors work with each other, may therefore be counter-productive in the long run." This is a strong conclusion that prompts us carefully to examine this new model without being blinded by the brilliance of its undeniable short-term performance.

**Private Markets for Basic Knowledge Function Badly**  Is the game worth the candle? The idea underlying a private market for basic knowledge and research tools is that firms patent their inventions and then sell licenses to other researchers who develop products. The discussion on the efficiency of this system can be taken further in two respects.

First, the efficiency of two industrial structures can be compared (Cockburn 2002). The vertically integrated structure is composed of a system of public sector research and big firms which capture a large part of innovation rents by combining various mechanisms: product patents, proprietary know-how, and brand names. The vertically disintegrated structure appears at the interface between public-sector research and the large integrated companies. A new class of companies is emerging and expanding. They are specialized in the production of research tools. The only way that these tool companies can lay claim to the benefits of innovation is by patenting the tools they develop. The vertically integrated structure is clearly an efficient solution to a set of economic problems corresponding to an R&D situation (financing and management of multiple uncertain, risky, complex, and long-term projects that are costly to run efficiently). This structure is therefore adequate when coupled to powerful public sector research with generous externalities toward industry.

Yet industrial history abounds with phenomena of vertical disintegration corresponding to specialization rationales in certain stages of production, which can create efficiency especially when the specialization concerns tools and equipment. This is the case of the appearance in the nineteenth century of a sector specialized in machines and industrial tools, from a situation where all tool manufacturing was integrated (Steinmueller 2000b). Thus, efficient vertically disintegrated structures exist. Yet the following conditions must be met: strong intrasegment horizontal competition; specialization that reduces costs; prices that reflect marginal costs; and simple and efficient contractual arrangements. In the case of organization of R&D, the latter two conditions are not met.

This brings us to the second point concerning the efficiency of the system. An essential difference between the appearance of a specialized tool and machine sector in the nineteenth century and the appearance of a specialized biotechnology tool sector is that in the latter the economy of the sector is based entirely on patents and exclusivity rights to generic knowledge. But patents on generic knowledge and research tools involve high social costs for the system (see chapter 7) due to

• monopoly on the exploitation of a research tool, the generic and cumulative value of which is thus lost. Social costs derive from the fact that exclusive licenses and refusal to grant licenses deprive the system of potential benefits generated when several firms with different capacities and perceptions of a problem are mobilized;
• increase in delays and costs involved in negotiation and litigation;
• possible blockages (anti-commons).

On the other hand, the market has so many shortcomings in the area of basic research (uncertainty and difficulty in appropriating knowledge, despite the use of patents) that commercial success is rare. Anecdotal evidence and the relatively low stock market returns from research tool companies support this pessimistic view. This reflects what Nelson (1959) called "the simple economics of basic research." As argued by Cockburn (2002, 10): "Patents or no patents, capturing the value that ultimately derives from fundamental early stage research is extraordinarily difficult for profit-oriented organizations." In particular, the definition and observance of property rights on this basic knowledge are virtually impossible. The results of early surveys on researchers' behavior regarding research tools protected by patents are surprising (Walsh, Arora, and Cohen 2000). First, the lack of awareness as to risks of infringement is dominant, for several reasons. At this stage of basic research, each researcher is often guided by the "do it yourself" principle and is therefore unaware that application of a particular method is illegal. Use of the research exemption clause is naturally also widespread (even if it were legally more restrictive than most researchers seem to think; see chapter 7).[26]

Second, the impression of impunity needs to be taken into consideration. Very often academics ignore (in the sense of failing to obey) the law, and firms are reluctant to sue them. Infringement also corresponds to a logic of discovery in this sector: "One has to try a million things for just one to work; it's only when you've found that one thing, that you think about property rights" (qtd. in Walsh, Arora, and Cohen 2000, 13).

Hence, there is the difficulty of making a private market function and ensuring property rights are respected when economic activity is centerd primarily around the creation of scientific objects. Firms either anticipate bad appropriability of their knowledge, by granting licenses on a large scale, or simply tolerate infractions, especially by academic researchers. Walsh, Arora, and Cohen (2000, 27) conclude: "Universities and firms simply infringe and patent holders tacitly tolerate this."

Economists can rationalize positively this failure of patent holders to have their rights respected by considering it as a form of price discrimination of the Ramsey rule. Economic theory suggests that such discrimination can enhance social welfare if the infringement, which is tolerated, does not reduce the value of the tool for users who are prepared to pay for access to it.

This conclusion suggests that the model of the small firm that invents a tool, patents it, and hopes to obtain income by granting licenses to other researchers who will pay only in case of success, functions only very rarely. Thus, the game is not worth the candle. Most of the forms of organization associated with what we called the *science-based innovation model* (chapter 3) are therefore still to be invented.

### The Revival of Public Property: To Keep the 3 E's!

The scientific revolution under way has unequalled potential to produce tools for development in the fields of agriculture, agri-food, and health. But this scientific revolution is historically the first to be essentially private, a situation that generates problems of access to and acquisition of knowledge, as well as problems of priorities regarding research programs (Foray 1999; Foray and Kazancigil 1999).

The end of chapter 7 is devoted to regulations that the intellectual property system must implement to control its own excesses. This is a crucial issue. Patent policy is extremely important in opening new fields of commercial opportunities. When research results become patentable, as a result of court and patent office decisions, expected private profitability increases substantially and many activities can be taken care of by the private sector. That is typically the case today in many areas of the life sciences. Thus, a fine and controlled patent policy is a key to regulating the tendency toward privatization (see chapter 7).

But it is also a matter of a revival of public property. It is therefore important to restructure the rationale supporting public property in the domain of basic knowledge. I propose to restructure it under the three E's: externalities, equity, expertise.

**Externalities** One important part of basic research is carried out under an open principle: providing an effective mechanism for ensuring fast and extensive dissemination of new knowledge. The institution of open science has demonstrated its effectiveness as an incentive system (see chapter 8). Thus, more than ever, standards of conduct regarding the disclosure and efficient distribution of knowledge should be top priorities in scientific research.

**Equity** The second type of public action involves the optimal use of knowledge for the benefit of future generations and for protecting the well-being of certain nonsolvent consumers, namely, those without financial resources to purchase critical goods such as drugs to combat infectious diseases. Many issues related to finding "equitable solutions" to difficult problems of resource allocation among research "priorities" fall into this category. Private markets are as a rule short-sighted and tend to direct resources toward investment projects offering profit streams that have a high present value. The result is the tendency to underfund not only projects with longer-term horizons, but also those targeted to the needs (or simply the tastes) of social minorities, as well as the low-income, developing economies. Generating and disseminating knowledge that is relevant to solving problems affecting the welfare of future generations is therefore an important societal objective. Future generations have the right to demand a "knowledge legacy," just as we currently benefit from knowledge produced by past generations. But these are not tasks that the private sector can be expected to perform unassisted.

**Expertise** A final category of action involves the provision of conditions in society that nurture the formation of independent communities of "expertise" in complex scientific, technological, and possibly cultural matters such as historical studies and the arts. It is unrealistic to expect profit-seeking private entities that must survive in competitive markets to subsidize the work of communities of experts whose opinions cannot be controlled and who might reach conclusions that adversely affect an "altruistic" business sponsor or benefit a rival company. An obvious difficulty in this area, however, is that the same mechanisms to control the pronouncements made by expert authorities on matters of a controversial political nature may exist in government circles as well. Sources of independent expertise are thus a form of public good that governments are unlikely to be able to supply by means of direct provision.

**Government Controlled and "Inherently Public" Properties** As mentioned in chapter 6, public intervention in such activities need not, of course, take the form of direct provision. Subsidies for commercially-oriented private producers, or procurement contracting by the public sector, are important alternatives that can coexist with direct public production of public goods. And apart from forms of public property which are "government-controlled," it is necessary to identify a distinct class of "inherently public property" which is controlled neither by government nor by private agents (Rose 1986). It is probably this category of public property that constitutes the framework for the revival of the public domain in the context of knowledge-based economies, since that is where we find the knowledge communities described in chapter 8, from open science to all the modes of collective production set up by users.

### Knowledge Depreciation: Education, Labor Market, and Public Policy

As I approach the end of this book, many public policy issues could be examined, particularly those concerning the promotion of innovation, the creation of business, and the liberalization of markets. However, I limit myself to the social issues directly related to problems posed by the increased rate and speed of knowledge creation and depreciation, mentioned in chapter 2.

### New Exclusions
Costs of adjustment and complementary investments accompanying the establishment of knowledge-based economies primarily concern the improvement of human capabilities and skills. From the point of view of equity, it is therefore important to determine who has (and who doesn't have) access to the skills required to develop prosperity in knowledge-based economies.

At least two sets of skills need to be distinguished. First, there are those that are directly linked to the use of ICT and that pose problems of complementarity between people and computers. Second, there are those that enable people to survive and prosper in a world of innovation and constant change. These relate to mobility, adaptability and, entrepreneurship. The two sets of skills are obviously closely interrelated, but it is useful to untangle them because the issues involved are not the same. "Technological" skills associated with the use of ICT are the object of real political debate based on unanimous recognition of increasing needs for education, training, and apprenticeship. On the other hand, skills related to the ability to deal with change are most often reduced to the ability to stand the negative effects of flexibility. They are not seen as a real qualification that can be obtained, enabling economic agents to understand and anticipate the rapid changes in their environment.

**ICT-Related Skills**   In leading countries in terms of quality of education and training programs related to ICT, the fact remains that some categories of the population do not have easy access to that education. The people concerned here are primarily the unemployed, including some women, jobless young people, and the aged, for the most important skills are those acquired in a working environment (Steinmueller 2002a). Moreover, some data on ICT in schools are misleading since having the equipment is only part of the story. While more than 80 percent of U.K. secondary schools are connected to the Internet, this does not mean that the children in these schools have access to it. The extent to which ICT is actually used and taught is less dependent on the number of computers than on the number of teachers with the training and motivation to exploit these resources in their lessons (Valentine, Holloway, and Bingham 2002).

Finally, despite the quality of education systems, a fringe of the population—essential skills in a knowledge-based economy—has difficulties in reading and writing (one out of ten young people in France have serious reading problems).

In this respect, the famous distinction of apologists of the information society, between those who have access to information and those who do not, is largely untrue. It leads people to believe that free access to the network and a terminal in each home will solve all problems, when in fact the real problem is not necessarily information but knowledge as a capacity to learn.

This obviously leads us to problems in less-developed countries, confronted very directly with the problem of exclusion. Not everyone is part of the global village, as a recent World Bank report (1998) pointed out. The information infrastructure is so derisory in certain countries that from their point of view the "Internet planet" seems to belong to another galaxy altogether. In this respect it was interesting to see 133 less-developed countries ask the United Nations to maintain the radio and other traditional media as a means of dissemination of information since exclusive use of the Internet would exclude millions from the flow of information. Furthermore, basic skills, such as reading and writing, are lacking.

**Skills Concerning the Control of Change** As Hatchuel and Weil (1995) clearly show (see chapter 2), the skills that enable individuals to confront constant change are related to learning capacities which far exceed control of ICT. Favereau (2001) shows how comprehension, memorization, and inference are at the heart of learning capacities. It is the acquisition of these abilities that enables individuals to implement strategies to deal with the unexpected and with change. The acquisition of "learning-to-learn" abilities (rather than a specific repertoire of technical skills) becomes a key objective in education and training in knowledge-based economies.

**Policy Issues: Acquisition of Knowledge and Access to Information** Education and training are obviously at the heart of problems of adjusting skills and abilities to the constraints of the knowledge-based economy. But the skills to acquire are multiple and, in any case, do not amount simply to "knowing how to use a computer." It is, more globally, the acquisition of cognitive and interactive competencies that has to be facilitated. Hence, a policy focused exclusively on the role of the school would probably be too limited (Bresnahan 1999). Many other institutions have a role to play in the acquisition of new skills. Moreover, education and training programs must also involve people who are either temporarily or definitively unemployed.

Universal access poses serious problems and, above all, raises the question of opening social institutions, such as schools and libraries, via the possibilities of electronic distribution of information. This problem of universal access is not only a matter of installing enough terminals; the financing of equipment, maintenance, and training also must be taken into consideration.

These two main objectives—the acquisition of knowledge and access to information—raise the question of an appropriate public or private institution for providing the service.

It is almost unanimously recognized (Booth and Snower 1996) that the need for training (not to mention education) can be satisfied only partially by the market, that is, by incentives for employers and employees to bear costs associated with these investments. The market is even less able to satisfy the training needs of jobless people. Thus, as the knowledge-based economy creates considerable opportunities for training for all age groups, the public sector must play a key role in the exploitation of these opportunities in order to help everyone to acquire the necessary skills and knowledge.

If the private sector were to play a key role in the construction of the information infrastructure and the deployment of ICT, the privatization of access would pose huge problems. Economists have probably not yet realized the impact of ICT on certain aspects of daily life, but this impact will certainly be very strong. It is therefore important to think about whether it is advisable to leave the market and commercial interests to control access to the services of institutions such as voluntary associations, representative government, education, religion, or even the family (Steinmueller 2002a). Each of these clearly constitutes a space for the deployment of ICT. By underestimating the changes under way, society runs the risk of allowing service provision by these institutions to be bound to commercial interests. Here again, the market must not take charge of everything.

### Memory, Integration, Search, and Trust

The way in which these different functions were fulfilled in the old economy can no longer be applied to solve the problems that arise in present circumstances. New infrastructures—institutions and technologies—are therefore necessary. Here again, the public dimension is important.

### Memory

Today's younger generations might never experience the emotions aroused on rediscovering old books or toys in the attic that still work. Future machines may never be able to bring back to life the equivalent of our elders' wooden horses and toy soldiers. Earlier versions of the Playstation are already impossible to use on the latest computers. Our societies are confronted with an almost paradoxical situation, for whereas we have never before had such powerful storage and memorization technologies at our disposal (chapter 4), memory itself appears to be threatened. The unit costs of short-term storage and data retrieval may have fallen, but significant problems remain with respect to memorizing, filing, and accessing old documents.

These uncertainties are clearly expressed in the observation that it is still possible today to read the Dead Sea Scrolls whereas a 15-year-old CD-Rom has become illegible (because the appropriate hard- and software no longer exists). In this respect, the continuity afforded by natural languages and paper-type mediums can be contrasted with the discontinuity linked to generations of electronic technologies.

Two problems are beginning to emerge. First, information technologies do not save documents but sets of instructions that need to be interpreted and managed by the right hardware and software. As a result, any lack of attention paid to the complementary components of a codified knowledge system (continuity of languages, keeping programs that enable access to older files) runs the risk of irremediably altering society's overall memory. The new electronic storage media are not all that stable; indeed, they are unstable in comparison with the low-acid paper on which good books were printed for a long time. Furthermore, the artificial languages used to encode information for computer processing are also comparatively less stable insofar as they are more likely to become suddenly obsolete, requiring the corpus of stored information to be periodically "migrated" to a new code that new programs are able to read. This has made "storage" of information in the digital age less a matter of archiving than a process of repeated renewal, a cultural task for which literate societies turns out not to be well-prepared.

Second, given the exponential growth of all types of document, does everything really need to be kept? If not, then what does? On what medium (electronic, paper)? Between 1968 and 1984 the Library of Congress destroyed 300,000 books. The criteria on which this selection was based are unclear. The rule of Simon (1982, 178), that we need to store only the fraction needed to predict the rest, still applies: "With each important advance in scientific theory, we can reduce the volume of explicitly stored knowledge without losing any information whatsoever."

**Integration**

There is a natural tendency for knowledge to fragment as it becomes subject to more in-depth division and dispersion. The division of knowledge stems from divisions of labor and increasing specialization.

Its dispersion is the outcome of increasingly diffuse sources of innovation. It is probably indisputable that the division of knowledge is increasing (specialization), raising the marginal cost of knowledge integration. The "dispersion" trend is less obvious, but is likely to increase as knowledge production becomes more broadly distributed. The result is an extremely fragmented knowledge base, which makes it difficult to form a broad and integrated view of things. The structures of knowledge constantly need to be rebuilt and the cost of integration is increasing dramatically.

This amounts to a matter of knowing how to integrate and organize fragmented, scattered, and thinly spread knowledge. Moreover, problems of integration of knowledge concern not only the field of basic knowledge but also the industrial domain, which creates increasingly complex technological systems composed of multiple modules whose assemblage is becoming a critical phase in the production process (see chapter 3). These issues also concern the daily lives of citizens, who need integrated knowledge to be able to form an opinion on a particular topic, for example, on questions of safety concerning the environment, food, or a sport.

The famous economist Alfred Marshall raised basically the same question, albeit with respect to industrial activities: how can one organize and coordinate highly specialized activities within a context marked by an extreme social division of labor? The answer, according to Marshall, lay in two main factors: a reduction in transport costs and local concentrations of activity clusters, with each locality creating the right conditions for integrating knowledge (Loasby 1989). So the whole question revolves around the capacity of the new information technologies to enable better integration of knowledge by helping to bring down the cost of transporting it and paving the way for local concentrations of virtual activities.

Under certain conditions, the new technologies clearly favor the low-cost transmission of knowledge and the creation of virtual communities. Some researchers, however, argue that the use of powerful communication technologies, such as the Internet, may promote uniformity to the detriment of diversity (Van Alstyne and Brynjolfsson 1996). Time spent on on-line interaction with members of one's own, preselected community leaves less time available for actual encounters with a wide variety of people. If physicists, for example, were to concentrate on exchanging email and electronic preprints with other physicists around the world working in the same specialized subject area—as indeed researchers today generally are—they would likely devote less time, and be less receptive to, new ways of looking at the world, to which they would otherwise be exposed by chance meetings and lunchtime conversations with colleagues working in other disciplinary fields. Facilitating the voluntary construction of highly homogeneous social networks of scientific (or other, say, political) communication therefore allows individuals to filter the potentially overwhelming flow of information. But the result may be the tendency to overfilter it, thus eliminating the diversity of the knowledge circulating and diminishing the frequency of radically new ideas. In this regard, even a journey through the stacks of a real library can be more fruitful than a trip through today's distributed virtual archives, because it seems difficult to use the available "search engines" to emulate efficiently the mixture of predictable and surprising discoveries that typically result from a physical shelf-search of an extensive library collection. New technologies are not automatically going to resolve the issue of knowledge integration. Establishing and developing interdisciplinary communities made up of a heterogeneous range of members needs to happen. In such cases, the sound "Marshallian" properties of information technologies really can serve to support the integration of knowledge.

**Search**
The tilting of our economies into a "Simonian" world in which it is no longer information and knowledge which are scarce, but rather attention, also forces companies to develop specific skills for managing attention and filtering information (Simon 1982). While the probability of knowledge existing and being stored somewhere is great, that of it not being found is just as great. Most often, searches for relevant information are localized, that is, limited to the firm's closest contacts. They are only rarely carried out throughout the entire potential space in which the knowledge in question might exist. The wealth of information combines with the increasing dispersion of knowledge (linked to the countless number of local and specific sites where information is produced) and to the increase in the division of knowledge (associated with the increasing division of labor in the production of knowledge and, thus, to specialization in various fields) to create a huge stockpile through which it is very hard to maneuver.

Searching for information and codified knowledge and screening and selecting it are becoming activities of growing economic importance for the performance of the knowledge-based economy. The increase in the productivity of processes used to search for existing information and knowledge (reference standards, artificial agents, transfer science) and the economy of cognitive resources in an information-rich environment ("intelligent" screening devices; new concepts for virtual filing) are the two main requirements for the improvement of both the richness of the knowledge environment and the ability of economic agents to survive and prosper in that environment (Steinmueller 1992).

**Trust**
Fraudulent behavior, forgery, and pretense have obviously not suddenly been spawned by the virtual world. Questions concerning the original and the copy (Eco 1992), not to mention the evaluation of goods that are the object of commercial transactions, have given rise to the problem of trust and have highlighted just how crucial trust-building mechanisms have been to the functioning of markets and communities since the beginning of time. But the development of virtual relations has given the trust issue a new edge. What is at stake here is the entire range of mechanisms that will facilitate interpersonal and interorganizational transactions, given the new conditions for knowledge transactions and exchanges: increasing specialization, increasing asymmetrical distribution of information and assessment capabilities, greater anonymity among interlocutors, and more opportunities for forgery of identity. Clearly, new methods need to be devised to "certify" the knowledge circulating on the Internet within a context where inputs are no longer subject to control (unlike the knowledge disseminated by scientific journals, for example, whose quality and reliability are validated through the peer review process). Issues of trust impinge upon the organization of new distance learning systems, where a significant problem is that of creating ways of certifying the competence of "teachers" and validating new curricula introduced by distance learning organizations. Another big issue concerns regulation and social behavior, and the formation of cooperation based upon "trust" and shared ethos/identity in virtual communities.

**Address to Economists: Knowing the Knowledge Economy Better**

The last challenge, the last test, is one facing economists and statisticians. Here we simply need to consider the questions in this book that have remained unanswered and the arguments that are still incomplete, to get an idea of the size of the gap between what economists want to understand and what they are able to observe.

In chapter 2 I focused on change, for it has become the main economic activity, and this development has significant repercussions. But basic statistics do not distinguish the costs of change. The systematic calculation of these costs is almost impossible, at least in the short term. In this respect, Carter (1994b) argues for the launching of wide-ranging surveys on the costs of change in the different sectors.

In several chapters I emphasize the importance of learning as a source of knowledge. But learning is still not taken into account in statistics on the production of knowledge. This is a serious shortcoming that will require a lot of time and effort to remedy.

Recent empirical studies on learning (chapter 3) are nevertheless cause for optimism, for it is still a set of good empirical studies that constitutes the prelude to the development of new indicators.

Economists are still far from mastering basic indicators on stocks and flows of knowledge. While measuring the stock of physical capital is a colossal task, measuring the stock of knowledge capital seems virtually impossible. Even limited to current science and technology indicators, this measurement will be introduced only if techniques for dealing with the question of obsolescence are developed. Moreover, does the measurement of a stock of knowledge have any meaning if problems pertaining to its location and access were not taken into account? An even more difficult task would be to measure flows of knowledge or the share of the stock of knowledge that enters into the economy during a given period. Measurement of embodied diffusion (i.e., the introduction into production processes of elements incorporating a new technology) and disembodied diffusion (i.e., transmission of knowledge in the form of patent licenses or know-how) are the two aspects today that are relatively well under control. But here again, they cover only a small part of all knowledge flows.

Finally, I need to emphasize the fact that indicators of the knowledge-based economy have, on the whole, been based on existing statistics that primarily concern science and technology. The most recent publication by the OECD on the subject makes this point very clear (OECD 1999b). The light that these indicators shed on the subject is therefore more relevant for some fields than for others. In certain cases it is satisfactory—the case of science-based industries—but in others these indicators illuminate an almost empty stage, for the economics of knowledge happens elsewhere, in an area that our indicators still leave in the dark. That is typically the education sector, where R&D plays a small role or at least where it is of secondary importance compared to experimental learning in school and the diffusion of tacit knowledge produced in these conditions (chapter 9). Thus, it is the center of gravity of the knowledge base that differs largely from one sector to the next. And when this center of gravity moves too far away from R&D and the diffusion of codified knowledge, our indicators do not shed light on very much at all.

**Networks, Alliances, Communities: The New Public Economy**

All the elements considered in this chapter—the necessary revival of the knowledge public domain; the question of education and learning faced with the rapid depreciation of knowledge; the implications of questions of memory, integration, information searches, and trust; and even the problem of creation of new indicators—have a common point. They all make it possible to restructure and revive the rationale for public support and public property in our economies. For each of those problems there are critical policy processes involving the subsidization or direct production (provision) of some of the crucial public goods in the knowledge-based economy. There is a clear economic rationale for public intervention where competitive markets are expected to do a particularly bad job in producing and distributing knowledge and information. Salient cases involve exploratory science, R&D that is expected to yield very substantial knowledge spillovers, access to training and learning for the unemployed (including jobless young people and the aged), the provision and support of information infrastructures, and so forth.

An economy centered around the production and distribution of a public good (in the economic sense of the word as defined in chapter 6) is an economy which constantly has to struggle against the dominant tendency of competitive private markets to conquer new domains in which the expected private profitability seems great. However, by nature these markets do not fulfill all the functions characteristic of these domains, and they impose forms of organization that run counter to the public nature of the goods studied here:

• private markets for basic knowledge are probably efficient in a specific niche but overlook questions of long-term research and the implications of intergenerational and interpopulation equity, and reduce knowledge externalities;

• private markets for information storage and security appear but neglect functions of archiving and memory—issues that can only be addressed in an intergenerational equity framework;

• private markets for training are proliferating but they exclude training services for certain categories of the population.

It is therefore the responsibility of experts and politicians to fully grasp the importance of the public dimension of knowledge-based economies.

The success of knowledge management practices designed to construct a new rationality for knowledge sharing (chapter 9), and the revival of collective forms of organization (networks, alliances, consortia) intended to solve problems of research and integration (chapter 3), show that this public dimension is constantly being born and reborn everywhere. Moreover, the amazing success of forms of knowledge openness (chapter 8) clearly shows that new forms of complementarity between the public and the private spheres are coming into being. These highly effective but extremely fragile forms of openness clearly constitute the future of knowledge-based economies and, more generally, of capitalism.

# Conclusion

My conception of knowledge-based economies is not an "extended" one, in that it claims not to explain all the issues and problems of the contemporary world economy, such as the rise of fundamentalism or the new threat of terrorism, but rather to provide a coherent frame based on an original discipline (the economics of knowledge; cf. chapter 1) for linking up all the changes related to the production and distribution of knowledge in modern societies.

1. These changes concern, above all, the sources of knowledge-based economies. One of the most noteworthy trends relates to the massive increase in resources devoted to the production, transmission, and management of knowledge (education, training, R&D, and management); another concerns a major technological event, the advent of information technology which has impacted the production, codification, and distribution of knowledge and information (chapter 2). These are long-term transformations that profoundly change the characteristics of the "mediums" and instruments of knowledge. From this first level readers already see that certain countries and groups do not have access to knowledge-based economies, simply because they do not fully benefit from these two developments.

2. For the economies that benefit from them, the encounter between the long-term trend and the technological revolution has basically led to a significant transformation of the system of knowledge production and diffusion, defined in a narrow sense as: the increase in the contribution of science to innovation and the appearance of new "roles" such as that of users, along with the growing importance of collaboration (chapter 3); the greater role of codification as a method for managing and reproducing knowledge, which propels the constant expansion of the areas in which the cost of marginal reproduction of knowledge is

very low (chapter 4); and, lastly, the combination of technological and institutional conditions favorable to the generation and exploitation of knowledge spillovers (chapter 5).

At this stage of my observation I have the impression of "the factory of the little chemist" which will henceforth function at full capacity. Stills, retorts, and tubes are used for the most interesting compositions to "distill" new knowledge. Owing to the changes mentioned, the "knowledge factory" never stops working and the pace of creation and depreciation of knowledge accelerates. However, in this factory some retorts have not yet been connected to the other instruments and some tubes are blocked. There is even a still that a little chemist has claimed for himself, and those who want to use it have to pay, while others have built a collective retort.

3. The third main area of change concerns institutions for the purpose of allocating resources for the production and distribution of this particular economic good (chapter 6). At this level, the increasing use of intellectual property (chapter 7) and the extension of new forms of public property (said to be "inherently public") (chapter 8) oppose forces at play.

These sets of transformations generate the need for additional technological, organizational, and institutional innovations, to solve many problems and meet numerous challenges identified at the end of the book (chapters 9–11).

If a "new economy" exists, it is clearly in the sense of the knowledge-based economy which crystallizes the unique articulation between a long-standing trend toward the increase in resources devoted to the production and transmission of knowledge and the advent of a new technological system. It is an economy in which knowledge creation and externalities are potentially strong but where the costs of creative destruction are higher than ever.

The effects of the knowledge-based economy spread throughout many economic activities, particularly science, industry and services, education and culture, health, and public administration, in various ways: exploitation of high productivity gains (especially on the codification and transmission of knowledge); creation of new activities; and elaboration of new organizational models. Everywhere, these trends are reinforced by the new abilities of the economic and financial world to enhance the value of knowledge-related performance.

The very high growth rate of the United States during the last decade is probably due to the fact that, for each of these modalities, the U.S. economy and society have provided coherent answers in the framework of a particular institutional trajectory:

• the productivity potential is exploited through U.S. firms' investments in computer technology which have grown spectacularly since 1993;

• the creation and development of new sectors have been facilitated in particular by the decisive role of the public sector and universities in providing the critical technologies, and by a legal, tax, and financial environment favorable to business creation and the emergence of new activities (Mowery and Simcoe 2001);

• in the United States the environment is favorable to the creation of new forms of organization allowed by ICT, particularly outsourcing, as a result of the restructuring and reengineering programs launched very early on, during the 1980s;

• finally, more than anywhere else, U.S. financial markets have been able to create appropriate mechanisms for extracting value from intellectual creation and knowledge capital.

The U.S. example prompts me to consider the question of whether there is one or several possible trajectories toward the knowledge-based economy. A number of signs point to the possibility of different trajectories:

• there is real disparity among countries regarding the structure of investments in knowledge (different levels of public spending on education and training; different levels of investment by companies in terms of R&D, software, advertising) (chapter 2);

• there is a wide variety of uses of intellectual property rights, various possible balances between the public and private research sectors, and unequal attention paid to the collective production of knowledge—all of which mean that knowledge-based economies can find themselves on relatively different trajectories.

The U.S. option is to leave private markets to determine the trajectory of this economy. We can therefore expect a fast rate of technological change, supported by a strong intellectual property right system, and a marked emphasis on the commercial goals and values of the knowledge-based economy. But we can also expect unbridled privatization of knowledge bases as well as a widening gap between the most privileged citizens and the rest of the population (Steinmueller 2002a).

Can we talk similarly of a European trajectory? Probably not, for the disparities among countries are too wide, depending on the different criteria (structure of investments in knowledge, sharing between public and private sector, and so on).

It is certain, however, that several roads lead to the new economy, and that the costs and benefits of current transformations will depend on the choices made in this respect. It is therefore essential for countries to decide, in all conscience, on the best road to take, namely, on whether to spend more or less on education and training, to devote more or less public and private resources to tangible and intangible investments (software, computer technology, R&D), which intellectual property rights policy to opt for, what place to reserve for open knowledge and public research, and so on. Each decision counts in the establishment of a knowledge-based economy from which everyone stands to gain.

# Postscript

This morning on a French radio station an expert on AIDS, participating in the international congress in Barcelona (July 2002), noted that young people know less today about the disease and the mechanisms of its transmission than they did in the 1990s. The expert affirmed this with alarming evidence: a substantial proportion of today's youth has no idea as to how the HIV virus is transmitted. In other words, knowledge has deteriorated even though it has not become obsolete and its private and social value is as important as ever. It is the social processes guaranteeing its memorization and transmission that have functioned less well. This example is useful for contrasting the performance and force of processes of scientific knowledge creation (possibly incorporating patients' competencies) that lead to new, more effective therapies and nurture hopes in a vaccine, with the fragility of common knowledge that society is responsible for maintaining and transmitting. The former, even if they seem to provide complete solutions (a vaccine) do not replace the latter in any way whatsoever; it is simply irreplaceable.

At the beginning of this conclusion, I said that I wanted a framework of analysis that was not too broad and not intended to explain everything. Yet simply the observation of the expert on the deterioration of knowledge on AIDS opens a vast field, that of the change from a knowledge-based economy to a knowledge society: a society in which not only the production and circulation of scientific and technological knowledge function, especially in professional communities, but also in which the memorization of common knowledge and its absorption by everyone is guaranteed; a vast new area that the main concepts and tools discussed here should help to clarify.

# Notes

1. An evaluation of the positive effects of access to knowledge on efficiency, quality, and equity is at the heart of the economics of knowledge as a discipline (see chapters 5 and 8).

2. Chapter 2 draws on Foray and Lundvall (1996) and David and Foray (2002).

3. In the chapter 3, I consider the creation of norms and standards as one of the fundamental processes of innovation in knowledge-based economies.

4. Although Nelson (1999) recognizes that some sciences are not experimental, he is right to point out that most of the strong fields of empirical science have involved experiments in an essential way.

5. As Rosenberg showed (1992), the first corporate R&D laboratories did not perform activities that could be regarded as research. Rather, they were engaged in a variety of routine and elementary tasks such as the grading and testing of materials, assaying, quality control, writing of specifications, and so on.

6. Chapter 4 draws on Cowan and Foray (1997), Cowan, David, and Foray (2000), Cowan and Foray (2001), and Foray and Steinmueller (2003a).

7. Chapter 5 draws on Foray and Mairesse (2002).

8. Chapter 6 draws on David and Foray (1995) and Cassier and Foray (2001).

9. Even if this norm is not coercive, it constitutes a general frame that strongly influences behaviors.

10. Chapter 7 draws on Foray (2002).

11. Directive 98/44/EC of the European Parliament and of the council on the legal protection of bio-technological inventions.

12. Amendments to U.S. patent law in 1999 revised this principle. Publication now takes place eighteen months after registration of the application.

13. Machlup made a rather similar argument a few years later: "If we did not have a patent system, it would be irresponsible on the basis of our present knowledge of its economic consequences, to recommend instituting one. But since we have had a patent system for a long time, it would be irresponsible, on the basis of our present knowledge, to recommend abolishing it" (Machlup 1958).

14. For example: USPTO: 5 851 117, 1998 (granted): *Building Block Training Systems and Training Methods*: The patent describes how an experienced person can teach a novice by using an illustrated publication, such as a training manual.

15. Directive 96/9/EC of the European Parliament and of the council on the legal protection of databases.

16. U.S. Patent and Trademark Office/European Patent Office.

17. See earlier in the chapter, for an analysis of the structure of this problem.

18. Chapter 8 draws on Foray and Hilaire Perez (2000); Foray and Zimmerman (2001); and David and Foray (2002).

19. Chapter 9 draws on Foray and Hargreaves (2003).

20. I am aware that such an argument conveys the risk of overgeneralization (see chapter 5 for a development of the argument that very few research results and scientific inventions are formalized from the start to the point of being a "simple" set of codified instructions so that experiments and results can be reproduced by scrupulously following the codified instructions). However, the nature of pecuniary and nonpecuniary rewards in scientific research produces strong incentives for knowledge codification, articulation, and clarification once it has been created since the rewards accrue from publication and dissemination (see chapter 8 and Dasgupta and David 1994).

21. I focus on primary school teachers where pedagogical content knowledge (how to teach, how to structure the teaching of the subject so that children learn) is considered the core of the professional knowledge base whereas subject knowledge (mathematics or history) is of secondary importance.

22. Statistical studies of course provide significant results (such as the relation between the education and the income of a pupil's parents), but as Nelson (1999) correctly points out, such a correlation gives no information on how to improve the performance of schools, given the background of the students.

23. This section has been written by David Hargreaves for a joint paper (Foray and Hargreaves 2003).

24. Chapter 10 draws on Foray (2001) and Foray and Gault (2003).

25. Chapter 11 draws on David and Foray (2002).

26. "Academic researchers are often shocked to discover that, except for some very limited statutory exemptions that do not generally apply to them, there is no general research exemption in the United States for using other people's patented technologies. . . . As a rule, the Federal Circuit only found exemptions when use was for idle curiosity or purely philosophical pursuits. In this landscape, research at a university, even if performed without any profit motive, would be infringing, as it is difficult to imagine research that is outside the scope of business interests of an organization" (Nottenburg, Pardey, and Wright 2001, 12).

# References

Abramovitz, M. 1989. *Thinking about growth.* Cambridge: Cambridge University Press.

Abramovitz, M., and P. David. 1996. "Technological change, intangible investments and growth in the knowledge-based economy: The U.S. historical experience." In *Employment and growth in the knowledge-based economy*, ed. D. Foray and B. A. Lundvall, 35–60. Paris: OECD.

Adler, P., and K. Clark. 1991. "Behind the learning curve: A sketch of the learning process." *Management Science* 37(3): 267–281.

Aghion, P., and P. Howitt. 1998. *Endogeneous growth theory.* Cambridge, MA: The MIT Press.

Agrawal, A., and L. Garlappi. 2001. "Public sector science and 'the Strategy of the Commons.'" NBER workshop on productivity, Cambridge.

Allen, R. 1983. "Collective invention." *Journal of Economic Behavior and Organization*, no. 4: 1–24.

Alper, J. 1999. "L'envol des logiciels libres." *La Recherche* 319 (April): 27–29.

Alter, N. 2000. *L'innovation ordinaire.* Paris: PUF.

Amendola, M., and J. L. Gaffard. 1988. *The innovative choice. An economic analysis of the dynamics of technology.* Oxford: Blackwell.

Antonelli, C. 1999. *The microdynamics of technological change.* London: Routledge.

Antonelli, C. 2001. *The microeconomics of technological systems.* Oxford: Oxford University Press.

Aoki, M. 1988. *Information, incentives and bargaining in the Japanese economy.* Cambridge: Cambridge University Press.

Aoki, M., and H. Takizawa. 2002. "Modularity: Its relevance to industrial architecture." Working paper, Saint Gobain Centre for Economic Research, Paris.

Appleyard, M. 1996. "How does knowledge flow? Interfirm patterns in the semiconductor industry." *Strategic Management Journal* 17 (Winter): 137–154.

Argote, L., S. Beckman, and D. Epple. 1990. "The persistence and transfer of learning in industrial settings." *Management Science* 36(2): 140–154.

Arora, A. 1995. "Licensing tacit knowledge: Intellectual property rights and the market for know-how." *Economics of Innovation and New Technology* 4(1): 41–59.

Arora, A., A. Fosfuri, and A. Gambardella. 2001. *Markets for technology: The economics of innovation and corporate strategy.* Cambridge: The MIT Press.

Arrow, K. J. 1962a. "Economic welfare and the allocation of resources for inventions." In *The rate and direction of inventive activity: Economic and social factors,* ed. R. R. Nelson, 609–626. Princeton: Princeton University Press.

Arrow, K. J. 1962b. "The economic implications of Learning By Doing." *Review of Economic Studies* 29(April): 166–170.

Arrow, K. J. 1969a. "Classificatory notes on the production and transmission of technological knowledge." *American Economic Review, Papers and Proceedings,* 29–35.

Arrow, K. J. 1969. "Political and economic evaluation of social effects and externalities." In *Frontiers of quantitative economics,* ed. M. D. Intriligator, 3–31. Amsterdam: North-Holland.

Arrow, K. J. 1974. *The limits of organization.* New York: Norton.

Arthur, B. A. 1989. "Competing technologies, increasing returns, and lock-in by historical events." *The Economic Journal* 99(394): 116–131.

Arundel, A., and I. Kabla. 1998. "What percentage of innovations are patented? Empirical estimates for European firms." *Research Policy* 27: 127–141.

Atkinson, A. B., and J. Stiglitz. 1969. "A new view of technical change." *The Economic Journal* (September): 573–578.

Audrestch, D., and M. Feldman. 1996. "R&D spillovers and the geography of innovation and production." *American Economic Review* 86(3): 630–640.

Audrestch, D., and P. Stephan. 1996. "Company-scientists locational links: The case of biotechnology." *American Economic Review* 86(3): 641–652.

Baldwin, C., and K. B. Clark. 1997. "Managing in an age of modularity." *Harvard Business Review* (September–October): 84–93.

Barton, J. 2000. "Reforming the patent system." *Science* 287 (5460): 1933–1934.

Barzel, Y. 1968. "Optimal timing of innovations." *Review of Economic Statistics* 50 (August): 348–355.

Bessy, C., and E. Brousseau. 1999. "Technology licensing contracts: Features and diversity." *International Review of Law and Economics* 18 (December): 451–489.

Boldrin, M., and D. Levine. 2002. "The case against intellectual property." *American Economic Review* 92(2): 209–212.

Boldrin, M., and D. Levine. 2003. "Why Napster is right." Available online at <www.econ.umn.edu/~mboldrin/Issues/Napster/napster1.html>.

Booth, A., and D. Snower. 1996. *Acquiring skills: Market failures, their symptoms and policy responses.* Cambridge: Cambridge University Press.

Bouveresse, J. 1996. "Robert Musil, le sens du possible et la tâche de l'école." *Biennale des Sciences de l'Education* (Avril): 1–29.

Bradshaw, J. 1997. "An introduction to software agents." In *Software Agents*, ed. J. Bradshaw, 3–7. Cambridge, MA: The MIT Press.

Bresnahan, T. 1999. "Computerization and wage dispersion." *The Economic Journal* 109(456): 390–415.

Bresnahan, T., A. Gambardella, and A. Saxenian. 2002. " 'Old economy' inputs for 'new economy' outcomes: cluster formation in the new Silicon-Valley." Paper presented at the DRUID Summer Conference, Copenhagen Business School.

Brown, K. M. 1998. *Downsizing science.* Washington, DC: The AEI Press.

Brynjolfsson, E., and B. Kahin. 2000. *Understanding the digital economy.* Cambridge, MA: The MIT Press.

Callon, M. 1994. "Is science a public good?" Fifth Mullins Lecture. *Science, Technology and Human Value* 19(4): 395–423.

Callon, M. 1999. "The role of lay people in the production and dissemination of knowledge." Mimeo. Ecole Nationale Supérieure des Mines de Paris, Centre de Sociologie de l'Innovation.

Callon, M., and D. Foray. 1997. "Nouvelle économie de la science ou socio-économie de la recherche scientifique?" *Revue d'Economie Industrielle*, no. 79: 13–35.

Cantley, M., and D. Sahal. 1980. "Who learns what? A conceptual description of capability and learning in technological system." IIASA Working Paper 80–42.

Carlsson, B., and R. Stankiewicz. 1991. "On the nature, function and composition of technological systems." *Journal of Evolutionary Economics* 1(2): 93–118.

Caron, F. 1997. *Les deux révolutions industrielles du XX° siècle.* Paris: Albin Michel.

Carter, A. P. 1994a. "Production workers, metainvestment and the pace of change." Working paper, no. 332, Brandeis University, Department of Economics.

Carter, A. P. 1994b. "Change as economic activity." Working paper, no. 333, Brandeis University, Department of Economics.

Carter, A. P. 1996. "Measuring the performance of a knowledge-based economy." In *Employment and growth in the knowledge-based economy*, ed. D. Foray and B. A. Lundvall, 61–92. Paris: OECD.

Cassier, M., and D. Foray. 2000. "Public knowledge, private property and the economics of high-tech consortia." *Economics of Innovation and New Technology* 11(2): 123–132.

Cassier, M., and D. Foray. 2001. "Economie de la connaissance: Le rôle des consortiums de haute technologie dans la production d'un bien public." *Economie & Prévision* 4/5(150–151) :107–122.

Cassier, M., and J. P. Gaudillere. 2001. "La recherche biomédicale au coeur des marchés economiques." In *Second French Health Economists Conference*. Paris: CNAM.

Chandler, A. 1992. "Organizational capabilities and the economic history of the industrial enterprise." *Journal of Economic Perspectives* 6(3): 79–100.

Chartier, R. 1994. "Du codex à l'écran: les trajectoires de l'écrit." *Solaris.* Presses Universitaires de Rennes, 1. Available online at <www.info.unicaen.fr/brum/selec/Solaris/d01/1Chartier.html>

Chartier, R. 2000. "Edition numérique: Révolution dans la révolution." *Le Monde*, May 13.

Clavier, J. P. 1998. *Les catégories de la propriété intellectuelle à l'epreuve des créations génétiques*. Paris: L'Harmattan.

Coase, R. 1937. "The nature of the firm." *Economica* 4: 386–405.

Coase, R. 1960. "The problem of social cost." *Journal of Law and Economics* 3: 1–44.

Coase, R. 1974. "The lighthouse in economics." *Journal of Law and Economics* (October).

Cockburn, I. 2002. "O brave new industry, that has such patents in it! Reflections on the economics of genome patenting." Mimeo. Boston University and NBER.

Cockburn, I., and R. Henderson. 1995. "Racing to invest? The dynamics of competition in ethical drug discovery." *Journal of Economics and Management Strategy* 3(3): 481–519.

Cockburn, I., and R. Henderson. 1997. "Public-private interaction and the productivity of pharmaceutical research." Working Paper Series, WP 6018, National Bureau of Economic Research.

Cockburn, I., R. Henderson, and S. Stern. 1999. "The diffusion of science driven drug discovery: Organizational change in pharmaceutical research." Working Paper Series, WP 7359, National Bureau of Economic Research.

Cohen, W., and D. Levinthal. 1989. "Innovation and learning: The two faces of R&D." The *Economic Journal* 99 (September): 569–596.

Cohen, W., R. Nelson, and J. Walsh. 1997. "Appropriability conditions and why firm patent and why they do not in the American manufacturing sector." Mimeo. Carnegie Mellon University.

Cohen, W., R. Florida, L. Randazzese, and J. Walsh. 1998. "Industry and the academy: Uneasy partners in the cause of technological advance." In *Challenge to the research university*, ed. R. Noll, 171–179. Washington, DC: Brookings Institution.

Cottereau, A. 1997. "The fate of collective manufactures in the industrial world: The silk industries of Lyons and London." In *Flexibility and mass production in Western industrialization*, ed. C. Sabel and J. Zeitlin, 75–152. Cambridge: Cambridge University Press.

Cowan, R. 2001. "Expert systems: Aspects of and limits to the codifiability of knowledge." *Research Policy* 30.

Cowan, R., and D. Foray. 1995. "Quandaries in the economics of dual technologies and spillovers from military to civilian R&D." *Research Policy* 24(6): 851–858.

Cowan, R., and D. Foray. 1997. "The economics of knowledge codification and diffusion." *Industrial and Corporate Change* 6(3): 595–622.

Cowan, R., and D. Foray. 2001. "On the codifiability of knowledge: Technical change and the structure of cognitive activities." In *Economics and information*, ed. P. Petit, 155–165. Boston: Kluwer Academic Publishers.

Cowan, R., P. A. David, and D. Foray. 2000. "The explicit economics of knowledge codification and tacitness." *Industrial and Corporate Change* 9(2): 211–253.

Cowan, R., E. Fauchart, D. Foray, and P. Gunby. 2002. "Learning from disaster." Mimeo. University Paris Dauphine.

Dagognet, F. 1995. "La communication: Métaphore ou métascience." In *Vers la société de l'information*, ed. R. Delmas and F. Massit-Folléa, 177–185. Rennes: Edition Apogée.

Dasgupta, P., and P. A. David. 1994. "Toward a new economics of science." *Research Policy* 23(5): 487–521.

Davenport, T., and L. Prusak. 1998. *Working knowledge: How organizations manage what they know*. Cambridge: Harvard Business School Press.

David, P. A. 1987. "New standards for the economics of standardization in the information age." In *Technology policy and economic performance*, ed. P. Dasgupta and Stoneman, 206–239. Cambridge: Cambridge University Press.

David, P. A. 1988. "Information technology, social communications, and the wealth and diversity of nations." Working paper, CEPR publication no. 148, Stanford University.

David, P. A. 1991. "Computer and dynamo: The modern productivity paradox in a not-too-distant mirror." In *Technology and productivity: The challenge for economic policy*, 315–347. Paris: OECD.

David, P. A. 1993. "Knowledge, property and the system dynamics of technological change." In *Proceedings of the World Bank Annual Conference on Development Economics 1992*, 215–248. Washington, DC: World Bank.

David, P. A. 1994. "Positive feedbacks and research productivity in science: Reopening another black box." In *Economics of technology*, ed. O. Grandstrand, 65–89. Elsevier Science.

David, P. A. 1997. "International cooperation and the economics of access to large-scale research facilities." Paper presented at the International Workshop on the Global Science System in Transition, International Institute for Applied System Analysis (IIASA), Austria.

David, P. A. 1998a. "Common agency contracting and the emergence of open science institutions." *The American Economic Review* 88(2): 15–21.

David, P. A. 1998b. "Communication Norms and the Collective Cognitive Performance of 'Invisible Colleges.'" In *Creation and transfer of knowledge*, ed. G. Navaretti, P. Dasgupta, K. Mäler, and D. Siniscalco, 115–163. Heidelberg: Springer.

David, P. A. 1998c. "Knowledge Spillovers, Technology Transfers and the Economic Rationale for Public Support of Exploratory Research in Science." European Committee for Future Accelerators.

David, P. A. 1999. "Path dependence and varieties of learning in the evolution of technological practice." In *Technological innovation as an evolutionary process*, ed. J. Ziman, 118–133. Cambridge: Cambridge University Press.

David, P. A. 2000a. "Understanding digital technology's evolution and the path of measured productivity growth: Present and future in the mirror of the past." In *Understanding the digital economy*, ed. E. Brynjolfsson and B. Kahin, 49–95. Cambridge, MA: The MIT Press.

David, P. A. 2000b. "A Tragedy of the Public Knowledge Commons? Global Science, Intellectual Property and the Digital Technology Boomerang." Working Paper 00–16, Department of Economics, Stanford University.

David, P. A. 2001. "Digital technologies, research collaborations and the extension of protection for intellectual property in science: Will building 'good fences' really make 'good neighbors'?" In *IPR Aspects of Internet Collaborations*, Final Report, Eur 19456, European Commission.

David, P. A., and D. Foray. 1994. "Dynamics of competitive technology diffusion through local network structures: The case of EDI document standards." In *Evolutionary economics and chaos theory*, ed. L. Leydesdorff and P. van den Besselaar, 63–78. London: Pinter.

David, P. A., and D. Foray. 1995. "Accessing and expanding the science and technology knowledge base." *STI Review* 16: 13–68. Paris: OECD.

David, P. A., and D. Foray. 2002. "An introduction to the economy of the knowledge society." *International Social Science Journal* (March) (171): 13–28.

David, P. A., and S. Greenstein. 1990. "The economics of compatibility standards: an introduction to recent research." *Economics of Innovation and New Technology* 1(1&2): 3–41.

David, P. A., and W. E. Steinmueller. 1996. "Standards, trade and competition in the emerging global information infrastructure environment." *Telecommunication Policy* 20(10): 817–830.

David, P. A., and G. Wright. 1999. "General Purpose Technologies and Surges in Productivity: Historical Reflections on the Future of the ICT Revolution." Paper presented at the International Symposium on Economic Challenges of the 21st Century in Historical Perspective, Oxford.

David, P. A., D. C. Mowery, and W. E. Steinmueller. 1992. "Analyzing the economic payoffs from basic research." *Economics of Innovation and New Technology* 2(1): 73–90.

David, P. A., D. Foray, and W. E. Steinmueller. 1999. "The research network and the new economics of science: from metaphors to organizational behavior." In *The organization of inventive activity in Europe*, ed. A. Gambardella and F. Malerba, 303–342. Cambridge: Cambridge University Press.

Dosi, G. 1996. "The contribution of economic theory to the understanding of a knowledge-based economy." In *Employment and growth in the knowledge-based economy*, ed. D. Foray and B. A. Lundvall, 81–92. Paris: OECD.

Dosi, G., D. Teece, and S. Winter. 1992. "Toward a theory of corporate coherence: Preliminary remarks." In *Technology and enterprise in a historical perspective*, ed. G. Dosi, D. Teese, and S. Winter, 185–211. Oxford: Clarendon Press.

Eamon, W. 1985. "From the secret of nature to public knowledge: the origin of the concept of openness in science." *Minerva* 23(3): 321–347.

Eco, U. 1992. "The Original and the Copy." *Understanding Origins*, ed. F. Varela and J. P. Dupuy. Boston: Kluwer Academic Publishers.

*The Economist.* 2000. "Untangling economics." *The Economist*, September 26.

Edquist, C. 1997. *Systems of innovation.* London: Pinter.

Eisenstein, E. 1980. *The printing press as an agent of change.* Cambridge: Cambridge University Press.

Eliasson, G. 1990. "The knowledge-based information economy." In *The knowledge-based information economy*, ed. Eliasson et al., 9–87. Stockholm: Almqvist & Wiksell International.

Encaoua, D., D. Guellec, and C. Martinez. 2003. "The economics of patents: From natural rights to policy instruments." EPIP Conference, European Patent Office, Munich.

Epstein, S. R. 1998. "Craft guilds, apprenticeship, and technological change in preindustrial Europe." *The Journal of Economic History* 58(3): 681–713.

Ergas, H. 1992. "A future for mission-oriented industrial policies? A critical review of Development in Europe." Draft. Paris: OECD.

Farrell, J. 1989. "Standardization and intellectual property." *Jurimetrics Journal.*

Fauchart, E. 2003. "Knowledge sharing pattern among rural firms and safety performance." Working Paper 2003-1, Laboratoire d'Econometrie, CNAM, Paris.

Favereau, O. 2001. "Theory of information: From bounded rationality to interpretative reason." In *Economics and Information,* ed. P. Petit, 93–120. Boston: Kluwer Academic Publishers.

Feldman, M. 2002. "The Internet revolution and the geography of innovation." *International Journal for Social Sciences* 171 (March): 53–64.

Feldman, M. and J. Francis. 2001. "Entrepreneurs and the formation of industrial clusters." John Hopkins University, Baltimore.

Fitz-Gibbon, C. 2001. "What's all this about 'Evidence'?" *Learning and Skills Research* (Autumn): 27–29.

Foray, D. 1999. "Science, technology and the market." *World Social Science Report,* 246–255. UNESCO. London: Elsevier.

Foray, D. 2001. "Continuities and ruptures in knowledge management practices." In *Knowledge management in the innovation process,* ed. J. de la Mothe and D. Foray, 43–52. Boston: Kluwer Academic Publishers.

Foray, D. 2002. "Intellectual property rights." In *The IEBM handbooks of economics,* ed. W. Lazonick, 75–83. London: Thomson.

Foray, D., and C. Freeman. 1992. *Technology and the wealth of nations.* London: Pinter.

Foray, D., and F. Gault. 2003. *Measuring knowledge management in the business sector: First steps.* Paris: OECD and Statistics Canada.

Foray, D., and D. Hargreaves. 2003. "The development of knowledge of different sectors: A model and some hypotheses." *London Review of Education* 1(1): 7–19.

Foray, D., and L. Hilaire Perez. 2000. The Economics of Open Technology: Collective Organization and Individual Claims in the "Fabrique Lyonnaise" during the Old Regime. Conference in Honor of Paul A. David, Turin.

Foray, D., and A. Kazancigil. 1999. *Science, economics and democracy: Selected issues.* Discussion paper, MOST-UNESCO.

Foray, D., and B. A. Lundvall. 1996. "The knowledge-based economy: from the economics of knowledge to the learning economy." In *Employment and growth in the knowledge-based economy,* ed. D. Foray and B. A. Lundvall, 11–32. Paris: OECD.

Foray, D., and J. Mairesse. 1998. *Innovations et performances des firmes: Approches Interdisciplinaires.* Paris: EHESS.

Foray, D., and J. Mairesse. 2002. "The knowledge dilemma and the geography of innovation." In *Institutions and systems in the geography of innovation*, ed. M. Feldman and N. Massard, 35–54. Boston: Kluwer Academic Publishers.

Foray, D., and W. E. Steinmueller. 2003a. The Economics of Knowledge Reproduction by Inscription. *Industrial and Corporate Change* 12(2): 299–319.

Foray, D., and W. E. Steinmueller. 2003b. "On the economics of R&D and technological collaborations—Insights and results from the Project Colline." *Economics of Innovation and New Technology* 12(1): 77–97.

Foray, D., and J. B. Zimmerman. 2001. "L'économie du logiciel libre." *Revue Economique* 52 (special issue): 77–93.

Freeman, C., and L. Soete. 1997. *The economics of industrial innovation*, 3d ed. London: Pinter.

Garrouste, P. 2001. "Learning in economics: The Austrian insights." Working Paper Series, 25/2001, ICER, Turin.

Gibbons, M., C. Limoges, H. Novotny, S. Schwartzman, P. Scott, and M. Trow. 1994. *The new production of knowledge*. London: Sage.

Gille, B. 1978. *Histoire des Techniques*. Encyclopédie de la Pléiade. Paris: Gallimard.

Goody, J. 1977. *The domestication of the savage mind*. Cambridge: Cambridge University Press

Gordon, R. 2000. "Does the 'new economy' measure up to the great inventions of the past." *Journal of Economic Perspectives* 14(4): 49–72.

Greenan, N., and J. Mairesse. 2000. "Computers and productivity in France: Some evidence." *Economics of Innovation and New Technology* 9(3).

Greenan, N., Y. L'Horty, and J. Mairesse. 2002. *Productivity, inequality, and the digital economy*. Cambridge: Cambridge University Press.

Griliches, Z. 1995. "R&D and productivity: Econometric results and measurement issues." In *Handbook of the economics of innovation and technological change*, ed. P. Stoneman, 52–89. Oxford: Basil Blackwell.

Grindley, P., and D. Teece. 1997. "Managing intellectual capital: Licensing and cross-licensing in semiconductors and electronics." *California Management Review* 39(2): 1–34.

Guellec, D. 1996. "Knowledge, skills and growth: Some economic issues." *STI Review*, 17–38. Paris: OECD.

Hall, B., and R. Ziedonis. 2001. "The patent paradox revisited: An empirical study of patenting in the U.S. semiconductor industry, 1979–1995." *Rand Journal of Economics* 32(1): 101–128.

Hansen, M. 1999. "The search-transfer problem: The role of weak ties in sharing knowledge across organisation subunits." *Administrative Science Quarterly* 44 (March): 82–111.

Hansen, M., N. Nohria, and T. Tierney. 1999. "What's your strategy for managing knowledge?" *Harvard Business Review* (March–April): 106–116.

Hardin, G. 1968. "The tragedy of the commons." *Science* 162(13): 1243–1248.

Hargreaves, D. 1999. "The production, mediation and use of professional knowledge among teachers and doctors: A comparative analysis." In *Knowledge Management in the Learning Society*, 219–238. Paris: OECD

Harhoff, D., J. Henkel, and E. von Hippel. 2000. "Profiting from voluntary information spillovers: How users benefit by freely revealing their innovations." MIT Sloan School of Management, Cambridge, MA.

Hastings, George W. 1865. "Is the granting of patents for inventions conducive to the interests of trade?" *Transactions of the National Association for the Promotion of Social Science* 661–665.

Hatchuel, A., and B. Weil. 1995. *Experts in organizations: A knowledge-based perspective on organizational change.* Berlin: de Gruyter.

Hatchuel, A., P. Le Masson, and B. Weil. 2002. "From knowledge management to design oriented organization." *International Journal of Social Sciences* 171 (March): 29–42.

Hayek, F. 1945. "The use of knowledge in society." *The American Economic Review* 35(4): 519–530.

Heller, M. 1998. "The tragedy of the anticommons: Property in the transition from Marx to markets." *Harvard Law Review* 111(3): 622–688.

Heller, M., and R. Eisenberg. 1998. "Can patents deter innovation? The anticommons in biomedical research." *Science* 280: 698–701.

Henderson, R., A. Jaffe, and M. Trajtenberg. 1998. "University patenting amid changing incentives for commercialization." In *Creation and transfer of knowledge*, ed. G. Navaretti, P. Dasgupta, K. Mäler, and D. Siniscalco, 87–114. Heidelberg: Springer.

Hicks, D. 1995. "Published papers, tacit competences and corporate management of the public/private character of knowledge." *Industrial and Corporate Change* 4(2): 407–424.

Hilaire Perez, L. 2000. *L'invention technique au siècle des lumières.* Paris: Albin Michel.

Hirsch, W. Z. 1952. "Manufacturing progress functions." *Review of Economics and Statistics* 34(2): 143–155.

Hirshleifer, J. 1971. "The private and social value of information and the reward to inventive activity." *American Economic Review* (September): 561–574.

Howitt, P. 1996. "On some problems in measuring knowledge-based growth." In *The implications of knowledge-based growth for micro-economic policies*, ed. P. Howitt, 9–37. Calgary: University of Calgary Press.

Huberman, M. 1992. "Teacher development and instruction mastery." In *Understanding teacher development*, ed. D. Hargreaves and M. Fullan. Cassell: Teachers College Press.

Imri. 2001. *Choix d'investissement dans les projets de rupture technologique et formes organisationnelles.* Institut pour le Management de la Recherche et de l'Innovation, Université Paris Dauphine.

Jackson, P. W. 1968. *Life in classrooms.* New York: Holt, Rinehart & Winston.

Jaffe, A. 1989. "Real effects of academic research." *American Economic Review* 79: 957–970.

Jaffe, A. 1999. *Measuring knowledge in the health sector.* OECD/NSF high-level forum, NSF, Washington, DC.

Jaffe, A. 2000. "The U.S. patent system in transition: policy innovation and the innovation process." *Research Policy* 29: 531–557.

Jaffe, A., and J. Lerner. 1999. "Privatizing R&D: Patent Policy and the Commercialization of National Laboratory Technologies." NBER working paper, no. 7064.

Jaffe, A., and M. Trajtenberg. 1996. "Modelling the flows of knowledge spillovers." In *Conference on New S&T Indicators for the Knowledge-Based Economy*. Paris: OECD.

Kahin, B. 2002. "Codification in context: Infrastructure and policy for the knowledge economy." Paper presented at the DRUID Summer Conference, Copenhagen.

Keely, L., and D. Quah. 1998. *Technology in Growth*. Discussion Paper 391, Center for Economic Performance, London School of Economics.

Kendrick, J. W. 1994. "Total capital and economic growth." *Atlantic Economic Journal* 22(1): 1–18.

Khan, M. 2001. "Investment in knowledge." *DSTI Review*, 19–47. Paris: OECD.

Kitch, E. 1977. "The nature and function of the patent system." *Journal of Law and Economics* 20: 265–290.

Kline, J., and N. Rosenberg. 1986. "An overview of innovation." In *The positive sum strategy*, ed. R. Landau and N. Rosenberg, 275–305. Washington, DC: National Academy Press.

Knorr Cetina, K. 1999. *Epistemic cultures*. Cambridge: Harvard University Press.

Konrad, K., and M. Thum. 1993. "Fundamental standards and time consistency." *Kyklos* 46(4): 545–567.

Kortum, S., and J. Lerner. 1997. *Stronger protection or technological revolution: what is behind the recent surge in patenting?* Working Paper 98–012, Harvard Business School.

Kremer, M. 1997. "Patent buy-outs: a mechanism for encouraging innovation." NBER working paper, no. 6304.

Kremp, E., and J. Mairesse. 2002. "Knowledge management in the manufacturing industry." *Les 4 Pages des statistiques industrielles*, SESSI, Ministère de l'Economie, des Finances et de l'Industrie, Paris, no. 169.

Laffont, J. J. 1989. *The economics of uncertainty and information*. Cambridge, MA: The MIT Press.

Lakhani, K., and E. von Hippel. 2003. "How open source software works: 'Free' user-to-user assistance." *Research Policy* 32(6): 923–943.

Lam, A. 2000. "Tacit knowledge, organisational learning and societal institutions: an integrated framework." *Organizational Studies*, 21(3): 487–513.

Lecuyer, C. 1998. "Academic science and technology in the service of industry: MIT creates a 'permeable engineering school.'" *American Economic Review* 88(2): 28–33.

Le Goff, J. 1985. *Les intellectuels au Moyen Age*. Collection Histoire-Point. Paris: Seuil.

Lenoir, T. 1998. "Revolution from above: The role of the state in creating the German research system, 1810–1910." *American Economic Review* 88(2): 22–27.

Lerner, J. 1994. "Patenting in the Shadow of Competitors." Working paper, Division of Research, Harvard Business School, April.

Leslie, S., and R. Kargon. 1993. *Imagined geography: Princeton, Stanford and the spatial dimension of knowledge in postwar America*. Stanford University: STEW.

Lita, S. 2001. "Debunking the Bayh-Dole myth: Forgotten contributors to the rise of academic capitalism." Mimeo., The Elliot School of International Affairs, George Washington University.

Loasby, B. 1989. *The mind and method of the economist*. London: Edward Elgar.

Long, P. 1991. "The openness of knowledge: An ideal and its context in 16th century writings on mining and metallurgy." *Technology and Culture*, 318–355.

Lortie, D. 1975. *Schoolteacher*. Chicago: University of Chicago Press.

Love, H. 1993. *Scribal publication in seventeenth century England*. Oxford: Clarendon Press.

Lundvall, B. A. 1992. *National systems of innovation: Towards a theory of innovation and interactive learning*. London: Pinter.

Lundvall, B. A., and P. Nielsen. 1999. "Competition and transformation in the learning economy." *Revue d'Economie Industrielle* 88: 67–88.

Machlup, F. 1958. *An economic review of the patent system*. Study no. 15 of Committee on Judiciary, Subcommittee on Patents, 85th Congress, 2D Session.

Machlup, F. 1962. *The production and distribution of knowledge in the United States*. Princeton: Princeton University Press.

Machlup, F. 1984. *Knowledge, its creation, distribution and economic significance*, vol. III. Princeton: Princeton University Press.

Mackenzie, D., and G. Spinardi. 1995. "Tacit knowledge, weapons design and the uninvention of nuclear weapons." *American Journal of Sociology* 101(1).

Mahjoub, J. 2000. *Le télescope de Rachid*. Arles: Actes Sud.

Mairesse, J. 1998. "Sur l'économie de la recherche technique." In *Des sciences et des techniques: Un débat*, ed. R. Guesnerie and F. Hartog, 321–340. Editions de l'Ecole des Hautes Etudes en Sciences Sociales.

Mairesse, J., G. Cette, and Y. Kocoglu. 2000. "Les technologies de l'information et de la communication en France: Diffusion et contribution à la croissance." *Economie et Statistiques* 339–340(9/10): 117–128.

Malerba, F., and L. Orsenigo. 1996. "The dynamics and evolution of industries." *Industrial and Corporate Change* 5(1): 51–87.

Mangolte, P. A. 1997. "La dynamique des connaissances tacites et articulées: une approche socio-cognitive." *Economie Appliquée* 50(2): 105–132.

Mansel, R., and U. When. 1998. *Knowledge societies*. Oxford: Oxford University Press.

Mansfield, E. 1977. "Social and private rates of return from industrial innovation." *Quarterly Journal of Economics* 363(2): 221–240.

Mansfield, E. 1985. "How rapidly does new industrial technology leak out?" *Journal of Industrial Economics* 34(2): 217–223.

Mansfield, E. 1995. "Academic research underlying industrial innovations: Sources, characteristics and financing." *Review of Economics and Statistics* 77: 55–65.

Maunoury, J. L. 1972. *Economie du savoir*. Paris: Armand Collin, Collection U.

McSherry, C. 2001. *Who Owns Academic Work?* Cambridge: Harvard University Press.

Merges, R., and R. Nelson. 1994. "On limiting or encouraging rivalry in technical progress: The effect of patent scope decisions." *Journal of Economic Behavior and Organization* 25: 1–24.

Metcalfe, J. S. 1998. *Evolutionary economics and creative destruction*. New York: Routledge.

Metcalfe, J. S. 1999. "Restless capitalism: increasing returns and growth in enterprise economies." CRIC working paper, June.

Minne, B. 1996. "Expenditures in relation to the knowledge-based economy in 10 OECD Countries." In *Conference on New S&T Indicators for the Knowledge-Based Economy*. Paris: OECD.

Mokyr, J. 2000. "The rise and fall of the factory system: Technology, firms, and households since the Industrial Revolution." Paper presented at the International Conference on Technological Policy and Innovation, Paris.

Mowery, D. C. 1990. "The development of industrial research in U.S. manufacturing." *American Economic Review* 80(2)(May): 345–349.

Mowery, D. C., and T. Simcoe. 2001. *Is the Internet a U.S. invention? An economic and technological history of computer networking*. Washington, DC: Council on Foreign Relations.

Mowery, D. C., R. R. Nelson, B. Sampat, and A. A. Ziedonis. 1998. "The effects of the Bayh-Dole Act on U.S. university research and technology transfer: An analysis of data from Columbia University, the University of California, and Stanford University." Kennedy School of Government, Harvard University.

Mulligan, M. 1994. "Speeding up the appliance of science." *Financial Times*, April 18.

Murnane, R., and R. R. Nelson. 1984. "Production and innovation when techniques are tacit: The case of education." *Journal of Economic Behaviour and Organisation* 5: 353–373.

Myers, M., and R. Rosenbloom. 1998. "Rethinking the role of research." *Research, Technology, Management* (May–June): 14–18.

Nelson, R. R. 1959. "The simple economics of basic scientific research." *Journal of Political Economy* 67: 297–306.

Nelson, R. R. 1993. *National systems of innovation: A comparative study*. Oxford: Oxford University Press.

Nelson, R. R. 1994. "An agenda for formal growth theory." IIASA Working Paper 85.

Nelson, R. R. 1999. "Knowledge and innovation systems." In *Knowledge management in the learning society*, OECD/CERI, 115–124. Paris: OECD.

Nelson, R. R., and S. Winter. 1982. *An evolutionary theory of economic change*. Cambridge: The Belknap Press of Harvard University Press.

Nelson, R. R., and G. Wright. 1992. "The rise and fall of American technological leadership: The postwar era in an historical perspective." *Journal of Economic Literature* 30 (December): 1931–1964.

Nightingale, P. 2000. *Physics on Wall Street: Science, risk and system's control.* CoPS Centre, SPRU, University of Sussex.

Nottenburg, C., P. Pardey, and B. Wright. 2001. "Accessing other people's technology: Do non-profit agencies need it? How to obtain it? EPTD Discussion Paper no. 79, International Food Policy Research Institute, Washington DC.

Nuvolari, A. 2002. "Collective invention during the British Industrial Revolution: The case of the Cornish pumping engine." Eindhoven Center for Innovation Studies.

OECD. 1996. *Technology, productivity and job creation,* vol. 2, Analytical report. Paris: OECD.

OECD. 1998. *Science, technology and industry outlook.* Paris: OECD.

OECD. 1999a. *Knowledge management in the learning society,* Center for Educational Research and Innovation, OECD, Paris.

OECD. 1999b. *The knowledge-based Economy: Facts and figures.* Paris: OECD.

Oliner, S., and D. Sichel. 1994. "Computers and output growth revisited: How big is the puzzle?" *Brookings Papers on Economic Activity* 2: 273–332.

Olson, G., and J. Olson. 2003. "Mitigating the effects of distance on collaborative intellectual work." *Economics of Innovation and New Technology* 12(1): 27–42.

Ordover, J. 1991. "A patent system for both diffusion and exclusion." *Journal of Economic Perspective* 5(1): 43–60.

Ostrom, E. 1990. *Governing the Commons: The evolution of institutions for collective action.* New York: Cambridge University Press.

Penrose, E. 1951. *The economics of the international patent system.* Baltimore: Johns Hopkins University Press.

Penrose, E. 1959. *The theory of the growth of the firm.* Oxford: Basil Blackwell.

Perriault, J. 1993. "The transfer of knowledge within the craft industries and trade guilds." In *The use of tools by human and non-human primates,* ed. A. Berthelet and J. Chavaillier, 341–350. Oxford: Clarendon Press.

Pigou, A. C. 1932. *The economics of welfare.* New York: Macmillan.

Pisano, G. 1996. "Learning-before-doing in the development of new process technology." *Research Policy* 25: 1092–1119.

Polanyi, M. 1966. *The tacit dimension.* New York: Doubleday.

Polanyi, K. 2001. *The great transformation.* Boston: Beacon Press.

Porat, M., and M. Rubin. 1977. *The information economy.* Washington, DC: Government Printing Office.

Prusak, L. 2001. "Practice and Knowledge Management." In *Knowledge management in the innovation process,* ed. J. de la Mothe and D. Foray. Boston: Kluwer Academic Publishers.

Quah, D. 1999. "The weightless economy in economic development." LES Economic Department, London.

Richardson, G. B. 1960. *Information and investment.* Oxford: Oxford University Press.

Romer, P. 1993. "The economics of new ideas and new goods." In *Proceedings of the World Bank Annual Conference on Development Economics 1992*. Washington, DC: World Bank.

Rose, C. 1986. "The Comedy of the Commons: Custom, Commerce and Inherently Public Property." *The University of Chicago Law Review* 53(3): 711–781.

Rosenberg, N. 1976. *Perspectives on technology*. Cambridge: Cambridge University Press.

Rosenberg, N. 1982. *Inside the black box: Technology and economics*. Cambridge: Cambridge University Press.

Rosenberg, N. 1992. "Science and technology in the twentieth century." In *Technology and Enterprise in a Historical Perspective*, ed. G. Dosi, R. Giannetti, and P. A. Toninelli, 63–96. Oxford: Clarendon Press.

Rosenberg, N., and R. Nelson. 1993. *American universities and technical advances in industry*. CEPR publication no. 342, Stanford University.

Rossi, P. 1999. *La naissance de la science moderne en Europe*. Paris: Seuil.

Rubin, M., and M. Huber. 1984. *The knowledge industry in the United States, 1960–1980*. Princeton: Princeton University Press.

Saxenian, A. 2001. "Transnational technical communities and regional growth in the periphery." Saint Gobain Centre for Economic Research, Paris.

Schön, D. A. 1983. *The reflective practitioner*. New York: Basic Books.

Schumpeter, J. 1942. *Capitalism, socialism and democracy*. New York: Harper.

Schwerin, J. 2000. The dynamics of sectoral change: Innovation and growth in Clyde Shipbuilding, c. 1850–1900. 8th International J. A. Schumpeter Society Conference, Manchester.

*Science*. 1999. "Companies battle over technology that's free on the Web." *Science* 286 (October 15): 446.

Scotchmer, S. 1991. "Standing on the shoulders of giants." *Journal of Economic Perspectives* 5(1): 29–41.

Severi, C. 1994. "Paroles durables, écritures perdues. Réflexions sur la pictographie cuna." In *Transcrire les mythologies*, ed. M. Detienne. Paris: Albin Michel.

Shapiro, C. 2000. "Navigating the patent thicket: Cross licenses, patent pools and standard-setting." NBER workshop on innovation policy and the economy.

Shapiro, C., and H. Varian. 1998. *Information rules*. Boston: Harvard Business School Press.

Sherman, C. 2001. "Music on the Internet." *Brookings Review* 19(1)(Winter): 35–37.

Simon, H. 1982. *Models of bounded rationality: Behavioural economics and business organization*, vol. 2. Cambridge: The MIT Press.

Slaughter, M. M. 1985. *Universal languages and scientific taxonomy in the seventeenth century*. Cambridge: Cambridge University Press.

Smith, A. 1995. *An inquiry into the nature and causes of the wealth of nations*, ed. W. Playfair. London: William Pickering.

Smith, K. 1995. "Interactions in knowledge systems: Foundations, policy implications and empirical methods." *STI review*, no. 16, OECD.

Smith, K. 2000. "What is the 'knowledge economy'? Knowledge-intensive industries and distributed knowledge bases." Paper presented at the DRUID Conference, Aalborg, June 15–17.

Steinmueller, W. E. 1992. "The economics of production and distribution of user-specific information via digital networks." In *The Economics of Information Networks*, ed. C. Antonelli, 173–194. Amsterdam: North-Holland.

Steinmueller, W. E. 1996. "Technological Infrastructure in Information Technology Industries." In *Technological Infrastructure Policy: An international perspective*, ed. M. Teubal, D. Foray, M. Justman, and E. Zuscovitch, 117–138. Boston: Kluwer Academic Publishers.

Steinmueller, W. E. 1997. "Do we all become programmers now?" Working paper, SPRU, University of Sussex.

Steinmueller, W. E. 2000a. "Will new information and communication technologies improve the 'codification' of knowledge?" *Industrial and Corporate Change* 9(2).

Steinmueller, W. E. 2000b. Learning in the Knowledge-based Economy: The Future as Viewed from the Past. Conference in Honor of Paul A. David, Turin.

Steinmueller, W. E. 2002a. "Networked knowledge and knowledge-based economies." *International Journal of Social Sciences* 171 (March): 159–173.

Steinmueller, W. E. 2002b. *Collaborative innovation: Rationale, indicators and significance*. In *Networks, alliances and partnerships in the innovation process*, ed. J. de la Mothe and A. Link, 29–43. Dordrecht: Kluwer Academic Publishers.

Stoke, D. 1994. "The impaired dialogue between science and government and what might be done about it." *AAAS Science and Technology Policy Yearbook*. Washington, DC: AAAS.

Styroh, K. 2001. *New and old economics in the "new economy."* New York: Federal Reserve Bank of New York.

Tassey, G. 1992. *Technology infrastructure and competitive position*. Norwell, MA: Academic Publishers.

Teece, D. 1998. "Capturing value from knowledge assets." *California Management Review* 40(3)(Spring): 55–79.

Teubal, M., D. Foray, M. Justman, and E. Zuscovitch, eds. 1996. *Technological infrastructure policy: An international perspective*. Boston: Kluwer Academic Publishers.

Thomas, S. M. 1999. "Les brevets en surrégime." *Biofutur* 191(July–August): 28–42.

Thomke, S. 2001. "Enlightened experimentation." *Harvard Business Review* (February): 67–75.

Thomke, S., and E. von Hippel. 2002. "Customers as innovators." *Harvard Business Review* (April): 74–81.

Thomke S., E. von Hippel, and R. Franke. 1998. "Modes of experimentation: an innovation process—and competitive—variable." *Research Policy* 27: 315–332.

Trajtenberg, M. 1990. *Economic analysis of product innovation*. Cambridge: Harvard University Press.

Tyre, M., and E. von Hippel. 1997. "The situated nature of adaptive learning in organizations." *Organization Science* 8(1): 71–83.

UNCTAD. 1996. *The TRIPS Agreement and developing countries*. New York and Geneva: United Nations Publication.

Valentine, G., S. Holloway, and N. Bingham. 2002. "The digital generation? Children, ICT and the everyday nature of social exclusion." *Antipode* 34: 296–315.

Van Alstyne, M., and E. Brynjolfsson. 1996. "Could the Internet Balkanize science?" *Science* 274(5292): 1479–1480.

Vicenti, W. 1990. *What engineers know and how they know it*. Baltimore: Johns Hopkins University Press.

von Hippel, E. 1988a. *The sources of innovation*. Oxford: Oxford University Press.

von Hippel, E. 1988b. "Trading trade secrets." *Technology Review*, (February/March): 58–64.

von Hippel, E. 1994. "Sticky information and the locus of problem solving: implications for innovation." *Management Science* 40(4): 429–439.

von Hippel, E. 1998. "Economics of product development by users: The impact of 'sticky' local information." *Management Science* 44(5): 629–644.

von Hippel, E. 2001a. "Perspective: User toolkits for innovation." *The Journal of Production Innovation Management* 18: 247–257.

von Hippel, E. 2001b. "Learning from open-source software." *MIT Sloan Management Review* (Summer).

von Hippel, E., and M. Tyre. 1995. "How Learning By Doing is Done: Problem Identification in Novel Process Equipment." *Research Policy* 24.

von Hippel, E., and G. von Krogh. 2003. "Open source software and the "private-collective innovation model: Issues for organization science." *Organization Science* 14(2): 209–223.

Wadman, M. 2001. "Testing time for gene patent as Europe rebels." *Nature* 413 (4 October): 443.

Walsh, J., A. Arora, and W. Cohen. 2000. *The patenting of research tools and biomedical innovation*. Washington, DC: Science, Technology and Economic Policy Board of the National Academy of Sciences.

Weizenbaum, J. 1976. *Computer power and human teason*. New York: W. H. Freeman.

Wenger, E. 1998. *Communities of practice: Learning, meaning and identity*. Cambridge: Cambridge University Press

The World Bank. 1998. *Knowledge for development*. Oxford: Oxford University Press.

Wright, G. 1936. "Factors Affecting the Cost of Airplanes." *Journal of Aeronautical Sciences* 3(4): 122–128.

Zucker, L., and M. Darby. 1998. "The economists' case for biomedical research." In *The future of biomedical research*, ed. C. Barfield and B. Smith, 42–66. Washington, DC: The AEI Press.

Zucker, L., M. Darby, and J. Amstrong J. 1994. Intellectual capital and the firm: the technology of geographically localized knowledge spillovers. NBER working paper, no. 4946.

# Index

Abramovitz, M., 13, 22–23, 27
Absorptive capacities, 95–96
Allen, R., 175, 180–181
Alter, N., 44
Amendola, M., 43
Antonelli, C., 91, 100
Aoki, M., 53, 66
Appleyard, M., 91–182
Appropriability mechanisms, 137–146
Arora, A., 139, 142, 150, 153, 213, 232–233
Arrow, K. J., 2, 8, 59–60, 82, 114, 124, 173
Arthur, B. A., 43
Audrestch, D., 101

Baldwin, C., 66
Bessy, C., 139
Boldrin, M., 146, 172
Bresnahan, T., 46, 101, 237
Brousseau, E., 139
Brown, K. M., 127, 230
Brynjolfsson, E., 34, 196

Callon, M., 64, 68, 98, 174
Carlsson, B., 13
Caron, F., 141, 211
Carter, A. P., 11, 37–39, 42, 243
Cassier, M., 57, 171, 229
Change as an economic activity, 37–45
Chartier, R., 86–87, 161
Clark, K. B., 59, 66
Clavier, J. P., 157, 160
Clusters, 101–103
Coase, R., 33, 118
Cockburn, I., 124–125, 171–172, 187, 194, 215, 225, 230–232
Cohen, W., 95, 124, 137, 142, 230, 232–233

Collaboration in R&D, 56–57, 67, 69, 118
Collective action, 30
Collective invention, 174–175
Collocation, 101–103
Communities
  epistemic, 195–196, 199
  knowledge, 37, 182–187
  and the new public economy, 244
  of practices, 195
  virtual, 30
Competition
  and innovation, 40
  winner-take-all, 148
Copyright, 132
Cowan, R., 17, 88, 122, 223
Creative destruction, 42–43

Darby, M., 97, 128
Dasgupta, P., 120, 125, 172, 174, 177, 179–180, 185
David, P. A., 16, 22–23, 27, 29, 31–33, 41, 43, 47, 51, 57, 60, 67, 87, 93–94, 110, 119, 120, 121, 123, 125, 147, 158, 166, 169–170, 172, 174, 177, 179–180, 185, 205
Discovery versus invention, 14
Distance learning 28–29. See also Remote access
Dosi, G., 13
Duby, G., 29

Eamon, W., 77, 99, 109, 136
Economic growth in the United States, 23, 249
Edquist, C., 13
Education and training, 23–25, 45, 235–238

Education sector, 196–205
Eisenberg, R., 155–156
Eisenstein, E., 29, 87
Eliasson, G., 8, 26
Encaoua, D., 159
Epstein, S. R., 83, 108, 132, 208
Equity, 234
Ergas, H., 121
European Community's directive
  for the legal protection of data bases,
  147
  on the patentability of living organisms,
  134
European Patent Office (EPO), 149–150
Expert system, 75–76, 88–89

Farrell, J., 148
Fauchart, E., 181
Favereau, O., 5, 237
Feldman, M., 29, 101, 103
Fitz-Gibbon, C., 55, 197, 204
Foray, D., 13, 32, 37, 41, 56–57, 85, 122,
  166, 171, 174, 203, 205, 222–223
Fosfuri, A., 150, 153, 213
Freeman, C., 13, 31–33

Gaffard, J. L., 43
Gambardella, A., 101, 150, 153, 213
Garrouste, P., 3
Gault, F., 222
General-purpose technology, 32, 35,
  47
Gille, B., 30, 41, 57
Goody, J., 76–80
Gordon, R., 35, 47
Greenan, N., 34
Griliches, Z., 114
Guellec, D., 40, 159

Hall, B., 153
Hansen, M., 216–221
Hardin, G., 167–168
Hargreaves, D., 198–203, 254
Hatchuel, A., 44, 73, 75, 87, 209, 237
Hayek, F., 2, 124
Health sector, 200–203
Heller, M., 143, 155–156
Henderson, R., 11, 124–125, 154, 171–172,
  187, 194, 215, 230
Hicks, D., 123, 215
Hilaire Perez, L., 175–177, 180
Hirshleifer, J., 19, 115, 170

Incentives
  lack of, 114–115
  provided by patents, 136
  to reveal knowledge, 179–181, 199,
  205
ICT
  economic effects of, 27
  and efficient markets, 40
  and employment, 46
  and intellectual property rights, 161–162
  and knowledge flows, 36–37
  as a knowledge instrument, 28–30
  as a knowledge investment, 24
  and knowledge management, 214, 220
  upheaval of, 30–35
ICT-related skills, 236–237
ICT skepticism, 34–35
Increasing returns, 57
Industrial architecture, 66
Innovation
  capacity for, 209–210
  geography of, 101–103, 107–108
  and knowledge management, 222–223
  measurement of, 38–39
  models of, 67–69
  public dimension of, 124–126
  systemic, 41
Intangible
  evaluation of, 214
  understanding the world of the, 215–217
Intangible capital, 22–23
Intangible investments, 23
Intellectual property rights, 109, 120,
  131–163, 213–215
Internal labor market, 83–84, 208–209

Jaffe, A., 11, 125, 138, 152, 154

Kahin, B., 34, 67
Kendrick, J. W., 22–23
Khan, M., 25
Kendrick, J. W., 22–23
Kitch, E., 170
Knorr Cetina, K., 195
Knowledge
  acquisition of, 98–99, 106
  as a cumulative good, 16, 94–95, 99–100,
  146–147
  as a joint product, 15, 60
  as a nonexcludable good, 15, 91–92,
  96–97
  as a nonrival good, 15, 92–94, 98–99

as a public good, 113–129, 181
codification of, 5, 36, 73–83, 85–90,
    96–97, 197–198, 218–221
cost structure of, 103–104
creation/production of, 29, 49–69,
    191–192
definition of, 3–5
depreciation and obsolescence of, 17,
    43–44, 235–238
dispersion and division of, 18, 239–240
growth of, 35–36
integrative, 36, 49, 67, 221, 239–241
measurement of, 9–12, 242–244
memorization and persistence of,
    100–101, 208–209, 238–239
privatization of, 226–233
reproduction of, 4, 71–90, 104–106
search for, 99, 241–242
sharing of, 91–113, 182, 209
tacit, 17, 71–73, 96–97
transfer of, 17–18, 63
uneven development of, 189–206
Knowledge-based economy, 21–47, 111,
    247–250
Knowledge-based sectors, 25–27, 39
Knowledge dilemma, 113–118
Knowledge externalities and spillovers,
    24, 36–37, 91–113, 114–115, 122,
    179–181, 192–193, 204–205, 234
Knowledge instruments, 28–30, 36
Knowledge management, 207–224
Knowledge modeling, 79–81
Knowledge openness, 108–110, 165–187
Knowledge-related investments, 24
Knowledge workers, 39, 45–47
Kortum, S., 153–154
Kremer, M., 158
Kremp, E., 222–223

Lam, A., 83–84, 208
Learning
  by doing and by using, 8,15, 49, 58–66,
    198–199
  costs of, 44
  experimental, 8, 61–62, 23–24, 44
  interorganizational, 211–212
  intraorganizational, 210–211
  situated nature of, 63, 215–216
  to learn, 77
Learning program, 77, 198
Le Goff, J., 29, 87
Lerner, J., 150, 153–154

Levine, D., 146, 172
Levinthal, D., 95
Licensing
  compulsory, 157–158, 163
  technology, 136–139
  university, 227–228
Lita, S., 227–228
Loasby, B., 240
Long, P., 109
Lundvall, B. A., 13, 37, 46

Machlup, F., 2, 10, 18–19, 25, 95, 100, 116,
    157, 253
Mairesse, J., 31–32, 34, 114, 222–223
Malerba, F., 189
Mansel, R., 161
Mansfield, E., 92, 114, 125, 146
Market
  for basic knowledge, 231–233
  for ICT-based services, 238
  and the role of ICTs, 40
  transactions in connection with
    knowledge, 12, 213–214
Marshall, A., 240
Maunoury, J. L., 2, 57
Memory
  digital, 82
  organizational, 212–213
  paradox of, 238–239
Merges, R., 142
Metcalfe, J. S., 37
Modularity, 36, 66, 68
Mokyr, J., 107
Mowery, D. C., 23, 50–51, 57, 228, 249

Nelson, R. R., 13–14, 23, 50, 54, 82,
    137, 142, 189, 191, 196–197, 227, 232,
    253
Network
  of engineers, 180, 187
  as a metaphor in policy discussion,
    204–205
  as a new form of organization, 33
  and the new public economy, 244
Network externalities, 148
New economy, 47, 213–214, 248
Norms and standards, 44–45, 67, 176
Nightingale, P., 55

Oliner, S., 43
Olson, G., 29, 102, 108
Olson, J., 29, 102, 108

Open science, 147, 172–174
Open source, 178, 185
Open technology, 174–177
Ordover, J., 139
Organisation for Economic Cooperation and Development (OECD), 5, 24–26, 45, 111, 222, 243
Organization and the productivity paradox, 32–34
Orsenigo, L., 189

Patent
  abuse of, 145
  advantages of, 135–140
  and cumulative knowledge, 142–143, 146–147
  economics of, 14, 132–163
  scope of a, 142
  shortcomings of, 140–144
  social cost of, 140–141, 154–156, 229, 232
  thicket, 159
  university, 227–228
Patent buy-out, 158
Patent institutions, 134–135, 151–152
Patent office, 145, 151–152, 159
Patent race, 169
Pavitt, K., 215
Penrose, E., 1, 144, 157
Pisano, G., 59
Polanyi, K., 168
Polanyi, M., 4, 71
Price discrimination, 158
Productivity
  ICT and, 27
  knowledge management and, 222–223
  paradox of, 31–35
  R&D and, 114
Prusak, L., 207–208
Public dimension of the knowledge economy, 225–245
Public property, 129, 233–235
Public sector and private sector, 124–129, 229–231

Quah, D., 9, 14, 93, 178

Remote access, 28–29. See also Distance learning
Research and development, 7, 22–25, 49–58

Richardson, G. B., 2
Romer, P., 93
Rose, C., 17, 124, 235
Rosenberg, N., 8, 41, 53–54, 57, 62, 95, 227–228

Saxenian, A., 101, 103
Science, 36, 54–56, 68, 197, 204
Scotchmer, S., 142
Script, 72–73, 75
Secrecy, 132–133
Shapiro, C., 148, 159
Sichel, D., 43
Simon, H., 1, 74, 239, 241
Skills, 42, 45–47, 236–238
Smith, A., 50, 61
Smith, K., 27, 56
Soete, L., 31–33
Solow, R., 31
Statistics Canada, 222
Steinmueller, W. E., 27, 33, 46, 49, 51, 56–57, 66–67, 82, 85, 90, 96, 205, 210, 212, 214, 230–231, 236, 238, 242
Stiglitz, J., 17, 100
Stoke, D., 52
Strategy of the commons, 181
Styroh, K., 35

Tassey, G., 51, 67
Teece, D., 13, 153, 156, 159, 213
Thomke, S., 56, 63, 216
Trade-Related Aspects of Intellectual Property Rights (TRIPs), 138, 149
Tragedy
  of the anticommons, 143–144
  of the commons, 16, 167–172, 184
Trajtenberg, M., 11, 114, 154
Trust, 184, 242

United Nations Conference on Trade and development (UNCTAD), 138
University, 226–229
U.S. Patent and Trademark Office (USPTO), 145, 149–150
Users as innovators, 62–64, 68, 185

Varian, H., 148
von Hippel, E., 15, 18, 59–60, 62–63, 92, 180, 182, 185, 187, 211, 215–216

Walsh, J., 137, 142, 232–233
Weil, B., 44, 73, 75, 87, 209, 237

Weizenbaum, J., 72
Wenger, E., 195
When, U., 161
World Bank, 128, 236
World Intellectual Property Organization
   (WIPO), 133, 152

Ziedonis, R., 153
Zucker, L., 97, 128